Ethnic Identities in a Transnational World

Recent Titles in
Contributions in Political Science
Series Editor: Bernard K. Johnpoll

Ethnic Identities in a Transnational World

Edited by JOHN F. STACK, Jr.

CONTRIBUTIONS IN POLITICAL SCIENCE, NUMBER 52

GREENWOOD PRESS
WESTPORT, CONNECTICUT • LONDON, ENGLAND

Library of Congress Cataloging in Publication Data

Main entry under title:

Ethnic identities in a transnational world.

    (Contributions in political science ; no. 52 ISSN 0147-1066)
    Bibliography: p.
    Includes index.
    1.   Pluralism (Social sciences)—Addresses, essays, lectures.   2.   Ethnicity—Addresses, essays, lectures.
3.   Ethnic relations—Addresses, essays, lectures.
4.   International relations—Addresses, essays, lectures.
I.   Stack, John F.   II.   Series.
HN18.E83   305.8   80-1199
ISBN 0-313-21088-8 (lib. bdg.)

Library of Congress Catalog Card Number: 80-1199
ISBN: 0-313-21088-8
ISSN: 0147-1066

First published in 1981

Greenwood Press
A division of Congressional Information Service, Inc.
88 Post Road West, Westport, Connecticut 06881

Printed in the United States of America

10 9 8 7 6 5 4 3 2 1

To the memory of Fred A. Sondermann

Contents

Figures and Table

Foreword

In the past two years, thousands of Vietnamese "boat people" have landed, or attempted to land, on the beaches of the east coast of Malaysia. Does it add anything to our understanding of the Vietnam War or its prolonged aftermath to know that two-thirds of these refugees are Vietnam's ethnic Chinese? One of the celebrated contemporary German films, Fassbinder's "Ali—Fear Eats the Soul," is about a touching but unlikely affair between a sixty-year-old German cleaning woman and a young Moroccan *Gastarbeiter*. The Moroccan mentions casually that he is not just Moroccan; he is Berber. Does it matter, in our analysis of the effects of foreign-worker migration in West Germany and France, that we usually ignore the interethnic distinctions between Berbers and Arabs among Algerian and Moroccan workers?

In the chapters that follow, John Stack and his colleagues push us to take explicit account of ethnicity in our analyses of international system dynamics. Their studies should shake the mental sets of both students of ethnicity and of international political economy. Best of all, perhaps they will prompt those of us in each subdiscipline to share data and theoretical hunches with each other more systematically in the future. It is becoming more and more clear that the mobilization and demobilization of ethnic groups are profoundly affected by the levels of international integration, whether in the form of state-to-state cooperation (often strengthening the ethnic groups that control each state, while undermining ethnic groups that lack state access) or in the form of World Bank or multinational-corporation loans and investments. To comprehend what it means to be a Kalinga in the hills of Luzon in the Philppines, one has to delve into the World Bank's loans for a dam in their region. To estimate the capacity of "Navajo" to remain a genuinely salient, subjective identity for certain inhabitants of the American Southwest, one has to go beyond ethnography or even interest-group analysis; one must take explicit account of the international political economy of oil and coal.

But it is not simply ethnicity specialists who will be provoked to think new thoughts and open new mental windows as a result of reading this book. Analysts of international politics and economy should find themselves addressing new questions, taking account of previously overlooked variables. The international system is not, as John Stack makes so clear in Chapter 1, simply a routinized pattern of interaction and dependency between states (usually masquerading as nation-states). If there is something accurately termed an international "system" in the late 1970s and 1980s, it is fueled by extrastate interactions and dependencies (typically asymmetrical) as well.

In fact, this may be the special advantage of investigating the international system from the ethnic vantage point. It reveals a para-doxical, coterminant rise both in interstate integration (UNCTAD, OECD, ASEAN, IMF, EEC, OPEC) and in extrastate and cross-state integration (labor migration into North America, the Persian Gulf, and Western Europe; the Trilateral Commission; multinational bank consortia; interethnic liberation movements' trading of arms and information). The paradox is that the growing interstate integra-tion should, theoretically, suppress or squeeze out extrastate inte-gration; through their growing capacities for deliberate cooperation, state elites should be able to monopolize the arena where international actions occur. Some of the studies in this volume underscore this paradox. Others suggest that the paradox can be unraveled if we look at who actually determines the ground rules for and controls the vehicles through which such seemingly extrastate international activities occur. Ethnic groups may reveal the persistent limitations of state power, or they may show us how even apparently extrastate mobilizations serve state interests—or at least the interests of particular states. To understand, then, *under what conditions* international integration is bypassing conventional states or is in fact reinforcing such political hierarchies, we have to examine ethnic groups directly.

Cynthia H. Enloe
Clark University

Acknowledgments

I would like to acknowledge my gratitude to a number of scholars who contributed to the realization of this volume. Without the continuing support of James P. Piscatori this book could not have been completed. Cynthia H. Enloe generously gave her time and enthusiasm through every phase of the manuscript's preparation. I have benefited from Mark B. Rosenberg's challenging criticisms. In addition, I am grateful for the help that was given to me by Paul R. Brass, Ralph S. Clem, Judson M. DeCew, Jr., Joyce R. Lilie, Anthony P. Maingot, James A. Mau, and Mark D. Szuchman.

I owe a large debt to the contributors—Pierre-Michel Fontaine, David B. Kanin, John P. Paul, James P. Piscatori, and Martin Slater—and am especially appreciative of the support they have given me.

Margaret Brezicki of the Greenwood Press was a constant source of enthusiasm and assistance throughout the production of this volume.

Judy Green and Maria Hildago typed several sections of the manuscript. Roberta McLaughlin provided patient and careful assistance in the preparation of the manuscript.

Finally, this book is dedicated to the memory of the late Fred A. Sondermann, who humanized my life as his student and who infused a conspicuously needed human element into the study of international politics.

J. F. S.

Ethnic Identities in a Transnational World

JOHN F. STACK, JR.

Ethnicity and Transnational   1
Relations: An Introduction

For the past decade, students and practitioners of international affairs have pointed to fundamental realignments of the international system. The central change that has been identified is the declining importance of the nation-state and the concomitant rise of such transnational actors and processes as multinational corporations, international nongovernmental organizations, transgovernmental actors (particularly bureaucracies), global communication and transportation networks, technological transfers, and patterns of economic interdependence. Indeed, the increasing importance of transnational actors and processes has become something of a truism in international-relations theory.[1]

Ethnic groups appear to be increasingly important transnational actors, but their role in international politics has been given only sporadic attention.[2] There appears to be a strong correlation between ethnic conflict and international instability in a number of regional subsystems: Western Europe—Ireland, Belgium, Switzerland, France, and Spain; Eastern Europe—Yugoslavia and the Soviet Union; the Mediterranean and the Middle East—Cyprus, Turkey, Lebanon, and Israel; Africa—virtually every nation; Asia—from Pakistan to the Philippines; and the Americas—from Canada throughout the Caribbean. Despite this apparent correlation, there has been little systematic examination of the intersection of international-relations theory and ethnicity. We have a number of empirically rich, but theoretically limited, case studies.[3]

ETHNICITY, POLITICS, AND THE GLOBAL SYSTEM

This book addresses the central question, how does the concept of transnationalism clarify the roles played by ethnicity and ethnic groups in world politics? The question raises two distinct observations: (1) the essential political quality of ethnicity; and (2) the changing structure of the international political and economic system.

First, if the international dimensions of ethnicity are ignored, there is a tendency to overlook the dynamic and intensely political quality of ethnicity. As Rupert Emerson and Walker Connor have documented, ethnicity is intimately related to the evolution of the nineteenth- and twentieth-century state systems through the force of nationalism.[4] It is the *idea* of modern nationalism that predicts the most intensely politicized dynamics of ethnic affiliations with its emphasis on "we" and "they." Nationalism identifies a primary political and territorial community—the state with a common ethnic identity—the nation. Nationalism forges together a sense of peoplehood or belonging, real or imagined, based on common history, ancestry, culture, language, or region. Thus, the rise of the modern state system formally institutionalized the notion of the ethnic (national) group as the legitimate and, at times, exclusive participant in the political community (the state). Nationalism, therefore, is only the most visible and politicized manifestation of the phenomenon we call ethnicity.[5] Whether one looks to the overall territorial and cultural homogeneity of the French nation-state in the nineteenth century or to the more pluralistic, elastic dynamics of nationalism in the nineteenth-century American case, a sense of ethnic identity (real or imagined, voluntarily accepted or enforced) becomes a necessary and sufficient condition of modern state-building. Ironically, just as ethnicity and politics go hand in hand in the process of statebuilding in the nineteenth century, as European politics suggests, the political dynamics of ethnicity are manifest in the expansion and fragmentation of the twentieth-century state system.[6] During this period, trends toward integration (the establishment of the Common Market in Western Europe and the creation of states from former colonies in the Third World) and then fragmentation (in the North as well as the South) accentuated the salience of ethnicity. Indeed, the process of nation-building and nation-destroying as Connor conceptualizes it dramatically illustrates the interplay of ethnicity and politics both intranationally and internationally.[7]

Second, the analysis of the transnational dynamics of ethnicity point to the structural realignments of international political and economic systems in the post–World War II era. Increasing patterns of global interdependence in economic relations, communication and transportation systems, and the penetration of societies provide ethnic groups with unprecedented opportunities to enter the political processes of states, regions, and the global system.[8] Patterns of global interdependence and dependence heighten the sensitivity and vulnerability of actors in world politics, particularly states, thus permitting nonstate actors to play a more significant role.[9] Moreover, the complexity of global political and economic relations gives rise to new kinds of political actors. These range from domestic bureaucratic elites whose common interests transcend the policies of their respective governments to the dramatic increase in the number and kind of transnational activities in social, economic, technological, and welfare areas.

The number of studies devoted to the analysis of interdependence, dependence, dependency, and global dominance suggests the utility of a transnational perspective.[10] It is the evolving nature of patterns of complex interdependence that provide insights into the growing importance of transnational actors. These are defined in terms of: (1) multiple channels of political intercourse—through the formulation of a state's foreign policy, international organizations, direct intrasocietal contacts via mass communication and transportation networks, and nongovernmental actors; (2) the shifting hierarchy of issues in the international system—economic interdependence, trade policies, resource dependence, and state security policies; and (3) the declining salience of military force "in determining the outcomes of bargaining or conflicts."[11]

These trends are seen most explicitly in the ubiquitous presence of multinational corporations (MNCs). Multinational corporations are important actors because of the influence they wield in both formal and informal relations with states. The permeability of states, coupled with patterns of systemic interdependence and hence the diminishing control governments exercise over internal and external decisions, heighten the influence of multinational corporations and other transnational actors.[12] World politics is further complicated by prevailing inequalities in the distribution of resources—technology, industrial development, the quality of life, and the potential for economic growth—that bind states and transnational actors together in a shifting milieu.

ETHNICITY AND TRANSNATIONAL RELATIONS

Thus, this volume suggests that ethnicity is a significant force in world politics because it frequently bypasses formal state-authority patterns *and* because it encompasses, often simultaneously, different levels of analysis: from intrasocietal to worldwide processes. By specifying the interactions between ethnicity and world politics on more inclusive levels of analysis, this approach is an attempt to generate possible middle-range conceptual insights; hence the utility of a transnational orientation.

Whereas the evolving body of literature examining the conceptual aspects of transnational relations fails to articulate anything approaching a theory of global politics, studies of transnational relations, however, document global political relations in an era of profound transition.[13]

Initially, the study of transnational relations challenged traditional notions of international political and economic relations through its emphasis on the nature of transnational relations—"the transfer of tangible or intangible items across state boundaries when at least one actor is not an agent of government or an intergovernmental organization."[14] The idea of transnationalism freed us from the dogmatic assertion that states are the exclusive actors in world politics. Moreover, the idea of transnational relations conveys a more holistic approach to evaluate contemporary international political and economic relations. Indeed, the concept of transnationalism argues that the terms "international economics" or "international politics" are misnomers, that most of what we conventionally call international politics is in fact *interstate* politics.[15] Thus, transnational relations constitutes a place to begin an assessment of the actors and forces augmenting, modifying, perhaps even transforming interstate politics in the post-industrial era.[16]

The analysis of the nature and scope of transnational relations does not dismiss the influence that states exercise in the global environment. In fact, the interplay between the state and states elites on one hand and between transnational actors and processes on the other is a significant and crucial dimension of the conceptual and substantive concerns of this volume. Incidents of ethnic conflict throughout the world are often defined by the unique structural setting of states. As each chapter in this book points out, states are central structures that help to define the dynamics of ethnicity on state, regional, and global levels. This observation raises two questions relevant to the study of transnational relations: Do states feel threatened when they no longer monopolize world affairs? Do some states find it convenient to use nonstate actors?[17] The answer to the first question is difficult to predict because states are seldom unitary rational actors.[18] The second question, however, has a direct bearing on the conceptual and substantive concerns of this study, for if the rules of traditional interstate politics are being modified by transnational relations, then one would presume a more direct and tangible interplay between states and transnational actors. This book argues that ethnic groups increasingly occupy a significant place in contemporary global politics.

This study is not an exhaustive presentation of transnational relations. Rather, it attempts to come to grips with selective dimensions of the interplay between ethnic groups, states, and the evolving transnational, rather than interstate, system.

SUBSTANTIVE CONCERNS

In "Ethnic Groups as Emerging Transnational Actors," John F. Stack, Jr., argues that the transnational dimensions of ethnicity are most explicitly seen on three levels of analysis: intrasocietal (ethnic groups as reflections of the global system); state (ethnic groups as direct participants in world politics); and global (ethnicity as a transnational force). Stack argues that the transformation of global *structures* and *processes* in the post–World War II era heightened the transnational ramifications of ethnicity. That chapter offers a general conceptual and substantive overview of a number of themes that are examined in the following chapters: the fundamental importance of systemic interdependence; the permeability of states;

the structural inequalities between advanced industrial states and developing countries; the power of worldwide communication and transportation networks; and the interplay between states and ethnic groups on intrasocietal, state, and global levels.

"The Greek Lobby and American Foreign Policy: A Transnational Perspective" by John P. Paul evaluates the intrasocietal and external implications of transnational relations. On the surface, Paul's analysis would appear to be quite conventional. Foreign-policy decision making has traditionally been a primary object of ethnic-group politics in the United States.[19] What Paul does, however, is to suggest that states can give ethnic groups more transnational clout than they could ever achieve on their own. Because the Ford administration and the governments of Greece and Turkey insistently pointed to the domestic and international *leverage* of Greek-Americans, the Greek lobby (whose actual congressional influence in achieving the U.S. arms embargo against Turkey was small) gained considerable political mileage in the United States. Perception has traditionally been a key aspect of political relations between states.[20] The putative power of a transnational actor is no less significant, especially for Greek-Americans during the Cypriot crisis in 1974–1975, as Paul points out.

Martin Slater's "International Migration and French Foreign Relations" suggests the importance of transnational relations on intrasocietal and state levels. Historically, mass immigrations have been one of the most important manifestations of transnational activities linking the fatherland to the new country of adoption.[21] The European immigration to the Western Hemisphere in the nineteenth century enriched American culture, provided invaluable human capital to assist in the physical and socioeconomic construction of the United States, and tangibly affected the American political system.[22] An unanticipated outcome of the mass migration was the fascination that immigrants and their descendants would have for their lands of origin.

Mass migrations are no less significant in the 1970s.[23] In fact, accelerating patterns of societal interdependence, especially in the post-industrial states of Western Europe, infuse large-scale movements of people with explosive political, socioeconomic, cultural, and transnational ramifications. The case of foreign workers in France documents the political and economic tensions inherent in the structural relations between France and her former North African colonies. The conspicuous and brooding presence of foreign laborers in France under conditions of decreasing affluence and increasing nativism makes equitable political decisions more difficult. Conversely, the ethnic ties that bind North African workers to their homelands are reinforced by large economic remittances and frustrated psychocultural desires for achieving upward mobility in the host country.

The ethnic ties that link France to North Africa suggest further structural dimensions of contemporary transnational relations: Western European reliance on poor, underdeveloped labor-exporting states during periods of economic prosperity; and the political, social, and economic problems that foreign workers present to Western European democracies during periods of economic stagnation or recession.[24] Ethnicity not only complicates already strained economic and political ties between center states and periphery states, it also infuses these conflicts with the potential for mobilizing collective group fears against the "foreigners."

Like Slater's analysis of the problem posed by France's foreign workers, James P. Piscatori's "The Formation of the Saʿūdī Identity: A Case Study of the Utility of Transnationalism" documents the embracing and dynamic consequences of transnational relations in intrastate, state, and global contexts. Piscatori emphasizes the importance of transnationalism in the difficult process of state-building and the utility of transnational appeals in the external relations of states. Traditional and revisionist assessments of state-building in Europe underscore the significant role played by transnational forces in the creation of states between 1500 and 1900.[25] Piscatori demonstrates the utility of transnational tactics in the process of building political legitimacy and nationalistic aspirations as well as in the difficult tasks of consolidating a state's political-military infrastructure. The further elaboration and application of this approach to state-building following the process of decolonization in the South and the trends toward fragmentation in the North would yield fruitful political insights, I suspect.

The second dimension of Piscatori's chapter is an examination of the extraordinary value of transnational appeals in a regional context—the Middle East. Saudi Arabian elites skillfully harnessed pan-Islamic sentiments to neutralize the militant assertion of Egypt's pan-Arabism in the early and middle years of the 1960s. By 1969, and during the 1970s, however, the Saudis fused pan-Islamic and pan-Arab sentiments into mutually reinforcing symbols of rising Saudi Arabian preeminence in a regional, and later global, setting. The Saudi manipulation of pan-Islamic and pan-Arab transnational values did not occur in a vacuum, of course: political, economic, and psychocultural factors directly informed the transnational direction of pan-Islam. The interplay between pan-Islamic sentiments and politics defined transnational relations on three levels: intrasocietal (tribal); state (the formation of a Saudi state via the royal family); and global (Saudi Arabian external relations in the Middle East and, after OPEC, throughout the world). Indeed, as Piscatori implies in his concluding remarks, Saudi Arabia illustrates the importance of transnational relations in the contemporary global system by pointing to the inherently transnational effects of the process of modernization (urbanization, "technification," and political development) that may ultimately and ironically destabilize the royal elite that so effectively manipulated transnational relations to its advantage.[26]

"Transnational Relations and Racial Mobilization: Emerging Black Movements in Brazil" by Pierre-Michel Fontaine underscores the central role played by structural factors in the creation of transnational relations. Fontaine argues that Brazilian economic and technological dependence on the United States provides opportunities for the mobilization of black protest movements in Brazil. Hence, the increasing visibility of overt anti-black racism in Brazil is, in part, stimulated by the economic bonds that bind Brazil to the United States and to other advanced industrial societies. As Brazil develops economically, the disparities between the Brazilian myth of racial egalitarianism and the imperatives of modern industrialization that exploit Brazil's racially subordinant black population become apparent.

The setting of the global political economy—the structural inequalities between advanced industrial societies of the North and upwardly mobile Third World states personified by Brazil—establishes the broader transnational parameters in which the

Brazilian oligarchy operates. The ultimate irony of Brazil's structural subordinance to the United States is that America's mass-produced and mass-marketed export culture—movies and music—heightens the racial and political awareness of blacks. Thus, the importation of American pop culture, like the central role played by U.S. technology in Brazilian industrial development, has important transnational implications. From this perspective, one of the most important consequences is the potential basis for racial conflict via the mass mobilization and politicization of Brazilian racial-protest movements. While Fontaine is careful to illustrate how contemporary Brazilian culture tends to inhibit the politicization of Brazilian blacks, his analysis, like those of Stack, Slater, and Piscatori, points to the potentially destabilizing and revolutionary consequences of ethnic and racial transnational relations that bypass formal state-authority patterns and directly intrude in the political, social, and economic affairs of states and regions.

The final chapter, David B. Kanin's "Ethnicity and the Politics of Cultural Exchange: Transnational Sport in the International System," illustrates the global dimensions of ethnic transnationalism. In the wake of sophisticated transportation and communication networks, Kanin analyzes how ethnicity directly intrudes into world politics. By underscoring the symbolic dimensions of ethnicity, particularly within the context of sports, Kanin demonstrates how nonstate actors maneuver to project particularistic concerns into domestic, regional, and global arenas.

It is especially fitting that the most embracing and politicized dimensions of contemporary ethnic transnationalism—Third World attempts to isolate fully South Africa from symbolic relations with other states through participation in international sporting events—illustrate the limitations of transnational actors in the the world of states. This is not to suggest the impotence of transnational actors on state or global levels. However, it does illustrate that transnational actors are themselves products of prevailing patterns of power and influence in world politics, even as they work to challenge the state system.

Finally, we must conclude with a caveat. Ethnicity and transnationalism have been attacked as "trendy" concepts—the newest fads of social-science inquiry—with little depth and no explanatory power. Ultimately, the refutation of such accusations rests with those who are working with these concepts. Before propositions and hypotheses can be formulated, a more elementary task must be undertaken: basic questions about ethnicity and transnationalism and their mutual interactions must be raised. That is the objective this book sets out to tackle; consequently, it is designed to serve as a guidepost—to offer preliminary assessments, to direct research, and to contribute to the task of further inquiry.

NOTES

1. The literature on transnational relations is enormous. Among the most influential pieces are: Karl Kaiser, "Transnational Politics: Toward a Theory of Multinational Politics," *International Organization* 25, no. 4 (Autumn 1971):790–817; Robert O. Keohane and Joseph S. Nye, eds., *Transnational Relations and World Politics* (Cambridge: Harvard University Press, 1971), especially the introductory and concluding chapters; Samuel P. Huntington, "Transnational Organizations in World Politics," *World Politics* 25, no. 3 (April 1973):333–67; Robert O. Keohane and Joseph S. Nye, "Transgovernmental Relations and International Organizations," *World Politics* 27, no. 4 (October 1974):39–69; Robert W. Cox and Harold Jacobson, eds., *The Anatomy of Influence: Decision Making in International Affairs* (New Haven: Yale University Press, 1974); Lawrence Juda, "A Note on Bureaucratic Politics and Transnational Relations," *International Studies Notes* 4, no. 2 (Summer 1977): 1-3; Herbert C. Kelman, "The Conditions, Criteria, and Dialectics of Human Dignity: A Transnational Perspective," *International Studies Quarterly* 21, no. 3 (September 1977):529–52; Robert O. Keohane and Joseph S. Nye, *Power and Interdependence: World Politics in Transition* (Boston: Little, Brown, 1977); K. J. Holsti, "A New International Politics? Diplomacy in Complex Interdependence," *International Organization* 32, no. 2 (Spring 1978):513–30; Richard R. Fagen, "A Funny Thing Happened on the Way to the Market: Thoughts on Extending Dependency Ideas," *International Organization* 32, no. 1 (Winter 1978):287–300; Wolfram F. Hanrieder, "Dissolving International Politics: Reflections on the Nation-State," *American Political Science Review* 72, no. 4 (December 1978):1276–87.

2. The literature has increased dramatically in recent years: Daniel Bell, "Ethnicity and Social Change," in Nathan Glazer and Daniel P. Moynihan, eds., *Ethnicity, Theory and Experience* (Cambridge: Harvard University Press, 1975), pp. 141-70; Wendell Bell and Walter E. Freeman, eds., *Ethnicity and Nation-Building: Comparative, International, and Historical Perspectives* (Beverly Hills, Calif.: Sage Publications, 1974), Judy S. Bertelsen, ed., *Nonstate Nations in International Politics: Comparative System Analyses* (New York: Praeger Publishers, 1977); Walker Connor, "Nation-Building or Nation-Destroying," *World Politics* 24, no. 3 (April 1972):319–55; Walker Connor, "The Politics of Ethnonationalism," *Journal of International Affairs* 27, no. 1 (1973):1–19; Leo A. Despres, ed., *Ethnicity and*

Resource Competition in Plural Societies (The Hague: Mouton Press, 1975); Rupert Emerson, *From Empire to Nation: The Rise to Self-Assertion of Asian and African Peoples* (Cambridge: Harvard University Press, 1960); Cynthia H. Enloe, *Ethnic Conflict and Political Development* (Boston: Little, Brown, 1973); Harold Isaacs, *Idols of the Tribe: Group Identity and Political Change* (New York: Harper and Row, 1975); Werner Link and Werner Feld, eds., *The New Nationalism: Implications for Transatlantic Relations* (New York: Pergamon, 1979); Philip Mason, *Patterns of Dominance* (London: Oxford University Press, 1970); Alvin Rabushka and Kenneth A. Shepsle, *Politics in Plural Societies: A Theory of Democratic Instability* (Columbus, Ohio: Charles E. Merrill Publishing, 1972); Abdul A. Said, ed., *Ethnicity and U.S. Foreign Policy* (New York: Praeger Publishers, 1977); Abdul A. Said and Luis R. Simmons, eds., *Ethnicity in an International Context: The Politics of Disassociation* (New Brunswick, N.J.: Transaction Books, 1976); R. A. Schermerhorn, *Comparative Ethnic Relations: A Framework for Theory and Research* (New York: Random House, 1970); George W. Shepherd, *Anti-Apartheid: Transnational Conflict and Western Policy in the Liberation of South Africa* (Westport, Conn.: Greenwood Press, 1977); Tamotsu Shibutani and Kian Kawn, *Ethnic Stratification: A Comparative Approach* (New York: Macmillan Co., 1965); John F. Stack, Jr., *International Conflict in an American City: Boston's Irish, Italians, and Jews, 1935-1944* (Westport, Conn.: Greenwood Press, 1979); Astri Suhrke and Lela Noble, eds., *Ethnic Conflict in International Relations* (New York: Praeger Publishers, 1977); Pierre L. Van den Berghe, *Race and Racism: A Comparative Perspective* (New York: John Wiley and Sons, 1967); Vernon Van Dyke, "The Individual, the State, and Ethnic Communities in Political Theory," *World Politics* 29, no. 2 (April 1977):342-69; Crawford Young, *The Politics of Cultural Pluralism* (Madison, Wis.: University of Wisconsin Press, 1976).

3. There are four recent efforts to link ethnicity to world politics. See: Astri Suhrke and Lela Noble, "Introduction," in Suhrke and Noble, *Ethnic Conflict in International Relations*, pp. 1-20; Judy S. Bertelsen, "An Introduction to the Study of Nonstate Nations in International Politics," in Bertelsen, *Nonstate Nations in International Politics*, pp. 1-5; Abdul A. Said and Luis R. Simmons, "The Ethnic Factor in World Politics," in Said and Simmons, *Ethnicity in an International Context*, pp. 15-47; and Ronald M. Grant and E. Spenser Wellhofer, eds., *Ethno-Nationalism, Multinational Corporations, and the Modern State* (Denver: Graduate School of International Studies Monograph Series on World Affairs, University of Denver, 1979).

4. Emerson, *From Empire to Nation*; Connor, "The Politics of Ethnonationalism," pp. 1-10.

5. Isaacs, *Idols of the Tribe*, p. 184; Werner Link, "Introduction," in Link and Feld, *The New Nationalism*, pp. 2-5.

6. Isaacs, *Idols of the Tribe*, pp. 11-17; Connor, "Nation-Building or Nation-Destroying," pp. 330-32; Emerson, *From Empire to Nation*, p. 60; Bertelsen, "Introduction," p. 2; Said and Simmons, "The Ethnic Factor in World Politics," pp. 24-29.

7. Connor, "Nation-Building or Nation-Destroying," pp. 319-55; and Isaacs, *Idols of the Tribe*, pp. 11-17.

8. See Edward L. Morse, *Modernization and the Transformation of International*

Politics (New York: The Free Press, 1976), pp. 114–50, for a thorough and provocative analysis of the permeability of states under conditions of modernization.

9. The concepts of sensitivity and vulnerability attempt to define precisely the role of power in interdependence. "Sensitivity involves degrees of responsiveness within a policy framework—how quickly do changes in one country bring costly changes in another, and how great are the costly effects? . . . Sensitivity interdependence is created by interactions within a framework of policies. . . . in terms of the costs of dependence, sensitivity means liability to costly effects imposed from outside before policies are altered to try to change the situation. Vulnerability can be defined as an actor's liability to suffer costs imposed by external events even after policies have been altered. Since it is usually difficult to change policies quickly, immediate effects of external changes generally reflect sensitivity dependence. Vulnerability dependence can be measured only by the costliness of making effective adjustments to a changed environment over a period of time. Keohane and Nye, *Power and Interdependence*, pp. 12–13.

10. Keohane and Nye's *Power and Interdependence* is the most ambitious conceptual analysis of the idea of interdependence. Scholars have also been concerned with clarifying the meaning of dependence and dependency. James A. Caporaso suggests an important distinction in "Introduction to the Special Issue of *International Organization* on Dependence and Dependency in the Global System," *International Organization* 32, no. 1 (Winter 1978), pp. 1–5. Caparoso argues that dependence suggests "external reliance on other actors," whereas dependency refers to "the process of incorporation of less developed countries (LDCs) into the global capitalist system and the 'structural distortions' resulting therefrom." The concept of dependency reinforces a transnational perspective through its emphasis on processes and structures outside formal interstate relations. The essential transnational quality of dependency is superbly presented in Johan Galtung, "A Structural Theory of Imperialism," *Journal of Peace Research* 2 (1971):81–117. A review article by Harry R. Targ further emphasizes the transnational aspects of relationships of dependency in world politics by building on the works of the *dependencia* school and linking it to the studies of post-industrialism proposed by Daniel Bell, H. Hveem, Jacques Ellul, and Theodore Roszak. Targ argues that transnational relations are a fundamental component of an evolving global dominance system. See "Global Dominance and Dependence, Post-Industrialism, and International Relations Theory: A Review," *International Studies Quarterly* 20, no. 3 (September 1976):461–82.

11. Keohane and Nye, *Power and Interdependence*, pp. 24–29.

12. Joan Spero, *The Politics of International Economic Relations* (New York: St. Martin's Press, 1977), pp. 1–18; and Keohane and Nye, *Power and Interdependence*, pp. 23, 33.

13. Keohane and Nye, *Power and Interdependence*, pp. 221–42; even as forceful a critic of the concept of transnational relations as Hedley Bull concedes that the global political system has been modified in the last two decades. See *The Anarchical Society* (New York: Columbia University Press, 1977), pp. 277–81.

14. Robert O. Keohane and Joseph S. Nye, Jr., "Transnational Relations and World Politics: An Introduction," in Keohane and Nye, *Transnational Relations and World Politics*, p. xii.

15. Cynthia H. Enloe, personal letter, March 15, 1978.

16. An essay by Daniel Bell, "Ethnicity and Social Change," pp. 141–70, explicitly points to the linkages between ethnicity and post-industrial society in the post-World War II period. His analysis points to the utility of a transnational perspective.

17. Cynthia H. Enloe, personal letter, March 15, 1978.

18. Juda, "A Note on Bureaucratic Politics and Transnational Relations," p. 2.

19. Louis Gerson, *The Hyphenate in Recent American Politics and Diplomacy* (Lawrence, Kans.: University of Kansas Press, 1964), is the classic example of this approach.

20. Robert Jervis, *Perception and Misperception in International Politics* (Princeton: Princeton University Press, 1976).

21. See Milton M. Gordon, *Assimilation in American Life: The Role of Race, Religion, and National Origins* (New York: Oxford University Press, 1964); Marcus Lee Hansen, *The Immigrant in American History* (Cambridge: Harvard University Press, 1940).

22. Oscar Handlin, *The Uprooted* (Boston: Little, Brown, 1952; John Higham, *Strangers in the Land: Patterns of American Nativism 1860–1925* (New York: Atheneum, 1974); Richard Hofstadter, *The Age of Reform: From Bryan to F.D.R.* (New York: Vintage Books, 1955).

23. Nathan Glazer and Daniel P. Moynihan, "Introduction" in Glazer and Moynihan, *Ethnicity, Theory and Experience*, pp. 23–25.

24. Bell, "Ethnicity and Social Change," pp. 151–52; and William Petersen, "On the Subnations of Western Europe," in Glazer and Moynihan, *Ethnicity, Theory and Experience*, pp. 176–208.

25. See Immanuel Wallerstein, *The Modern World-System: Capitalist Agriculture and the Origins of the European World-Economy in the Sixteenth Century* (New York: Academic Press, 1976); Charles Tilly, ed., *The Formation of Nation States in Western Europe* (Princeton: Princeton University Press, 1975); and Bull, *The Anarchical Society*.

26. Morse, in *Modernization and the Transformation of International Relations*, presents the most extensive analysis of the revolutionary force of modernization in the contemporary global system.

JOHN F. STACK, JR.*

Ethnic Groups as Emerging Transnational Actors

2

In a recent volume attempting to demonstrate the significant role played by ethnic groups in world politics, Abdul A. Said and Luis R. Simmons suggest that:

As emerging actors in the international system, they [the ethnic group and the emerging neoethnic group] are indications that our perceptions of international relations and the causes of war and peace lag behind the consciousness of the men and nations we study. The ethnic nation cannot yet compete with the state in nuclear warheads and warships, but it continues to exercise formidable influence over the primary authority patterns of men. It is from this exercise of power that revolutions are born.[1]

Said and Simmons provide an essential insight when they correctly credit the ethnic group with the ability "to exercise formidable influence over the primary authority patterns of men." These primary authority patterns stand independent of the physical boundaries of nation-states. The "independence" of ethnic identity rests in its social-psychological dynamics and in the lack of congruence between ethnic nations and the geographical and political boundaries of states.[2] Thus, ethnic groups throughout the world offer their members two crucial elements usually identified with traditional

*I wish to express my gratitude to Cynthia H. Enloe, Joyce R. Lilie, James P. Piscatori, Mark B. Rosenberg, and the late Fred A. Sondermann for their comments on earlier drafts of this manuscript.

nineteenth-century European nationalism: an effective group identity; and the psychosocial sustenance of affective ties, a sense of peoplehood, self-esteem, and interdependence of fate.[3] This sense of belonging and/or peoplehood forms the basis of ethnicity. It is reinforced by racial, religious, linguistic, and cultural differences, providing group members with a distinctive identity or world view. Ethnicity is a subjective identity that clearly distinguishes between group members and outsiders. The ethnic group, therefore, comprises the realm of primordial identities to which men and women have increasingly turned throughout the 1960s and 1970s both in developing and in developed states.

Emphasis on the subjective aspects of the ethnic group should not obscure its relationship with the external environment. Specific conditions account for the resurgence of ethnic identity throughout the world. For example, the ethnic group is a significant basis for group cleavage in many advanced industrial societies because ethnic identity is an effective means of group mobilization. The ethnic group becomes an efficient vehicle for expressing demands for group advantage—power, status, and wealth—in the political system. In the face of increasingly technocratic and bureaucratic industrial societies, the ethnic group combines utilitarian interests with affective attachments. The salience of ethnicity is only heightened because other bases of group mobilization have declined in recent years (most notably, ideological and class ties). Consequently, the ethnic group has become a crucial social and political variable in many advanced industrial societies.[4]

In developing countries, strains of economic development and social mobilization underscore the key role played by ethnic groups. Political order and the continued viability of the state frequently depend on a delicate balance of power among competing ethnic groups. The internationalization of ethnicity—a process fueled by global economic, technological, and communication networks—heightens the salience of ethnic groups in both developed and developing societies.

Ethnic groups surely do not rival states in military capabilities or in the accouterments of coercive state power, though they can weaken or divert them. But ethnic groups do challenge the legitimacy heretofore reserved for states in a great many countries throughout the world. The strains that domestic ethnic groups impose on state authority transcend the formal boundaries of countries, thereby projecting ethnicity directly into the world political arena. The ethnic factor in contemporary world politics assumes its present transnational hue because of unprecedented levels of systemic interdependence.[5] "Ethnic groups are often shaped or influenced by the larger milieu (micro affected by macro) and . . . . ethnic considerations often transcend the traditional state boundaries and operate as at least quasi-independent variables in the international system (macro affected by micro)."[6] It is the vastly expanded scope and intensity of these multileveled interactions (micro and macro processes) that make ethnicity a suitable subject of transnational relations.[7]

The task confronting students of world politics is to begin thinking about these different levels of analysis from an explicitly transnational perspective. The challenge is a demanding one because it is no longer adequate merely to identify transnational actors. It is essential that we begin the task of analyzing the independent-dependent variable status of ethnicity in the contemporary global environment and relate it to those global structures and processes that interact with states. Therefore, the purpose of this chapter is to analyze the transnational dimensions of ethnicity on three levels.

First, the intrasocietal level alerts us to interactions between societies without the direct intervention of state decision-making elites. The intrasocietal level investigates the impact of global communication processes on the intensification of ethnicity within a state. For example, civil rights activists in Northern Ireland in the mid-1960s employed the protest techniques developed by American blacks in the United States during the 1950s and early 1960s. Moreover, the coverage of events in Northern Ireland by the world's mass media, especially the political and military repression of the Irish civil rights movement by the governments of Northern Ireland and Great Britain, legitimated the struggle for political rights while reestablishing ethnic linkages between the beleaguered Irish of Ulster and their ethnic brethren in England, Canada, and the United States.

Second, the state level conceptualizes ethnic groups as direct participants in world politics, particularly the ways in which ethnic groups interact with states and other international actors. An illustration of this process is the threat that ethnic terrorism poses to the sovereignty of states and the stability of international law. The reception accorded to Palestine Liberation Organization (PLO) leader Yasir Arafat by the United Nations General Assembly in 1974 is another example of how ethnic groups can directly participate in the state system (comprised of state and intergovernmental organizations) in the contemporary transnational political environment.

Third, the global level of analysis studies ethnicity as an independent transnational force. It is most concerned with how increasing levels of worldwide interdependence and dependence affect the prospects for the intensification or attenuation of ethnicity throughout the world. This level of analysis sees the evolution of a global transnational system as providing ethnicity with a significance, perhaps a quasi-independent variable status, that simply is not possible in a global system defined solely by the activities of states. Ultimately, this approach addresses a number of questions relating to the structural transformations of contemporary international politics. Will the salience of ethnic affiliations diminish as a global mass culture evolves based on increasingly powerful and sophisticated levels of technology? How does the widening gap in basic living conditions between the North and the South affect the nature of ethnic relations within and between these societies? How will ethnicity be manipulated by elites of the North and the South?

THE INTRASOCIETAL LEVEL: ETHNIC GROUPS AS REFLECTIONS OF AN EVOLVING TRANSNATIONAL SYSTEM

Scholars began to recognize the significant role played by ethnicity in world politics during the late 1960s and early 1970s. While few linked ethnicity to an explicitly transnational perspective, a number argued that the ethnic group constituted an increasingly important social and political variable throughout the world.[8]

Traditional analyses of international politics, by contrast, de-emphasized the global implications of ethnicity by exclusively focusing on the intrastate dynamics of ethnic groups.[9] From a transnational perspective, the resurgence of ethnicity throughout the world appears to be tied to the global environment in two respects: (1) through the politicization of global communication and transportation networks; and (2) in accelerating patterns of political and cultural fragmentation.[10] This is not to suggest that states are of little consequence in determining the dynamics of ethnicity, but rather to emphasize the increasing intrusion of the international environment in the domestic arena of states.

ETHNIC GROUPS AND THE GLOBAL MASS MEDIA

Dramatic increases in the scope and intensity of intergroup contacts via technological advancements help to transform contemporary world politics by facilitating the creation of networks of transnational ties among ethnic groups around the world. Vastly expanded communication and transportation networks reduce the control a state exercises over its internal environment. The extent of global penetration in domestic politics provides ethnic groups with greater opportunities for transnational interactions: the exchange of ideas, information, wealth, and political strategies. Undoubtedly, these highly politicized communication networks provide the basis for powerful demonstration effects to occur. During the late 1960s, television facilitated student protests throughout North America and Western Europe. The mass media focused attention on common problems and dissatisfactions, which resulted in a politicization of student protests on both continents.

There appears to have been an equally powerful demonstration effect at work among ethnic groups in the 1970s. As Walker Connor argues: "There is an inbuilt accelerator in the technological advances and other forces that causes a continuous 'shrinking of world' and the shrinking of its states as presently defined. The frequency and pervasiveness of intergroup contacts appear, therefore, to be fated to increase exponentially, regardless of the planner."[11] The proliferation of terrorist tactics among ethnic groups—Irish, Palestinian, Corsican, Croatian, Puerto Rican—documents the influence of a highly politicized mass media. The internationalization of the mass media has provided ethnic groups with a new tool for mobilization and for potential survival. The irony is that the very process (the internationalization of the mass media) that makes groups like Yugoslavs, Croatians or French Corsicans seem more "parochial" than ever is, in fact, a process that is giving them new life. Between

1949 and 1969, there were an average of five hijackings per year.[12] The number rose to more than sixty annually in the early 1970s.[13] Between 1970 and 1976, over five hundred major acts of international terrorism had been recorded.[14] For ethnic groups with limited resources, terrorist tactics are a cheap, effective strategy for articulating demands and grievances before a global audience.

Television gives the terrorist instant access to the world's living rooms, thereby enabling him to draw global attention to his cause. The mobility offered by the modern jet aircraft allows him to strike at will almost anywhere in the world and then move on to safe asylum. Hence, advances in technology have made it possible for a large society to be directly affected by a small band of terrorists.[15]

Quite aside from the existence of a powerful demonstration effect, the intensity and sophistication of the global mass media may stimulate and reinforce ethnic identities across state lines. Highly politicized communication networks provide groups with the attributes of ethnicity, not through a common historical tradition that usually includes the immigration experience, but through a more synthetic process of rapid ideological and political conversion. The Japanese Red Army perpetrated the infamous Lod Airport massacre of May 1972 in the name of Palestinian liberation.[16] The Croatian Ustasha terrorists have collaborated with the Macedonian IRMO.[17] A similar dynamic may have motivated the Hanafi Muslims' rampage in Washington, D.C., in May 1977. These transnational processes constitute a type of *psychological immigration* in which artificial images and self-perceptions replace more traditional components of ethnicity—a common culture rooted in historical experiences.

The Hanafi Muslims, for example, inherit some semblance of a common outlook from the Nation of Islam, a mass separatist movement of poor, urban black Americans established during the 1920s.[18] Unlike the genuinely pan-African orientation of Marcus Garvey's back-to-Africa movement, the Hanafi Muslim ties to viable pan-African and pan-Arab cultural traditions are tenuous at best.[19] Thus, the movement "psychologically" looked to Africa and the Middle East for cultural ties, but it remained predominantly a by-product of the disillusionment and dissatisfaction of a poor, urban black American culture. While the Hanafi Muslims do not possess a coherent, historically defined Islamic cultural tradition, they nonetheless share a profoundly "psychological" identification with Islam at the same time that they share extremist political values. The intensity of communication networks is sufficient to support claims to an ethnic "destiny" linking the Hanafi Muslims with terrorist groups throughout the world. Consciousness of kind, however synthetic, is a by-product of an instantaneous and visceral mass media—hence, the extraordinary spectacle of three Muslim ambassadors to the United States reading from the Koran and assisting in the release of the 134 hostages captured by the Hanafi terrorists.

While the politicization of transnational communication and transportation networks contributes to the heightening of ethnicity in world politics, it is not sufficient to explain the extent to which ethnicity is a significant variable in world affairs. As Connor points out: "Perhaps an even more important factor in explaining the recent upsurge of militant ethnic consciousness in advanced as well as less advanced states involves not the nature or density of the communications media, but the message."[20] Indeed, the substance of the message reveals much about the way that accelerating patterns of worldwide political and cultural fragmentation have resulted in rising ethnic consciousness throughout the world. With the establishment of Afro-Asian states in the late 1950s and early 1960s, two concurrent trends have characterized world politics: the steady increase in systemic interdependence;[21] and the progressive fragmentation of the world along political, cultural, and ideological lines. Ironically, technological developments simultaneously fuel trends toward systemic interdependence and fragmentation.[22]

The world is unquestionably more interrelated than ever before in economic relations, agricultural production, resource dependence, and technological developments. Trends toward global homogenization in these areas have proceeded at accelerating rates since World War II. One consequence of homogenization is a recognition of similarities as well as differences among collectivities, be they regions, states, or ethnic groups. Differences based on industrialization, wealth, ideology, or ethnicity become more obvious. Cognizance of these differences may generate situations in which expectations and demands cannot be fulfilled. Conflict is a likely end product.[23]

ETHNIC GROUPS AND GLOBAL POLITICAL FRAGMENTATION

Perhaps the most powerful rationale for political fragmentation lies in the ideological arena. The principle of self-determination serves as a justification for fragmentation based on ethnic diversity. This is a particularly acute problem in Third World nations that are multiethnic by definition since political borders were established by colonial administrators rather than by indigenous ethnic groups.[24]

In addition, the pace of political, economic, and social change throughout the Third World exacerbated ethnic cleavages. The quest for political order is a difficult struggle at best. Increasing communication and transportation networks heighten dissatisfactions with economic and social conditions while fueling rivalries among diverse groups; polarization among diverse groups is likely to occur.

Finally, urbanization, economic growth, social mobility, and the lack of it (marginalization) tend to destabilize a precarious balance of power among competing ethnic groups. The absence of a stable political order and of common cultural values makes prospects of political disintegration acute.

This fragmentation of human society is a pervasive fact in human affairs and always has been. It persists and increases in our own time as part of an ironic, painful, and dangerous paradox: the more global our science and technology, the more tribal our politics; the more universal our system of communication, the less we know what to communicate; the closer we get to other planets, the less able we become to lead a tolerable existence on our own; the more it becomes apparent that human beings cannot decently survive with their separateness, the more separate they become. In the face of an ever more urgent need to pool the world's resources and its powers, human society is splitting itself into smaller and smaller fragments.[25]

Unquestionably, this fragmentation has come at a high cost. One authority estimates that thirty-four major ethnic conflicts have occurred between 1945 and 1967. And it has been suggested that the number of deaths resulting from such conflicts surpassed the ten-million mark in 1974.

If we take the matter down in scale from open warfare or large-scale massacres to ethnic/cultural conflicts marked by sporadic riots, bombings, and other collisions and clashes, the list swells from scores into hundreds. If we add those situations around the world where tension and strain exist between and among groups producing acts of violence in new political settings, the number could hardly be guessed, for here we would have to include every country in which a changing political order has to try to strike new balances among contending tribal/racial/ethnic/religious/national groups. And this now means virtually every country on every continent.[26]

Ethnic conflicts are not confined to states undergoing the strains of modernization. Neither the modernization of the nation-state nor the modernization of the international order is a guarantee of ethnic conflict. Historically well-integrated nations and regions have witnessed the reintensification of ethnic attachments and outbursts of ethnic conflict. The very pace of industrialization in the West is itself a powerful transnational force. Additionally, a number of structural features of the global system contribute to the rise of ethnicity in advanced industrial countries.

First, technological innovations in communication and transportation processes bind advanced industrial societies together as never before. Not only is the impact of demonstration effects heightened, but the scope and intensity of intrasocietal penetration has reached unprecedented levels. As Daniel Bell writes:

I think it is more true because of a simple and fundamental structural change in the world community: new and larger networks and ties within and between societies have been woven by communication and transportation, shocks and upheavals are felt more readily and immediately, and reactions and feedbacks come more quickly in response to social changes.[27]

The evolving transnational dynamics of world politics transcend "mere" demonstration effects from an ethnic perspective, however. Intrasocietal penetration contributes to the strengthening of ethnicity throughout the global environment. French-Canadian separatists are not unmindful of the battles waged by Basque, Welsh, or Irish nationalists.

Moreover, transnational linkages supply ethnic groups with

vital resources necessary to carry on their struggles: information, money, weapons, and moral support. For example, the American civil rights movement served as a useful prototype for the civil rights movements in Northern Ireland during the mid-1960s. The tactics, strategies, and goals of the American movement were effectively utilized by Irish advocates of nonviolence to challenge the legitimacy of the Ulster regime.[28]

Second, the salience of ethnicity in advanced industrial states results from the steady expansion of "political boundaries and arenas."[29] There has been a progressive expansion of the political arena in advanced societies, particularly since World War II. Economics, social-welfare policy, and religious issues assume an intensely politicized dimension. Bell describes these characteristics of advanced industrial societies as." . . . the increase in the number of actors and claimants in a political arena; the challenges to present-day distribution of place and privilege; and the questioning of the normative justifications and legitimations which have sanctioned the status quo."[30] As the political arena becomes the central focal point of life in industrialized countries, the ethnic *group* becomes an essential vehicle for placing group demands on the political process. As the political process achieves more complexity, the ability of an individual to exert political influence in an advanced society decreases. Thus, the ethnic group becomes an instrumental or strategic device to protect and promote group interests. Moreover, the achievements of ethnic groups in one country reinforce the legitimacy of ethnic politics in another country.[31]

Third, the trend toward "more inclusive identities" in advanced industrial states reintensifies the search for communal attachments. Ethnic and regional groups have established their own lobbying offices in Brussels in order to have influence on the European Economic Community. Industrial societies are increasingly urban, bureaucratic, and remote from the masses of their citizens. As the necessity of communal mobilization to place demands on the political system becomes urgent, so, too, does the need to escape the alienation and rootlessness of modern life. The ethnic group is a repository of common traditions that can be tapped to provide affective and primordial dimensions of a group's life history. Ethnic identity, therefore, fulfills fundamental needs for a communal identity and serves as a viable strategy "to become a means of gaining place or advantage" in advanced industrial societies.[32] The very process of industrialization in the West since World War II constitutes a profoundly influential transnational force. Ethnicity is one consequence of those embracing transnational dimensions of modern industrial life.

THE STATE LEVEL: ETHNIC GROUPS AS DIRECT PARTICIPANTS IN WORLD POLITICS

The second level of analysis suggests that ethnic groups participate directly in world politics through their involvement with states and other international actors. The central assumption is that the structure and institutions of the state system facilitate the multiple roles played by ethnic groups as significant transnational actors. From this perspective, the state system establishes two conditions that provide ethnic groups with unprecedented influence in international politics. First, the state system legitimates ethnicity as a key social and political variable in world politics. Second, the progressive blurring of lines between a state's foreign policy and its domestic policy facilitates the prominence of ethnic groups as transnational actors.[33]

ETHNIC GROUPS AND THE SEARCH FOR LEGITIMACY

The interaction between the state system and ethnicity is accounted for by two specific factors: the collective legitimacy function of international organizations, particularly the United Nations; and the significance of ideology. The collective legitimacy function of internationational organizations has been analyzed in detail by Inis L. Claude.[34] The United States utilized the technique of creating enormous pluralities to support its anti-Communist stance throughout the 1950s during the most intense years of the cold war. The United States hoped that the General Assembly resolutions that it sponsored would come to be seen as the collective will of most of the world's states. Implicit within this perspective was the belief that international organizations could both generate and legitimate international norms and values. With the influx of "new" states into the United Nations in the wake of the decolonization process, especially between

1955 and 1966, the collective legitimacy function of the United Nations was increasingly, if not exclusively, utilized to the advantage of Third World states. It is within this context that the interplay between ethnic groups and international organizations is most explicit. The case of the Palestinians is perhaps the most suggestive because of the number and intensity of transnational interactions.[35]

The Palestinians have historically attempted to legitimate their political aspirations within the United Nations and other international organizations. Each major crisis in recent Middle East politics has raised the issue of the status of the Palestinians, but none more so than the 1973 Arab-Israeli War. Yasir Arafat, in the wake of the Rabat summit's endorsement of the PLO as the "sole legitimate representative of the Palestinian People," was triumphantly received at the United Nations when he addressed the General Assembly on November 13, 1974. The granting of observer status to the PLO at the UN and at several specialized agencies has enhanced the organization's position and has accelerated the process by which its legitimacy has been acknowledged by such other political actors as the European Economic Community. Although the General Assembly has refused to expel Israel from its ranks, it has symbolically expressed approval of Palestinian aspirations with its vote to equate Zionism with racism. By linking their demands to the anticolonialist stance of the General Assembly, and by asserting their claims to ethnic self-determination in the global arena, the Palestinians have contributed to the politicization of ethnicity transnationally. The UN, the Organization of African Unity (OAU), the Arab League, and other international and regional organizations have been effective forums for legitimating the Palestinian appeals throughout the global environment.

The manipulation of the state system through ideology has been a potent tool of ethnic groups in transnational struggles with states. Ethnic appeals are themselves legitimated by the state system at least "theoretically" rooted in such principles as self-determination and sovereignty. Indeed, ethnic groups very skillfully draw on symbols and images that lend themselves to ideological expression. Thus, ethnicity becomes an end in itself—the ultimate search for individual and collective identity. This perspective is suggested by Frantz Fanon's impassioned essay, *The Wretched of the Earth*. Fanon places the struggle for decolonization within the larger context of the search for individual and collective identities.[36] In so doing, Fanon provides an ideological rationale for ethnic conflict. The destruction of colonialism becomes an essential means of achieving an authentic sense of peoplehood. The IRA, Bengalis, Eritreans, Bantus, and South Moluccans have sought to justify their struggles because of the legitimacy of ethnic aspirations, be they racial, linguistic, religious, or nationalist.

ETHNIC GROUPS AMID THE CONVERGENCE OF A STATE'S DOMESTIC AND FOREIGN POLITICS

The manipulation of the state system through international organizations and ideology is one process that permits ethnic groups to serve as transnational actors in world politics. A second process is the progressive blurring of a state's foreign and domestic politics in both advanced industrial societies and Third World states. Distinctions between high politics (intensely politicized issue areas such as national defense, political stability, and economic autonomy) and low politics (primarily technical and bureaucratic concerns) are no longer valid.[37] Economic interdependence encompasses every area of a state's vital national interests: defense, political stability, and the quality of life generally. The mere existence of interdependence makes advanced industrial societies permeable and thus vulnerable to external manipulation. The outbursts of terrorism in Western Europe, especially West Germany and Italy, vividly document these trends. In Great Britain, the impact of the Irish Republican Army was facilitated by networks linking the IRA in Belfast, Dublin, and London. Cooperation between the governments of Britain and the Irish Republic has limited the actions of the IRA in recent years.[38] However, transnational ties among the Irish Republican Army and sympathizers in the United States, the Irish Republic, Northern Ireland, and Britain largely account for its survival in the face of intensifying governmental opposition in these states.[39] The activities of the IRA do not threaten the viability of the Irish Republic and the United Kingdom at the present time. The degree of interdependence among these societies does make them susceptible to manipulation by ethnic groups with transnational ties, particularly if terrorism is involved, as the activities of the IRA document. Thus, the structural interdependence of advanced industries societies provides ethnic groups with the means to become transnational actors.

Lines between foreign and domestic politics are also blurred in the Third World, and the reasons for the blurring differ from those of advanced industrial societies. Despite the difficulty of generalizing about the foreign-policymaking processes in the Third World, a number of structural features of world politics account for the interdependence of foreign and domestic politics.[40] In advanced industrial states, foreign and domestic politics intermesh because of the primacy of economic interdependence. In developing societies, foreign and domestic politics merge because of the centrality of the political arena in the process of development. Nearly every major problem confronting Third World political development has profound domestic and external consequences. The decolonization process affected every significant segment of Third World politics. Similarly, current demands by the Third World states for the establishment of a new international economic order have major implications for the conduct of foreign and domestic politics.

In this environment, ethnicity may play a critical role in both foreign and domestic policymaking. Intrastate and regional patterns of ethnic conflict impinge on the domestic politics of many Third World states. Racism and intensifying repression in South Africa and Rhodesia are salient issues in the foreign and domestic politics of every African country. Conversely, ethnic conflict in one country— Lebanon, for example—can become central foreign and domestic issues throughout regional and global systems. Similarly, Muslim unrest in the Philippines is a matter of grave importance for the foreign policies of many Arab states. Indeed, the convergence of foreign and domestic politics in the Middle East facilitates the rise of the Palestinians as transnational actors.

Historically, Arab governments have attempted to use Palestinian organizations for their own political ends. Because the Palestinians are a significant variable in the internal and external affairs of every Middle East country, Arab states have tried to control Palestinian organizations in order to maintain control over their own foreign and domestic politics.[41] The PLO was founded in 1964 by Egypt; it was designed to be "Nasser's docile instrument."[42] Syria and Egypt created the Popular Democratic Front for the Liberation of Palestine

(PDFLP) in December 1967.[43] Iraq established the Arab Liberation Front (FLA) in 1968. Syria promoted the establishment of Saiqa ("Lightening") in 1968.[44] In March 1970, the Communist parties of Jordan, Syria, and Iraq formed the "Partisan Forces" with Moscow's blessing.[45] Perhaps the best example of the convergence of international and domestic policymaking is Syrian's use of Saiqa to advance its own foreign-policy goals of creating a rough equilibrium in Lebanon.

The political fortunes of these Palestinian organizations were tied to the successes and failures of the Arab states. In the face of Israeli military and political victories in 1956, 1967, and 1973, Palestinian organizations have often dissociated themselves from the policies pursued by Arab governments. Moreover, the organizations have emerged with enhanced prestige among the Palestinian people throughout the Middle East. Conversely, during times when the Arab states have maintained the status quo, the Palestinian organizations have escalated the level of violence in order to influence the foreign and domestic policies of Arab states. The centrality of the Palestinian issue to the internal stability of Middle East states permits the Palestinians to exert formidable influence on domestic and foreign policy, particularly in Kuwait and Lebanon.[46]

Furthermore, the blurring of lines between foreign and domestic policy allows Palestinian organizations to "widen cleavages between and among states."[47] Ideological, political, and military cleavages divide Arab leaders and states, and the extent of the rivalry and competition enhances the influence of the Palestinians. Palestinian organizations, the PLO, for example, become crucial actors in the delicate balance of power between Egypt, Jordan, and Syria. These organizations often possess a freedom of action that contrasts with the foreign policies of Egypt, Syria, and other states.

The Palestinians have not restricted their political and military goals to the Middle East. They have participated in world politics by expanding the arena of the Middle East conflict to include the global environment through two strategies. First, the Palestinians have increasingly worked through the United Nations General Assembly.[48] With the support of Arab governments, the Palestinians have exploited Third World resentment with the West, particularly after the Arab oil embargo of 1973–1974. Second, Palestianian organizations have expanded the arena of the conflict to include third parties outside the Middle East.[49] It was the specter of the "hijacker-kidnapper" that symbolized the intensity of Palestinian frustration to the world.[50] With considerable success, Palestinian groups have resorted to terrorist tactics to keep the Palestinian issue before a captive world audience. The murder of Israeli athletes at the Munich Olympic Games (August 1972), the Lod Airport massacre (May 1972), the scheme to destroy oil depots in Singapore (January 1974), the kidnapping of OPEC officials (December 1975), and the Entebbe hijacking (August 1976) document these trends.[51] Moreover, collaboration with such radical terrorist groups as Black September and the Japanese Red Army expanded the Middle East conflict to embrace the world.

The attacks on targets other than Israel seemed designed to prevent nation-states outside the Middle East from dismissing the Palestinian Arabs as a "domestic problem" of Israel and her neighboring Arab states. Further, the moves seemed aimed at convincing all countries that the problem cannot be solved by either attacking or ignoring the Palestinian Arab goals.[52]

Systemic interdependence also links Palestinians with other ethnic groups such as the Irish, Basques, and Croatians. There remains the possibility of the further globalization of ethnicity if these organizations collaborate to launch further transnational strategies.

THE GLOBAL LEVEL: ETHNICITY AS A TRANSNATIONAL FORCE

The third level of analysis hypothesizes that ethnicity may be conceptualized as an evolving transnational force. Two trends in world politics, perhaps not fully developed at this time, promote ethnicity on a global level: (1) the proliferation of transnational actors, for example, multinational corporations; and (2) evolving patterns of interdependence, dependency, and global dominance throughout the world system.

ETHNICITY AND MULTINATIONAL CORPORATIONS

As important global actors, multinational corporations (MNCs) facilitate the rise of ethnicity as a transnational force. Multinational corporations are not restrained by the traditional attributes of state sovereignty, such as territoriality and nationalism. In contrast to states, MNCs are free-wheeling entities that directly interact with ethnic groups throughout the global system. In so doing, MNCs "have far reaching consequences for ethnic identities and interethnic distributions of power."[53] Multinationals suggest possible trends in world politics whereby transnational actors directly affect the political and economic stratification of ethnic groups within states and regions. Therefore, the internationalization of ethnicity underscores, not only the tangible political and economic roles played by ethnic groups, but also the legal and political standing of ethnicity as a transnational force in a world of states.

In the Third World, multinational corporations must deal with governments frequently dominated by one ethnic group whose main concern is to insure its own political and economic dominance.[54] As such, MNCs explicitly confront ethnic questions when they negotiate for licenses, for access to markets, and for exploitation of natural resources.[55] The superordinate ethnic group seeks to insure its position of political and economic dominance. The multinational corporation, therefore, becomes a vehicle for expanding the political and economic control of a country's ethnic elite. For example, multinational corporations require governmental support to exploit remote regions of a country. MNCs become a prime vehicle in extending governmental control over remote sections of a country as they open up demographic, economic, and technological lines of communication with the hinterland.[56] Moreover, MNCs provide governments with significant bases of political and economic power.

In Indonesia, for example, Japanese-, American-, European-, and Canadian-dominated multinational corporations exacerbate communal cleavages between groups as they search for natural resources in the islands outside central Java.[57] As MNCs penetrate isolated territories, political and economic power accrues to the Javanese-dominated central government.[58] When International Nickle

Corporation began mining operations in remote Sulawesi, Javanese-Sulawesi tensions increased.[59] Thus, the MNC became a potent vehicle for extending governmental control over a subordinate ethnic group.

Multinational corporations effectively manipulate ethnicity to advance their interests. Throughout Southeast Asia, Japanese MNCs have strengthened the economic power of the overseas Chinese.[60] Japanese-dominated multinational corporations view the Chinese as the "most competent businessmen" with whom to deal.[61] Moreover, the Chinese have earned the trust of the Japanese through years of association.[62] The Japanese-Chinese partnership in Southeast Asia increases ethnic tensions between the overseas Chinese and indigenous ethnic groups in Thailand, Indonesia, Malaysia, and the Philipines.[63] Nationalists in these countries charge that Japanese MNCs' involvement with the overseas Chinese breeds corruption and "bureaucratic anarchy" since the Chinese must pay off local governmental officials to advance the interests of multinational enterprises.[64] In Southeast Asia, multinational corporations effectively utilize ethnicity as a strategy for economic and, hence, political penetration of "soft" states such as Indonesia.

The case of South Africa illustrates how multinational corporations reinforce systems of domestic ethnic stratification while contributing to global, regional, and domestic instability. Despite the risks that overt racism imposes on the long-term stability of the South African regime, multinational corporations have continued to invest heavily in South Africa.[65] The economic and technological benefits of MNCs' investments in South Africa reinforce the tyrannical Afrikaner subjugation of the black masses.[66] By reinforcing a state of *de facto* slavery, multinational corporations support the regional leverage of the South African regime over neighboring poor black states. Furthermore, multinational corporations, because of their multilateral organization and worldwide networks, provide South Africa with access to the developed world in the face of increasing political isolation. Ultimately, the consequences of MNCs' support for the South African regime affect prospects of global stability.

Multinational corporations also have significant impact on fragile ethnic relationships in historically developed states. In Belgium, the investments of MNCs have profoundly affected political relationships between the Flemings and the Walloons.[67] The French-speaking Walloons of southern Belgium traditionally controlled the country's political and economic systems. Since World War II, Walloonia has experienced declining coal and steel industries as well as rising levels of economic unrest.[68] From 1950, American multinational corporations have invested heavily in Flemish-speaking Flanders.[69] Patterns of multinational investments help to account for the political and economic ascendancy of the Flemings. The shifting ethnic balance of power results in ethnic conflicts that threaten Belgium's political stability.[70] "To talk about growing tensions between Walloons and Flemings with reference only to birth rates and political party splits, and to make no mention of General Motors, Monsanto and Chemical Bank of New York, is to leave a gaping hole in our understanding of ethnic politics in Belgium."[71] Systematic investigations of MNCs' involvements in other advanced industrial states would probably provide further data on the interplay between multinational corporations and ethnicity.

From a broader perspective, the activities of multinational corporations may foreshadow the interactions between other transnational actors and ethnic groups in the future. MNCs are perhaps the most obvious examples because of their significant economic power, worldwide communication networks, and nonterritorial status. In a global system characterized by increasing levels of systemic interdependence among advanced industrial states, and of asymmetrical relations between them and the poor, underdeveloped countries of the third and fourth worlds, it becomes apparent that international organizations—intergovernmental; supranational (the European Economic Community, EEC, or the International Monetary Fund, IMF); and nongovernmental (MNCs, private research and development firms, and foundations)—are central actors with whom ethnic groups will increasingly interact. Patterns of ethnic stratification within regions and societies, therefore, are likely to become critical variables in assessing the political strategies of international organizations as well as of states.

ETHNICITY AND WORLD POLITICS IN TRANSITION:
INTERDEPENDENCE, DEPENDENCY, AND GLOBAL DOMINANCE

Evolving patterns of systemic interdependence, dependency, and global dominance constitute the second approach that illustrates the transnational dimensions of ethnicity in world politics.

Ethnicity and Interdependence

The recognition that the contemporary global system is moving toward greater levels of interdependence, particularly among advanced industrial societies, suggests the possibility that ethnicity may become an integral part of a more egalitarian world order. As we have pointed out throughout this chapter, trends toward interdependence affect ethnicity on intrasocietal, national, and global levels. The world system is increasingly (one might say irretrievably) interconnected, thus providing transnational actors with the potential for unprecedented influence if they mobilize effectively. This is not to suggest that transnational actors operate without constraints, but rather to emphasize the fluidity of global political relations under conditions of interdependence.

Robert O. Keohane and Joseph S. Nye are correct in arguing that patterns of "complex" interdependence alter traditional interstate politics in three areas: (1) multiple channels of communications by all types of actors—states, bureaucracies, nongovernmental actors, international organizations, and individuals; (2) the absence of a hierarchy of issues—specifically, the decline of military security issues and the increased importance of economic, technical, and social concerns; (3) the diminution of military force in determining outcomes of bargaining and conflicts.[72] The consequences of complex interdependence for central, state decision-making elites are that governments experience a loss of control and reduced effectiveness in the formulation of public policy.[73] Thus, complex networks of functional tasks restrict state sovereignty in economic, social, political, and foreign-policy areas. For example, the devaluation of the dollar, the mark, or the yen directly affects foreign and domestic policymaking in the United States, West Germany, Japan, among their closest allies and much of the world. Indeed, the aftershocks of devaluation intrude into the economic and political relations of all post-industrial societies. Conditions of complex interdependence suggest the possibility that the political salience of ethnic affiliations will intensify as state nationalism declines. These trends are evident in the process of regional integration in Western Europe.

The growth of large and complex transnational structures (the European Economic Community, EEC, and its associated organizations), the sprawling technocratic and social welfare bureaucracies characteristic of all advanced industrial societies, and the growing prevalence of huge nongovernmental organizations (ranging from multinational corporations to labor unions) reduce the effectiveness, and perhaps the meaningfulness, of nationalistic sentiments. The irony of regional integration in Western Europe is that the unprecedented affluence of the 1960s and 1970s, brought about in large part through the formal institutionalization of economic interdependence, stimulated the search for smaller, more intimate communities. Ethnicity, therefore, constitutes a counterweight to the alienation and anomie that is a by-product of life in advanced industrial societies.

The upsurge of ethnicity in Western Europe, however, is not so much an attempt to capture a primordial past as it is a way to cope with life in post-industrial societies on political, social, cultural, and psychological levels. It is within this context that ethnicity becomes a vehicle whereby the ethnic group seeks to participate in the political structures of the EEC and the states that comprise them. It is in their attempt to wield political influence through the mobilization of group resources (frequently transnationally) that ethnic groups will play an important intermediate role between individuals and states in the context of the advanced industrial societies of Western Europe. It is this recognition that prompts political scientists to emphasize the ethnic group as a key transnational actor in a number of issue areas.

Samuel Huntington has argued that "tribalism in politics" and "transnationalism in economics" are, in some respects, mutually reinforcing. He suggests that transnational relations may in fact democratize the global system by linking the political activities of individuals in one state to those in another. "The sovereignty of the government may, in this sense, be limited but the sovereignty of the people may be made more real by the fact that the 'sovereign' unit of government is smaller, closer, easier to participate in, and much easier to identify with."[74] Vernon Van Dyke suggests a similar perspective. He argues that ethnic groups should be recognized as legitimate "right-and-duty-bearing units" alongside the rights and status granted to "states," "nations," "peoples," and "individuals." The ethnic group, therefore, constitutes a legitimate basis of group organization and should be accorded a legal status commensurate with that standing.[75]

The steady increase in transnational linkages in advanced industrial societies, brought about in part by complex interdependence, provides ethnic groups with the capabilities for expanded political influence. Ultimately, the intensity of interdependence may increase the sensitivity and responsiveness of post-industrial societies to the demands of ethnic groups. This possibility is documented in the progressive expansion of international law from the level of states to the level of ethnic groups and individuals—a process that C. Wilfred Jenks referred to as the evolving "common law of mankind."[76] This trend is most evident in the growing body of international law devoted to human rights. These legal and political advancements are illustrated in the dramatic strides taken by the European Court of Justice in its sensitivity to state violations of individual and group rights.

The salience of ethnicity as a transnational force, however, transcends the arduous development of international law, even in as propitious a setting as contemporary Western Europe. Ethnicity forms an integral component of new ideological perspectives predicated on the further evolution of world politics. Systemic interdependence makes the realization of human dignity an imperative of global survival.[77] Hence, Herbert Kelman foresees a restructuring of the global system, insuring the protection of ethnicity as a fundamental step toward the realization of human rights worldwide. Kelman states:

The extensive cross-cutting links that characterize the contemporary world necessarily make violations of human rights in any country a matter of active transnational concern. As a result, such violations constitute sources of international tension and threats to international peace. The status of human rights everywhere thus becomes important, not only to those who specifically identify with victims of repression on ethnic or ideological grounds, but to the entire world community. It adds pragmatic support to the principled position that the protection of human rights is indivisible.[78]

The demise of exclusive state sovereignty, the building of global consensus, the redistribution of wealth, and the achievement of world peace are essential components of this blueprint.

Ethnicity and Global Asymmetries

If the fundamentally liberal, egalitarian, and neofunctionalist orientations of the interdependence perspective are modified by an emphasis on the fundamental political and economic asymmetries between advanced industrial centers of the North and poor, underdeveloped peripheries of the South, then the transnational dimensions of ethnicity are no less significant. Thus, dependency and global-dominance approaches underscore the worldwide implications of ethnicity.

The concept of dependency as used in this context refers to the process of "incorporation of less developed countries (LDCs) into the global capitalist system and the resulting 'structural distortions' resulting therefrom."[79] The term "global dominance" refers to a small number of elite institutions that direct the production, distribution, accumulation, and control of goods and services throughout the entire global system. Therefore, patterns of dependency and global dominance reinforce each other under specific conditions. Several scholars have argued that the structural distribution of power and influence in the contemporary global system so overwhelmingly favors the advanced industrial societies of the North that the evolution of a global-dominance system is a foregone conclusion.[80]

This futuristic system, perhaps resembling a 1984-type global society, is brought about by the systematic exploitation of the underdeveloped peripheries by the powerful centers. The center dominates its periphery through its control of such transnational processes as communication and transportation networks, the global economic system, and technology. The ultimate "integration of the global system into a unified hierarchy of control and accumulation is facilitated by the new technological expertise generated in post-industrial society."[81] A small group of managers and technicians skillfully utilize technology to dominate the entire system. Distinctions between international and domestic arenas merge as conditions of dependency and centralization heighten. States are preempted by efficient, powerful, and omnipresent centers of control.[82]

In this environment, ethnic groups become the lowest common denominators capable of exerting "formidable influence over the primary authority patterns of men."[83] In the face of an increasingly homogeneous global culture, ethnicity remains one of the last remnants of distinctive communal identities. Ethnic groups will remain viable as long as they prove to be useful to the global managers. It is questionable how long ethnic groups will persist as trends to global homogeneity increase in intensity. Thus, the ethnic group plays a vitally important, intermediate role as the object of elite manipulation between the demise of the state system and the establishment of a hierarchically ordered, homogeneous global-dominance system. The point of this analysis is not to reduce the utility of the dependency or global-dominance approaches to absurdity. Rather it is to underscore the ability of center-based actors—states, international organizations, and nongovernmental institutions—to manipulate ethnicity through transnational processes. It would at least seem plausible to conclude that the power of center-based actors will increase as long as advanced industrial societies direct the creation and refinement of technology.

Transnationalism, quite clearly, is not a normatively neutral concept, as our analysis of the interdependence, dependency, and global-dominance approaches suggests. It is significant, however, that ethnicity is identified as an important transnational force amid the structural transformation of the global system from two radically different conceptual orientations.

TRANSNATIONALISM AND ETHNICITY: AN ASSESSMENT

This chapter suggests that ethnic groups are emerging transnational actors in world politics. Moreover, we can specify three different levels of transnational activity: intrasocietal (ethnic groups as reflections of an evolving transnational system); state (ethnic groups as direct participants in world politics); and global (ethnicity as an independent transnational force). Each level of analysis suggests a number of conditions promoting transnational manifestations of ethnicity. In addition to the specific approaches already mentioned, we can make a number of general statements.

First, the emphasis on ethnic groups as emerging transnational actors departs from traditional approaches to the study of world politics. The transnational and ethnic dimensions of world politics offer an alternative to the realist, state-centric vision of global politics. States are the most important actors in world politics and are likely to remain so for many years. However, transnationalism provides us with a perspective to evaluate other important processes and actors as well as to assess extant theoretical assumptions. This volume hardly suggests that ethnic groups will challenge the primacy of states in the near future, but it does raise a number of significant questions about the validity of the realist approach to the study of world politics.

Second, the study of ethnicity and transnationalism provides insights into the ongoing dynamics of world politics. When ethnic groups are compared alongside the political, economic, and military might of states, the significance of ethnicity appears ludicrous. However, the strength of ethnicity does not rest on the attributes of state power as much as on the changing structures and processes of global politics. Systemic interdependence, dependency, and global dominance are all processes modifying the modern state system. Ethnic groups and other transnational actors draw their strength and viability from these changing global structures and processes.

Third, the dynamics of ethnicity and transnationalism must be further clarified. Because ethnicity and transnationalism are new concepts, there is a danger that the terms will become so inclusive as to be analytically useless. The case studies in this volume are attempts to operationalize both concepts.

At the beginning of this chapter, ethnicity was defined as a sense of belonging and/or sense of peoplehood based on language, religion, culture, or race. Although our definition is broad, ethnicity is an essentially specific phenomenon. Whether ethnicity is characterized by religion, language, culture, or race will depend on a number of factors to be specified by the researcher. Similarly, transnationalism must be operationalized under specific conditions as each case study in this volume demonstrates.

NOTES

1. Abdul A. Said and Luis R. Simmons, eds., *Ethnicity in an International Context: The Politics of Disassociation* (New Brunswick, N.J.: Transaction Books, 1976), p. 14.

2. Walker Connor, "The Politics of Ethnonationalism," *Journal of International Affairs*, 27, no. 1 (1973): 1–19.

3. Daniel Bell provides an excellent analysis of the instrumental and affective dynamics of ethnicity in "Ethnicity and Social Change," in Nathan Glazer and Daniel P. Moynihan, eds., *Ethnicity, Theory and Experience* (Cambridge: Harvard University Press, 1975), pp. 142–74.

4. Ibid., pp. 142–52, 160–72.

5. Indeed, the growth of transnational actors and processes is directly tied to increasing levels of systemic interdependence. For the complete presentation of this thesis, see Edward L. Morse, *Modernization and the Transformation of International Politics* (New York: The Free Press, 1976).

6. James P. Piscatori, personal letter, July 3, 1977.

7. Joseph S. Nye, Jr., and Robert O. Keohane define transnationalism as "the movement of tangible or intangible items across state boundaries when at least one actor is not an agent of government or an intergovernmental organization." "Transnational Relations and World Politics: An Introduction," *Transnational Relations and World Politics* (Cambridge: Harvard University Press, 1971), p. xii. For a thoughtful critique, see Samuel P. Huntington, "Transnational Organizations in World Politics," *World Politics* 25, no. 3 (April 1973):333–67. Although Huntington's article raises a number of penetrating questions, especially from a transgovernmental perspective, Nye and Keohane's definition of transnationalism provides the widest possible latitude in assessing transnational actors and processes. The study of transnationalism has been broadened by the work of students of dependency and global dominance.

8. See chapter 1, note 10 for an evaluation of the literature.

9. Walker Connor's critique of the literature in "Nation-Building or Nation-Destroying," *World Politics* 24 no. 3 (April 1972):319–55, is pathbreaking. See also David E. Apter, "Political Life and Cultural Pluralism," in Melvin M. Tumin and Walter Plotch, eds., *Pluralism in a Democratic Society* (New York: Praeger Publishers, 1977); and Roy Preiswerk, "Could We Study International Relations As If People Mattered?" (Genève: Institute universitaire des hautes études internationales, 1977).

10. Harold R. Isaacs, *Idols of the Tribe: Group Identity and Political Change* (New York: Harper and Row, 1975), pp. 11–25.

11. Connor, "Nation-Building or Nation-Destroying," pp. 352.

12. Andrew J. Pierre, "The Politics of International Terrorism," *Orben* 19, no. 4 (Winter 1976):1252

13. Ibid.

14. Ibid.

15. Ibid., p. 1253.

16. Walter Laqueur, *Terrorism* (Boston: Little, Brown, 1977), p. 194.

17. Ibid.

18. Theodore Draper, *The Rediscovery of Black Nationalism* (New York: Viking Press, 1969), pp. 69–85.

19. Ibid.

20. Connor, "Nation-Building or Nation-Destroying," p. 10.

21. Morse, *Modernization and the Transformation*, pp. 123–32.

22. Ibid., p. 179.

23. Cynthia H. Enloe, *Ethnic Conflict and Political Development* (Boston: Little, Brown, 1973), pp. 261–74; Connor, "Nation-Building or Nation-Destroying," pp. 327–32.

24. Connor, "The Politics of Ethnonationalism," pp. 1–19; Isaacs, *Idols of the Tribe*, pp. 11–17; and Rupert Emerson, *From Empire to Nation* (Cambridge: Harvard University Press, 1960), p. 60.

25. Isaacs, *Idols of the Tribe*, p. 2.

26. Ibid., p. 4.

27. Bell, "Ethnicity and Social Change," p. 142.

28. Owen Dudley Edwards, *The Sins of Our Fathers* (Dublin: Gill and MacMillan, 1970), p. 177.

29. Bell, "Ethnicity and Social Change," p. 142.

30. Ibid.

31. Ibid.

32. Ibid., p. 148.

33. See Morse's analysis of the transformation of the Westphalia state system through the merging of foreign and domestic policy in *Modernization and the Transformation*, pp. 77–114.

34. For a further elaboration of the concept of collective legitimacy, see Inis L. Claude, Jr., *The Changing United Nations* (New York: Random House, 1967), pp. 73–103.

35. My analysis of the Palestinians is substantially indebted to Judy S. Bertelsen's "The Palestinian Arabs," in Judy S. Bertelsen, ed., *Nonstate Nations in International Politics: Comparative Systems Analyses* (New York: Praeger Publishers, 1977), pp. 6–35; and extensive discussions with James P. Piscatori.

36. See Frantz Fanon, *The Wretched of the Earth* (New York: The Grove Press, 1965).

37. Morse, *Modernization and the Transformation*, pp. 84–88.

38. John F. Stack, Jr., "The City As a Symbol of International Conflict: Boston's Irish, Italians, and Jews, 1935–1944," (Ph.D. diss., University of Denver, 1977), pp. 102–104.

39. Ibid., pp. 97–103.

40. Morse, *Modernization and the Transformation*, p. 108.

41. Bertelsen, "The Palestinian Arabs," p. 30.

42. Eric Rouleau, "The Palestinian Quest," *Foreign Affairs* 53, no. 2 (January 1975): 274.

43. Ibid., p. 275.

44. Ibid.

45. Ibid.

46. Bertelsen, "The Palestinian Arabs," pp. 30–32.

47. Ibid., p. 31.

48. Ibid.

49. Ibid.

50. Laqueur, *Terrorism*, p. 192.

51. Ibid., p. 193.

52. Bertelsen, "The Palestinian Arabs," p.31.

53. Cynthia H. Enloe, "Multinational Corporations in the Making and Unmaking of Ethnic Groups," in Ronald M. Grand and E. Spenser Wellhofer, eds., *Ethno-Nationalism, Multinational Corporations, and the Modern State* (Denver: Graduate School of International Studies Monograph Series on World Affairs, University of Denver, 1979), p. 27.

54. Ibid., pp. 19–20.

55. Ibid.

56. Ibid., pp. 21–22.

57. Ibid., p. 14.

58. Ibid.

59. Ibid.

60. Franklin B. Weinstein, "Mutinational Corporations and the Third World: The Case of Japan and Southeast Asia," *International Organization* 30, no. 3 (Summer 1976):398.

61. Ibid., p. 399.

62. Ibid.

63. Ibid., p. 398.

64. Ibid., p. 399. As Weinstein points out: "Reinforcing an economic structure dominated by the overseas Chinese minority lends added support to the perpetuation of corruption. The Chinese, as a pariah minority, are under extraordinary pressure to pay off those with power. In Indonesia many of them have sought to neutralize a hostile environment by establishing relationships with army generals. These relationships give them security and access to those officials whose approval is needed if business activities are to proceed; in exchange, the Chinese help meet the financial needs of their military associates."

65. Enloe, "Multinational Corporations in the Making and Unmaking of Ethnic Groups," pp. 21–22. South Africa is attractive to corporate investors for a number of reasons: "political stability (in the form of the Afrikaner-led Nationalist Party), a convertible hard currency, an abundance of cheap labor and a large domestic market coupled with access to other markets nearby."

66. Ibid., p. 22.

67. Ibid., p. 20.

68. Ibid.

69. Ibid.

70. Ibid.

72. Robert O. Keohane and Joseph S. Nye, *Power and Interdependence: World Politics in Transition* (Boston: Little, Brown, 1977), pp. 24–29.

73. Joan E. Spero, *The Politics of International Economic Relations* (New York: St. Martin's Press, 1977), pp. 1–18.

74. Huntington, "Transnational Organizations in World Politics," p. 365.

75. Vernon Van Dyke, "The Individual, the State, and Ethnic Communities in Political Theory," *World Politics* 29, no. 2 (April 1977):369.

76. C. Wilfred Jenks, *The Common Law of Mankind* (New York: Praeger Publishers, 1958).

77. Herbert C. Kelman, "The Conditions, Criteria, and Dialectics of Human Dignity: A Transnational Perspective," *International Studies Quarterly* 21, no. 3 (September 1977):535.

78. Ibid., p. 542.

79. James A. Caporaso, "Introduction to the Special Issue of International Organization on Dependence and Dependency in the Global System," *International Organization* 32, no. 1 (Winter 1978):2.

80. Harry R. Targ, "Global Dominance and Dependence, Post-Industrialism and International Relations Theory: A Review," *International Studies Quarterly* 20, no. 3 (September 1976): 470-82.

81. Ibid., p. 479.

82. Ibid., pp. 478-80.

83. Said and Simmons, *Ethnicity in an International Context*, p. 14.

JOHN P. PAUL

The Greek Lobby and 3
American Foreign Policy:
A Transnational Perspective

Following the invasion of Cyprus by Turkish armed forces in July and
August 1974, Greek-Americans lobbied the United States Congress
and the Ford administration, helping to secure the suspension of
U.S. military and economic aid to Turkey. The Turkish arms embargo
stated that, under the provisions of the Foreign Assistance Act and
the Foreign Military Sales Act of 1961, Turkey disqualified herself
from receiving further U.S. military assistance from the moment she
used U.S.-supplied arms against Cyprus.

The response of the Greek-American community to the Turkish
invasion of Cyprus illustrates how a heretofore politically ineffective ethnic group transformed itself into a significant political actor
with transnational implications. Within a few months, Greek-
Americans became an influential political lobby within the United
States Congress. The successful political initiatives of Greek-
Americans helping to impose the arms embargo against Turkey had
ramifications that transcended national boundaries, influencing the
development of events in Cyprus, Greece, and Turkey, as well as
in the United States.

The congressionally imposed arms embargo also affected political
developments in the Mediterranean area. To the extent that Greek-
Americans influenced the U.S. Congress in imposing the embargo,
they were transnational actors. This chapter examines the Greek-
American lobby from a transnational perspective. The first section

gives a historical perspective of the 1974 Cypriot crisis. Section two explores the makeup and *raison d'être* behind the Greek lobby and the major reasons for its success—the Greek-Americans' strong sense of ethnicity. Section three presents an outline of the political dynamics involved in the embargo votes in the House during 1974 and 1975. The last two sections analyze the group's indirect influence on the development of events in the Mediterranean and assess the Greek lobby in the broader context of American foreign-policy and transnational relations.

THE SCENARIO: CYPRUS 1974

In the summer of 1974, pro-*enosis* EOKA-B terrorists (who desired the political union of Cyprus and Greece) intensified their activities in Cyprus. On July 2, President Makarios complained to the Greek government that the 650 officers commanding the Greek National Guard were planning to overthrow him, and he demanded their immediate recall. As early as February 1974, indisputable evidence revealed that a Greek contingent of the National Guard in Cyprus was indeed preparing a *coup d'état* against Makarios. By early June, the plot was somewhat of an open secret. As a result, the Greek foreign minister, Tetenes, his aides, and more than twenty Greek officers resigned.[1] On July 5, the Nicosia newspaper *Apoyevmatini* printed an account of the plot against Makarios and of the intention of the Greek officers and some EOKA-B members to kill Makarios and put a "puppet" in his place.[2]

Ten days later, on July 15, Greek officers, on instructions from the military junta ruling in Athens, overthrew the legitimate government of Cyprus. Nikos Sampson was appointed president. President Makarios, however, escaped death and was flown to London by the British. In London, and later at the United Nations, Makarios called for the restoration of the independence and sovereignty of Cyprus.

Most governments condemned the *coup*. Great Britain, one of the three guarantor powers of Cyprus's independence (the other two were Greece and Turkey), condemned Sampson and strongly urged the restoration of Makarios. The only exceptions were the governments of Greece and the United States. Greece denied any involvement and called the *coup* an internal affair of Cyprus. The United

States assumed a similar position, calling for "moderation" and a return to "constitutional arrangements."[3] Not until after the Turkish invasion of Cyprus did the U.S. government acknowledge that the Athens junta was responsible for the *coup* in Cyprus.

At the United Nations, U.S. Ambassador John Scali attempted to put the best possible face on the Greek Cypriot junta. On July 19, 1974, Scali told the UN Security Council, immediately after Makarios had made his own plea before the Security Council, that "the U.S. government has always opposed intervention in the internal affairs of one country by another, and to the extent that this was the case in Cyprus, the U.S. deplores it."[4] Thus, Scali and the U.S. government avoided labeling the Athens-inspired Sampson *coup* as "intervention" and essentially supported the Greek position.

During the five days between the *coup* and the Turkish invasion of Cyprus, the ambiguous statements emanating from the U.S. State Department were interpreted by Ankara as tacit acceptance by the United States of the new state of affairs on Cyprus. The United States neither condemned the *coup* nor recognized the Sampson regime, even after it had assumed effective control of the island. Furthermore, the State Department did not clearly define its view of Makarios's position as president of Cyprus.

From a Turkish perspective, Sampson's elevation to power and America's seeming acquiescence to Greek aims signaled the possibility of *enosis*. Ankara, therefore, prepared for a military solution to the problem. Turkish Prime Minister Bulent Ecevit flew to London in an effort to convince the British to take joint action with Turkey in Cyprus. Both countries were guarantor powers of Cyprus's independence, but Britain rejected Turkey's proposal.[5] Ecevit also demanded the recall of all Greek military officers and the establishment of a federal system of government on Cyprus.

Once again, the United States neither supported the Turkish position on Cyprus nor seriously warned the Turks that if they sought a military solution, the United States would at least consider stopping all military assistance to Turkey. Either stance by the United States might have significantly reduced the chances that Turkey would opt for military action.[6]

Turkey began landing troups on Cyprus on July 20, 1974. Fighting broke out soon thereafter, and the Greek Cypriots managed to limit initial Turkish gains to a slim corridor from Kyrenia to Nicosia. On the day of the invasion, the United Nations Security Council unanimously adopted the first of a series of strongly worded resolutions, Resolution Number 353, demanding an immediate cease-fire, the removal of all foreign troops from Cyprus, and the immediate resumption of negotiations by the guarantor powers—Greece, Turkey, and Great Britain.[7]

A cease-fire with U.S. mediation was set for July 22. From the outset, however, the Turkish government continued to increase its forces in the occupied northern corridor. During this time, the United States issued public statements referring to the buildup of Turkish troops in northern Cyprus as minor military actions.[8]

The Turkish invasion and the ensuing possibility of war between Greece and Turkey forced the Greek junta to recall former Prime Minister Constantine Karamanlis to form a civilian government. On the same day, July 23, Glafkos Clerides, Speaker of the Cypriot House of Representatives, replaced Nikos Sampson as the acting president of Cyprus.[9]

On July 30, under British leadership at Geneva, the three guarantor powers agreed to implement the UN-sponsored cease-fire on Cyprus. The second phase of the Geneva talks, which concerned political issues, began on August 8. The following day, Greece, Turkey, Cyprus, and UN military observers agreed upon a cease-fire line separating the two opposing forces on Cyprus.

At the conference, the Turks proposed, first, a federal system under which the Turkish Cypriots would have administrative control of nearly 38 percent of Cyprus and, second, a cantonal system under which the Turkish Cypriots would administer several smaller areas throughout the island.[10]

Cypriot Acting President Clerides requested thirty-six hours for the representatives to discuss the Turkish proposals with their respective governments; the negotiations were at an impasse. Turkey rejected Greece's request for a temporary adjournment to consider the proposals. The British described the Turkish position as "arbitrary and unreasonable." At this crucial juncture in the talks, the United States did not issue a statement that clearly supported the Geneva negotiations.

On August 14, 1974, Turkey invaded Cyprus for the second time on the grounds that her proposals had been rejected and that any delay would endanger the Turkish troops already on the island as well as the Turkish Cypriots. In three days, Turkey's overwhelming military forces sliced off at least 40 percent of Cyprus, which was slightly more than what the Turks had been demanding at the Geneva talks.[11]

For Cyprus, the consequences of the invasion were immense. The first was the presence of an occupation army of approximately forty thousand heavily armed Turkish troops. The second was a grave humanitarian crisis. Nearly half the population of the island, 282,000 Cypriots, were now refugees, civilian detainees, or prisoners of war. The loss of some $4.5 million per day in economic production only heightened the plight of the Cypriot people.[12]

In the United States, one of the major consequences of the invasion was the rapid political mobilization of the Greek-American community and the crystallization of the Greek lobby. The Hellenic community organized quickly to persuade the United States government to adopt a foreign policy suspending all U.S. aid to Turkey until Turkey had withdrawn her military forces from Cyprus.

THE EMERGENCE OF THE GREEK LOBBY

Although the Greek lobby appeared in 1974, its roots extend back to the formation of the Greek community in the United States. Indeed, the Greek immigrant first experienced the euphoria of nationalism in the United States. The force of American nativism lessened parochial distinctions among Greek immigrants based on region and village and forged a sense of common identity and purpose among Greeks in the United States. Undoubtedly, the small number of Greek immigrants in the United States (no more than 1.5 percent of the total immigrant population at any one time) reinforced their solidarity as an ethnic group. Thus, America's unique contribution to the Greek immigrants was to force them to think of themselves, not as Macedonians or Spartans, but as Greeks. This new sense of ethnic identity and unity helped the Greeks, and other immigrant groups as well, to organize along ethnic lines and work toward specific group-oriented goals. Most of these efforts were directed toward the foreign-policy arena since their group concerns focused primarily on events involving the homeland.[13]

From the 1890s until after World War II, Greek-Americans lacked the manpower and financial resources, as well as adequate knowledge of the American political system, to express their concern for Greece and Cyprus in effective political ways. Greek immigrants to the United States displayed loyalty to the homeland and to the goal of *enosis* by fighting with the allied forces in both world wars or by volunteering for the Greek army. Like most other ethnic minorities in the United States, Greek-Americans pressed for Greek territorial gains at both Versailles and Yalta. In these efforts, however, they were not successful.

Prior to the 1974 invasion of Cyprus, a unified and well-organized political effort on behalf of Cyprus did not exist. Greek-Americans were divided into rival factions reflecting contrasting political, social, economic, and ideological orientations on the issues of Greece and Cyprus, partially accounting for their inability to influence American foreign policy on behalf of Cyprus during the 1950s and 1960s.

Throughout the 1950s, Greek-Americans did little more than petition the United Nations and the United States government to encourage Great Britain to grant self-determination to the people of Cyprus. It was not pressure generated by Greek-Americans that forced England into granting independence to Cyprus in 1960, but the untenable political situation in Cyprus itself. The 1960s saw a series of complex internal problems in Cyprus over which Greek-Americans had little control.

Although Greek-Americans did not directly affect political events during the 1950s and 1960s, they acquired important political know-how, organizational skills, and financial resources that were drawn upon in July 1974. During this twenty-year period, the leaders of the Greek-American community succeeded in increasing the political consciousness of the Hellenic community in the United States with the ethnic, political, and economic issues surrounding Cyprus. Although the Greek lobby crystallized in the 1970s, it developed and evolved over a half-century of immigrant experience in the United States.[14]

Unlike previous crises in Cyprus, Greek-Americans perceived the Turkish invasion in the summer of 1974 as a direct threat to the survival of the state of Cyprus. It was no longer merely a case of championing *enosis* or self-determination. In 1974, Greek-Americans were confronted with a profoundly disturbing Turkish *fait accompli* —the invasion and occupation of 40 percent of Cyprus and one-quarter of a million Cypriot refugees—and with the threat of a Greco-Turkish war and the threat of harm to Greeks still living in Turkey, particularly the Patriarchate in Istanbul.

The immediate reaction of the Greek-American community was to condemn the Turkish action, demand a total withdrawal of Turkish forces from Cyprus, and insist upon the cessation of U.S. military and economic aid to Turkey. What made the 1974 situation unique from previous crises was that official U.S. policy and the political goals of Greek-Americans diverged sharply. For Greek-Americans, the 1974 lobby effort was the first major political push in their history.

To achieve an arms embargo against Turkey, Greek-Americans had to influence several political audiences: members of the U.S. Congress, the Ford administration, and public opinion. The efforts launched by the Greek-American community to change U.S. policy toward Cyprus gave them the potential to influence, not only the formulation of U.S. policy toward Cyprus, but also events in the Mediterranean.

Greek-Americans united quickly on the issue of Cyprus and formed one of the most effective ethnic lobbies in Washington. According to many political observers, the congressionally mandated cut-off of aid to Turkey in February and July of 1975 attested to the strength of the Greek-American political organization. The invasion and occupation of Cyprus spontaneously united the approximately three million people of Greek descent in America who had recently been divided over the military government in Greece.[15]

THE INITIAL ORGANIZATION OF THE LOBBY

The Greek Lobby functioned through many channels; key congressional members, fraternal organizations, and the Greek Orthodox Church formed the core of the lobby effort. In Congress, the Greek-American community worked primarily through Senators Paul Sarbanes of Maryland (then a U.S. Representative) and Thomas

Eagleton of Missouri, and Representatives John Brademas of Indiana and Benjamin Rosenthal of New York. Besides Brademas and Sarbanes, there were three other Greek-Americans in the Congress: Paul Tsongas of Massachusetts, Gus Yatron of Pennsylvania, and Louis Bafalis of Florida. These five Greek-American congressmen generated, coordinated, and lobbied for the embargo legislation from the introduction of the first embargo resolution in September 1974 to the embargo's reversal in October 1975.

AHEPA, the American Hellenic Educational Progressive Association, was the largest and most effective of the established fraternal organizations and one of the principal political actors in securing the arms-embargo legislation by organizing direct mail and telegram campaigns, visits with White House officials and with members of the House and the Senate, and conferences with Greek and Cypriot leaders. The Washington-based American Hellenic Institute (AHI) was organized as a result of the invasion and served as the Greek-American community's formal liaison with members of the U.S. Congress, monitoring and analyzing congressional votes and attitudes. Similarly, Archbishop Iakovos, as head of the Greek Orthodox Church in America, and its three million communicants exerted significant emotional influence over the Greek-American community. The established and extensive structure of the communication channels of the church throughout the country allowed for the quick and easy mobilization of the Greek community and gave the church the appearance of considerable political strength.

Initially, Greek-Americans responded to the Cypriot invasion on an intensely emotional level. There were two principal reasons for this reaction: (1) Cypriot territory, with strong historical and political ties to Greece, had been invaded; and (2) the invader was the traditional enemy of the Greeks. Moreover, Greek-Americans have always had a strong cultural identity with the people of Cyprus. For the first time in its history, the Greek-American community experienced an emotional and political crisis based on perceived U.S. support for Turkey. Thus, the strident ethnic response of Greek-Americans catapulted them into the role of transnational actors. This was how they were perceived by the Ford administration, members of Congress, and the governments of Cyprus, Greece, and Turkey.

As the Greek lobby evolved, Greek-Americans tried to deemphasize the explicitly ethnic dimensions of their campaign. By early September 1974, Greek-Americans launched an effort to secure an arms embargo against Turkey on legal grounds. The leadership of the Greek-American community argued that Turkey had violated the U.S. Foreign Assistance Act and the Foreign Military Sales Act, which prohibited the use of U.S.-supplied weapons for offensive purposes, as Turkey had done in the invasion of Cyprus. Thus, an initial ethnic reaction to the invasion was buttressed by strong legal arguments calling for the imposition of the embargo. The legal argument put forth by Greek-Americans was reinforced when the Rosenthal-DuPont Amendment passed in the House of Representatives on September 24, 1974, by a vote of 307 to 90. The amendment cut off military aid and arms sales to Turkey until the president certified that substantial progress toward an agreement on Cyprus had been made. The Rosenthal-DuPont Amendment was the first piece of legislation dealing with the Turkish arms embargo.

Notwithstanding the legal arguments of the pro-embargo advocates, unsavory images of narrow Greek self-interests characterized the popular reaction to the political initiatives of Greek-Americans. On July 9, 1975, ABC news commentator Howard K. Smith implied that Greek-American efforts to continue the arms embargo were motivated strictly by ethnic considerations. More importantly, however, Smith blamed the Greek-American lobby for the failure of negotiations between Greece and Turkey and for irreparable military and political damage suffered by NATO in the Mediterranean area as a result of the embargo.[16] Similarly, three days after the Turkish arms embargo was successfully reimposed by the U.S. Congress (July 24, 1975), Senate Majority Leader Mike Mansfield denounced the use of ethnic-group pressure on the members of Congress, particularly in the area of foreign affairs. Mansfield argued that the Turkish arms embargo threatened the national interests of the United States.[17] These statements were endorsed by both President Ford and Vice-President Rockefeller, who made statements in April singling out Greek-Americans as a particularly powerful as well as potentially harmful political influence on the formulation of U.S. policy regarding Cyprus.[18]

The vigorous, and at times virulent, opposition of high-ranking government officials may have ultimately contributed to the solidification of the lobby and its transnational ramifications. Unlike many ethnic groups who have attempted to influence U.S. foreign policy, Greek-Americans possessed the resources to mobilize quickly for political action. The core of the Greek lobby consisted of a network of fraternal organizations that effectively organized massive demonstrations, telephone and telegram campaigns, and a direct congressional lobbying operation. In 1974, there were approximately 155 Greek fraternal groups in the United States.[19] Most of these organizations were located in the large cities where the largest number of Greeks had settled. By drawing upon already existing manpower pools and by dealing with specific issues, Greek-Americans put together what appeared to many observers to be one of the most successful ethnic lobbies in recent American politics.

THE RELIGIOUS LOBBY

The Greek Orthodox Church is among the largest, best organized, and most influential institutions in the Greek-American community. For the average Greek, religion and ethnicity are synonymous, and most Greek-Americans readily identify with the church.[20] As a powerful national religion, Greek Orthodoxy in the United States has retained much of its ethnic character in terms of language and religious traditions. It is this type of ethnic environment that fostered continued close ties with Greece and with events concerning Greeks around the world.

With 431 parishes and approximately 1.5 million members in the United States, the church is an organized unit through which information can be disseminated easily and quickly. The church's ability to elicit a swift response from its communicants gave the Greek community the initial appearance of a highly organized interest group and contributed to the establishment of more formal lobby groups. Financial as well as human resources combined to make the church's efforts a significant factor in the passage of the arms embargo.

On July 30, 1974, Archbishop Iakovos, Primate of the Greek Orthodox Church in North and South America and the spiritual leader of three million Greeks in the United States, convened a combined meeting of the Archdiocesan Council of the Greek Orthodox Archdiocese of North and South America and the presidents of all Greek federations and societies in the United States. The purpose of the meeting was to coordinate the efforts of Greek-American organizations to assist the people of Cyprus. The committee resolved to request from the U.S. government the cut-off of all military aid to Turkey and the establishment of a channel for aiding the Greek Cypriot refugees. The committee appointed a representative in each state to help coordinate the national program.[21]

The church instructed all its members to send letters and telegrams to their elected officials in Washington urging them to support the imposition of an arms embargo against Turkey. In addition, church officials encouraged mass rallies and gatherings to convey the urgency of the situation and the great concern of the Greek community. However, the church in America feared that its political activities might provoke retaliation by the Turkish government against the Patriarchate in Istanbul, although the threat of reprisal did not prevent the church from taking an active role in the campaign.[22]

Archbishop Iakovos, by the very nature of his office, appeared to be a significant leader in the Greek-American community. For example, Osman Olcay, Turkish ambassador to the United Nations, described the archbishop as a highly influential and independent political actor. To substantiate this claim, Olcay cited the visits of Archbishop Iakovos with President Ford, Secretary of State Kissinger, several U.S. senators and congressmen, as well as his close relationship with Archbishop Makarios and Patriarch Athenagoras.[23] Yet, the archbishop's power was not unlimited. As the lobby evolved, Archbishop Iakovos complained to Secretary of State Kissinger and President Ford that his communicants no longer listened to him and had become increasingly more difficult to control.[24]

The visit of Archbishop Makarios to New York in October 1974, however, suggested the extent of the transnational dimensions of religious and cultural bonds.[25] Makarios represented the front-line resistance to Turkish demands over the Cyprus negotiations. Moreover, his visit rekindled the strong ethnic emotions inherent in the arms-embargo issue. Makarios openly acknowledged the political activities of Greek-Americans and praised them for their role in lobbying for the arms embargo. Makarios's visit to the United States reinforced the salience of ethnic ties between the Greeks of the

United States and Cyprus. It also contributed to the further political mobilization of the Greek-American community.

THE SECULAR CHURCH

The best-known and largest Greek-American organization is AHEPA, the American Hellenic Educational Progressive Association, founded in 1922 and claiming a current membership of seventy-five thousand.[26] AHEPA has adapted continually to changing times and thus has been the most successful Greek-American organization in terms of maintaining and increasing its membership. In many ways, AHEPA is the secular counterpart of the Greek Orthodox Church.[27] When the Cypriot crisis arose in 1974, AHEPA was able to organize a successful grass-roots campaign through effective and well-established communication channels. Local chapters of AHEPA exist in almost all states and are very strong in areas with the largest Greek populations such as New York, New Jersey, Illinois, Massachusetts Ohio, and California. The district governors and the Supreme Lodge in Washington, D.C., coordinate the political activities of all the districts and local chapters and represent a large portion of the Greek-American community to the outside world.

During the congressional-executive debate over Cyprus, AHEPA disseminated information to all its local chapters throughout the United States. If AHEPA's Washington office suspected that a congressman or senator was wavering, AHEPA members from those congressional districts and States were alerted so that personal telegrams, letters, and telephone calls could be dispatched stating the official Greek-American position on the Cyprus issue.

The Ford administration recognized the importance of AHEPA within the Greek-American community. On several occasions, AHEPA officials met with Secretary of State Henry Kissinger. In August 1974, during the annual National Supreme Convention of AHEPA in Boston, a delegation traveled to Washington, D.C., and met with Kissinger. President Ford reciprocated by sending the newly appointed U.S. ambassador to Greece, Jack B. Kubisch, to the convention to explain American policy in the Mediterranean.[28]

During 1974 and 1975, AHEPA officers repeatedly visited Cyprus on fact-finding missions and conferred with Archbishop Makarios and frequently consulted with Prime Minister Karamanlis of Greece.

Following the death of Archbishop Makarios in 1977, AHEPA established a close relationship with the new president of Cyprus, Spyros Kyprianou, and served as the direct contact between the government of Cyprus and the Hellenic community in the United States. By consulting with American officials in the Ford administration and the U.S. Congress, AHEPA established itself as a transnational actor.

In July 1975, Greek-Americans reared for their heretofore largest assault on Congress. Aside from the established institutions and organizations such as the church and AHEPA, considerable political pressure was generated by a number of newer groups. Most effective of these groups was the American Hellenic Institute (AHI), founded in the summer of 1974 in Washington, D.C., headed by attorney Eugene Rossides, a former Nixon-appointed Treasury Department official.

Because of its Washington location and administration and congressional contacts, the American Hellenic Institute was able to spearhead the lobby effort. Rossides and Leon Stavros, a former legislative aid to Representative John Brademas and second in command at AHI, brought their government experience to the institute. The AHI provided other organizations with information about activities and legislation on Capitol Hill and informed members of Congress and the White House staff about the institute's positions on developments in Cyprus and on pending U.S. embargo legislation.

In August 1974, Columbia University economics professor Phoebus Dhrymes founded the Hellenic Council of America (HCA) in New York City to enlist academic and professional people in the embargo campaign. Its immediate goal was to inform the American public and the Hellenic community about the Cyprus issue as well as to influence congressional and executive policies affecting Cyprus and Greece. The Hellenic Council operated its lobby in a similar fashion to most national interest groups. The HCA directed its initial efforts toward securing a cut-off of military aid to Turkey through campaigns in the press and other news media primarily in the New York City and Washington, D.C., areas and through mailings to congressional leaders and Greek-Americans across the country.

In June 1975, mailings were sent to all Greek Orthodox parishes in the United States and Canada. These mailings included instructions on the mailing of telegrams, which were prearranged through a computer service in Washington, D.C., computer printouts of past congressional voting records on the embargo issue, and copies of all HCA publications. It was hoped that these materials would provide Greek-Americans with the procedural information on how to contact their congressional representatives to begin grass-roots campaigns for the embargo throughout the United States.

Like the AHI, the Hellenic Council was active on Capitol Hill. Personal letters were sent to the members of the Senate Foreign Relations Committee and the House International Relations Committee expressing opposition to the lifting of the arms embargo. A five-page memorandum was issued to all committee members stating the arguments against HR 5918, which would have permitted a partial resumption of military aid to Turkey in July 1975. The bill was defeated. The memorandum included a detailed discussion of U.S. law pertaining to the granting of military aid to Turkey after the invasion, the role of U.S. military installations in Turkey, and Greece's participation in the NATO alliance. A delegation of HCA members visited Capitol Hill just before the July 24, 1975, vote on HR 5918 and spoke to nearly seventy congressional aides and had meetings with Representatives Bingham, Solarz, and Wolff, Democrats of New York. The HCA representatives also attended hearings of the House International Relations Committee and submitted their memorandum on HR 5918 as a permanent part of the committee's proceedings for July 9, 1975.

Each of the Greek-American organizations contributed time, money, and human resources to help secure the passage of the arms-embargo legislation in 1974 and 1975. However, the work of the Greek-American organizations is clarified by examining the nine major Turkish arms-embargo votes in the House of Representatives during this period. An analysis of these nine votes helps to determine the sources of support for the embargo and the political significance of the Greek lobby.[29]

THE GREEK LOBBY AND CONGRESSIONAL POLITICS

During 1974 and 1975, the members of the House of Representatives took nine major votes on the Turkish aid issue. Below is a summary of these votes:

1. On September 24, 1974, the Rosenthal-DuPont Amendment, which was attached to the continuing resolution on appropriations, passed by a vote of 307 to 90. The resolution cut off military aid and sales to Turkey until the president certified that substantial progress toward an agreement had been made.

2. On October 7, 1974, the House rejected the House Conference Committee language, and the Rosenthal Amendment passed 291 to 69.

3. On October 11, 1974, the Mansfield motion, HJ 247, was defeated 187 to 171. The Mansfield motion would have authorized the president to postpone the arms cut-off until December 15, 1974, if he determined that it would help the Cyprus negotiations.

4. On October 15, 1974, the House failed to override President Ford's veto of HJ Resolution 1131, 223 to 135 (sixteen votes short), and new legislation was required, causing concern among the embargo supporters. HJ 1131 prohibited funds for U.S. assistance to Turkey until the president certified that Turkey was in compliance with the Foreign Assistance Act of 1961 and that progress had been made in negotiations regarding the withdrawal of Turkish troops.

5. On October 16, 1974, the House passed Resolution 1163, which called for a continued military ban against Turkey. The president exercised his veto for the second time insisting that the continued imposition of the arms embargo was detrimental to the national security interests of the United States in the Mediterranean and that it only contributed to the deterioration of the political situation on Cyprus.

6. On October 17, 1974, the House sustained the president's veto of HJ 1163, 161 to 83, two votes short of passage. Then, the House passed, by voice vote, HJ 1167, which established December 10, 1974, as the cut-off date for military aid to Turkey. President Ford signed HJ 1167 into law on October 18, 1974.

7. On December 11, 1974, the Rosenthal-DuPont Amendment to the Foreign Aid Bill passed 297 to 98. This amendment cut off military aid and sales to Turkey immediately. On December 17, a compromise was reached with White House officials, which retained the cut-off of military sales to Turkey but delayed the effective date until February 5, 1975. The Foreign Aid Bill passed in Congress on December 17, 1974, and was signed by President Ford on December 30, 1974.

8. On July 24, 1975, HR 5918, which would have permitted a partial resumption of arms sales to Turkey, was defeated 223 to 206. The Ford administration sponsored and lobbied for the passage of HR 5918 and blamed the Greek-American community as the major factor in its defeat. The Greek lobby was at its strongest point with the defeat of HR 5918 in July 1975.

9. On October 2, 1975, the House passed S 2230 by a vote of 237 to 206, which gave Turkey access to military sales on a cash basis while preventing U.S. military aid to Turkey. This bill was the first major congressional defeat of the pro-embargo forces and witnessed the rapid deterioration of the Greek lobby.

The voting record of the U.S. representatives for each of these nine votes, excluding the 92 freshmen representatives, shows that on an average, 169 congressmen favored retaining the embargo against Turkey, while 171 were consistently unfavorable or neutral. If a congressman voted five or more times out of nine votes to retain the embargo, he was recorded as being pro-embargo. If a congressman voted for the embargo four times or less, or if he failed to vote at all, he was considered unfavorable or neutral by the Greek-American community and its supporters.

The 92 freshmen congressmen elected in November 1974 voted on only the two final embargo votes—July 24 and October 2, 1975. Of this group, 58 percent including 51 Democrats and 2 Republicans, voted for the embargo on both ballots, while only 24 of the freshmen representatives, composed of 11 Democrats and 13 Republicans, or 26 percent, voted both times against the embargo. The remaining 15 congressmen, including 13 Democrats and 2 Republicans, voted differently on each bill.

The Rosenthal-DuPont Amendment on September 24, 1974, received the highest pro-embargo vote of any of the nine votes, as Figure 1 illustrates. The overwhelming vote for the arms embargo, 307 to 90, was the first one following the invasion, and suggests that the congressmen were voting against the Turkish government for violating the conditions of the U.S. Foreign Assistance Act and perhaps also for humanitarian reasons.

Beginning with the third vote on October 11, the pro-embargo vote fell sharply, approximately 33 percent. This pattern held for votes three through six. Since there was no appreciable gain for the anti-embargo votes, except on vote three, most of this loss may be attributable to the high rate of absenteeism due to the November election campaigns. This is highlighted by the October 17 vote where 190 members were absent, 44 percent of the total. On the first vote following the elections, December 11, 1974, the pro-embargo vote soared to 60 percent of the total possible vote.

Figure 1
TOTAL HOUSE VOTE
ON TURKISH ARMS EMBARGO

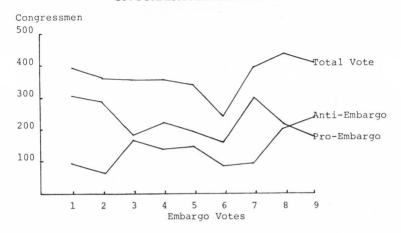

Figure 2
COMPARISON OF
PRO- AND ANTI-EMBARGO
DEMOCRATIC VOTE

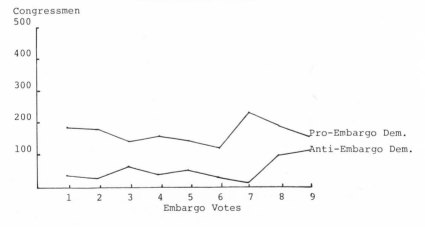

Figure 3
COMPARISON OF PRO- AND
ANTI-EMBARGO REPUBLICAN VOTE

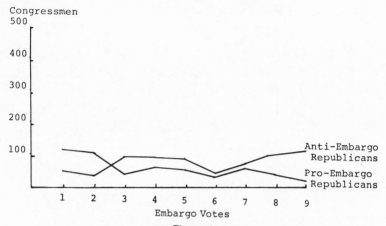

Figure 4
REPRESENTATIVES FROM METROPOLITAN AND
NONMETROPOLITAN DISTRICTS FOR AND AGAINST
THE TURKISH ARMS EMBARGO

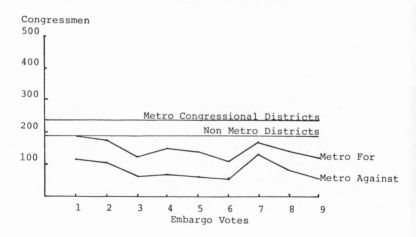

The final two House votes in 1975, HR 5918 and S 2230, showed a steady decline in embargo support. The July vote was won by only 17 votes. Many congressional members attributed the erosion of embargo support to extreme presidential pressure and the issue of national security. A changeover of 43 votes, including 26 Democrats and 17 Republicans, provided the margin of defeat on S 2230.

The voting on the arms-embargo issue was a highly partisan vote, with 58 percent of the Democrats voting for the embargo and against the administration and 85 percent of the Republicans voting against the embargo and with the Ford administration, as Figures 2 and 3 point out. This pattern remained fairly consistent on all nine votes, except for the first vote where 66 percent of the Republicans along with 83 percent of the Democrats voted for the imposition of the embargo. The first vote was the least partisan of the nine. On vote nine, the highest percentage of Republicans, 80 percent, and Democrats, 43 percent, voted against the continuation of the embargo. Of the 169 congressmen who voted consistently in favor of the embargo, 116 were Democrats and 53 were Republicans. Of the 171 congressmen voting against the embargo, 109 were Republicans and 62 were Democrats.

Most of the Democrats' strength, approximately 80 percent, came from the industrial states of the Northeast and the Midwest. Most of the southern Democrats voted against the continuation of the embargo—54 of 92 congressmen, or nearly 59 percent. However, representatives from southern congressional districts with sizable Greek-American communities, such as Texas's eighth district surrounding Galveston and Florida's seventh district including Tampa and districts 11, 13, 14, and 15, which surround and include the Miami area, voted consistently to retain the embargo.

According to the Bureau of the Census, there are 159 standard metropolitan statistical areas (SMSA), which include approximately 244 congressional districts. Each SMSA has a population of two hundred thousand or greater.[30] On the series of Turkish aid votes, 69 percent of the congressmen from the SMSAs voted pro-embargo, while 57 percent of the nonmetropolitan congressmen voted for the embargo. By the final vote, however, these percentages became 50 percent and 67 percent, respectively, illustrating a sharp rise in opposition to the embargo by both metropolitan and nonmetropolitan congressmen. See Figure 4. In 1974, the congressional districts represented by the SMSAs were 67 percent Democrat; in 1975, 74 percent had Democratic congressmen. Thus, congressional support for the embargo came largely from metropolitan districts with Democratic congressmen.

Determining which districts supported the embargo is crucial in the analysis of the Turkish aid issue. One method is to establish which congressional districts in the United States have the highest concentrations of Greek-Americans and then tabulate how the respective congressmen voted. Data on patterns of Greek-American residential distribution throughout the United States are not available. Questions of nationality and ethnic identity for the national census survey are directed only toward immigrants and first-generation Americans, leaving little accurate national data on the Greek-American community.

Church membership is one of the few measures available to obtain a representative sample of Greek-American distribution across the country. Although Church membership does not indicate the actual number of Greek-Americans in a particular area, it provides a reasonable estimate, allowing for comparisons to be made for congressional districts. Based on church membership, the number of Greek-Americans per district was determined, and then each district was ranked. An index of Greek ethnicity by congressional district was compiled and divided into those congressional districts falling into the top 25 percent and top 50 percent with the highest number of Greek residents, as presented in Figure 5.

In several of the large metropolitan areas in which there are many churches in the congressional districts, the total number of church membership was distributed evenly among the metropolitan congressional districts. For example, New York City is composed of 17 congressional districts. The total number of church members is listed as 9,291 giving each congressional district a rating of 547 and placing them in the top 25 percent. The hazard here is the possibility of assigning a high rating to a congressional district that has no significant Greek-American constituency. At the same time, districts with high concentrations of Greek-Americans may not be assigned their true value.

The congressional districts with the highest number of Greek-

Figure 5

PERCENTAGE OF REPRESENTATIVES FROM DISTRICTS WITH THE HIGHEST NUMBER OF GREEK-AMERICAN CONSTITUENTS VOTING FOR THE TURKISH ARMS EMBARGO ON NINE HOUSE VOTES

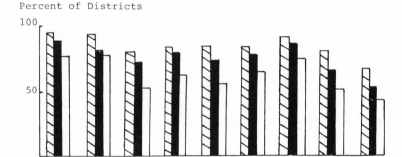

Percent of Districts

 Top 25%

 Top 50%

 Total Vote

American constituents—those in the top 25 percent and 50 percent
—voted overwhelmingly to continue the embargo. The pattern was
consistent on all nine votes. For instance, 80 percent and above of
the congressmen from the top 110 districts voted for the embargo
on the first eight votes, falling only to 69 percent on the final vote,
S 2230, which gave Turkey access to U.S. military sales on a cash
basis. Congressmen from the top 220 districts registered support of
70 percent or above on votes one through seven, slipping on votes
eight and nine to 67 percent and 54 percent respectively, but still
registering a majority.

The total affirmative vote for all districts was the most varied;
it included districts with high and low concentrations of Greek-
Americans, metropolitan and nonmetropolitan districts. However,
the overall affirmative vote was above 50 percent on all but the final
vote. Support for the embargo remained high even during the
October 1974 votes, when many congressmen were absent cam-
paigning for the November elections. Consequently, not only did a
consistently high level of support come from congressional districts
in the top 50 percent of the Greek districts, but from all districts in
general, showing that the U.S. Congress was well disposed toward
supporting the embargo on all nine votes.

Congressional support for the arms embargo was strongest in
districts with the highest levels of Greek-American population.
Twelve congressional districts are cited by the *Almanac of American
Politics* as having high concentrations of Greek-Americans. Three
of these districts are located in Chicago, districts 8 and 9 with 1 percent
Greek population and district 11 with 2 percent. In New York City,
districts 6 and 15 have 1 percent Greek population, and districts 8,
9, 10, and 20 have 2 percent each. In Massachusetts, districts 5
(Lowell) and 8 (Cambridge and Somerville) have 1 percent, and the
North Shore, district 6, has 2 percent Greek population.[31]

These twelve districts and their representatives share several
characteristics. On the nine embargo votes, all twelve congressmen
voted 100 percent in favor of the embargo. These congressmen were
all democrats, except for Massachusetts district 5, which was represented by Republican Michael Cronin in 1974; he was replaced
by Democrat Paul Tsongas in 1975. Each of these districts is located
in central city areas that have high concentrations of ethnic Americans

in general: Chicago—40 percent; New York—53 percent; and the state of Massachusetts as a whole—35 percent. Congressmen from districts with large ethnic populations are accustomed to ethnic appeals and acknowledge the political advantage and necessity in responding to ethnic issues.

Several of these congressmen singled out ethnic pressures from their Greek-American constituents as a significant factor in their decision to vote for the embargo. Included in this group were: Frank Annunzio (Ill–11), Lester Wolff (Ny–6), Benjamin Rosenthal (NY–8), Mario Biaggi (NY–10), Leo Zeferetti (NY–15), Bella Abzug (NY–20), and Paul Tsongas (Mass—5).

Five congressional seats in the 93rd and 94th Congresses were held by Greek-Americans. All five were Democrats and voted 97.3 percent in favor of the embargo on all nine votes. The only exception was Representative Skip Bafalis, a Republican from Florida's tenth district. He voted against the embargo on S 2230, listing national security as the reason for his change in position. Bafalis's district ranked in the lower half on the index of Greek districts. Representative Peter Kyros, Democrat of Maine, was replaced by David Emery in the 94th Congress who continued the district's pro-embargo position. The remaining Greek-American congressmen, John Brademas, Gus Yatron, Paul Sarbanes, and Paul Tsongas, represented districts in the top quarter on the Greek district index.

Of the 110 congressional districts with the largest Greek-American constituencies, 86 percent of the congressmen were Democrats, and approximately 80 percent of these districts were metropolitan. Of the top half of the Greek-oriented districts, 70 percent of the congressmen were Democrats and came from metropolitan districts. The congressional districts in the top 25 percent came from the following states: New York, New Jersey, Pennsylvania, Ohio, Illinois, Indiana, Michigan, Massachusetts, Connecticut, and California. Following closely in the second half were: Florida, North Carolina, Virginia, Texas, Minnesota, Wisconsin, and New Hampshire.

In summary, the data indicate that congressional support for the embargo came primarily from Democrats from metropolitan districts. Districts ranking in the top 50 percent on the index of Greek districts and coming from the above states, particularly the

Mid-Atlantic and Midwest regions, formed the core of this support. The higher the district ranked on the index of Greek ethnicity, the more likely its congressman supported the embargo. By example, solid support came from all five Greek-American congressmen and from the twelve congressmen representing the "Greek districts." With the exception of Representative Bafalis, all these congressmen were Democrats, represented a metropolitan district, and ranked in the top 25 percent on the index of Greek districts.[32]

THE GREEK LOBBY AND AMERICAN FOREIGN POLICY

Undoubtedly, the political pressure exercised by Greek-Americans was initially a salient factor in the decision by Congress to suspend aid to Turkey, but the pressure-group tactics of the Greek-American community fail to explain other, perhaps more significant dimensions of the Turkish embargo. The margin of defeat for the Ford administration was provided by Secretary of State Kissinger, who transformed the question of Turkish aid into an issue of who runs foreign policy—the State Department or Congress. In the House of Representatives where opposition to Turkish aid was strongest, the issue became a focus for criticism of Henry Kissinger. For example, Representative Abner Mikva, Democrat of Illinois, entered the congressional debate favoring aid to Turkey and left convinced that Kissinger intended to use the issue to drive Congress out of foreign-policy decision making.[33]

Even many stalwart Republicans feared that Kissinger was more interested in establishing executive-branch dominance over foreign policy than in helping to solve the Turkish problem. The 223 to 206 defeat of the July 24, 1975, Turkish aid bill in the House was authored by 39 Republicans, comprised of 27 conservatives, including the vanguard of the right wing: Representatives John Ashbrook of Ohio, John Rousselot of California, Robert Baumen and Marjorie Holt of Maryland, and Phillip Crane of Illinois.[34] On the October 2, 1975, vote on S 2230, 25 of the 39 conservative Republicans continued to vote against the Ford administration, still convinced of the administration's intention to assume complete control over foreign-policy decision making. Representative John Brademas observed that the success of the arms embargo went beyond the fact that there are more Greeks than Turks in the United States. "The Republicans share with the Democrats a sense of outrage at the defiance of law and contempt for Congress of the Watergate era."[35]

The fact that Turkey had violated U.S. law, necessitating the embargo, appeared to be secondary to the congressmen's concern with the perceived encroachment by the executive branch in the area of foreign policy. The Ford administration's adamant position on the executive's supremacy in foreign-policy decision making forced many Republicans to switch sides and vote for the embargo. By assuming this political posture, the Ford administration was more responsible for the success of the Turkish arms embargo in July 1975 than the Greek-American lobby. Additional factors contributing to the defeat of the Turkish aid bill included the weakening of the presidency after Watergate, Gerald Ford's pardon of President Nixon, and Congress's disenchantment with Secretary of State Kissinger.

Why did the Greek lobby first seem to win and then lose? Greek-Americans and the pro-embargo forces never had the upper hand over the administration on the fate of congressional bills HR 5918 and S 2230. Even in July 1975, HR 5918 was defeated by only 17 votes, while it passed in October with a sizable margin of 61 votes. The July victory was attributable, not to the congressmen's pressing concern for punishing Turkey for violating domestic and international law, although many legislators were concerned with these issues, but because of the 39 conservatives who voted for the embargo as a protest against the executive's assertion of supremacy over Congress in the formulation of foreign policy. These 39 Republicans were impervious to Greek-American and administration pressures and remained steadfast in their support of the embargo on the October vote, whereas 61 other congressmen changed their positions, suggesting that perceived national-security demands superceded the issue of who decides foreign policy or the arguments of the lobby.

Indeed, Greek-Americans generated support for the embargo by supplying the members of Congress with essential information on the Cyprus issue and by applying ethnic-group pressure. Their efforts helped to secure many of the votes that contributed to the July victory, but the overall effect of the Greek-American lobby effort was small. The successful passage of the embargo in July and the degree of political influence attributed by the administration to

Greek-Americans as the architects of that victory suggest that Greek-Americans were solely responsible for the imposition of the arms embargo against Turkey. Thus, the October repeal of the arms embargo appeared as though Greek-Americans had suffered a major political defeat, when it was only a more accurate indication of their political clout.

The passage S 2230 in October 1975 was only a partial victory for President Ford, who had sought for months to end the arms embargo against Turkey. The newly passed bill allowed for the delivery of already purchased arms and for military sales only on a cash basis, thus severely restricting military aid to Turkey.

To the Greek-American community, the passage of S 2230 indicated the limitations of ethnic-group pressure in influencing the formulation of U.S. foreign policy, and it was an acknowledgment of the Greek-American community's lack of sufficient financial and human resources to continue the lobby effort indefinitely. In addition, the embargo issue further highlighted the political obstacles that confront an ethnic group when it attempts to change attitudes and beliefs perceived by the majority to be in the best interests of the United States. On the arms embargo issue, members of Congress were influenced by, but did not yield to, ethnic pressures. The Greek-American lobby was only one of several factors in a representative's or a senator's decision to vote for or against the embargo. In addition, most of the bills concerning the embargo were attached to larger bills such as the Continuing Appropriations bill and were open to influences from other sources; therefore, they cannot be examined in a vacuum as if the Greek-Americans had the only input in the outcome of the final vote.

TRANSNATIONAL IMPLICATIONS

The Greek-Americans' concerted action to influence U.S. foreign policy toward Cyprus elicited a reaction, not only from domestic forces, but from transnational ones as well. Greece saw, in the political and economic success of Greek-Americans, a future lobby group for the Greek nation.

With great satisfaction we note the role played by Greek Americans in the decisions taken by the legislative bodies of the United States to halting U.S.

military aid to Turkey. This time—the Americans of Greek birth acted as "one body," in a dynamic way, and with the results for the support of their cause. They show how much strength they have when they want to act together and in a decisive manner. Welcoming this occurrence, we express the hope that it will not remain a one time event. We hope that in the future Greek Americans will manifest their support whenever a crisis confronts the Greek people.[36]

Greek-Americans did not disappoint their homeland in 1974 and 1975. Not only were Greek-Americans viewed domestically as having influenced the direction of U.S. foreign policy toward Cyprus, but this was the international perception as well. It is difficult to determine to what degree this perception was due to the role of the U.S press or to the insistence of the Ford administration and the Turkish government that Greek-Americans were the decisive factor in the embargo. It does illustrate, however, the transnational status Greek-Americans achieved during the crisis.

To the extent that Greek-Americans influenced the passage of the arms embargo and to the extent that the arms embargo affected the development of events in the Mediterranean, Greek-Americans had some indirect influence on these international developments. This is the linkage between Greek-Americans as an ethnic lobby within the American political arena and Greek-Americans as transnational actors. Relations between the United States and Turkey and the United States and Greece were altered in three areas as a result of the suspension of U.S. military aid to Turkey.

First, as a result of the congressional action, the Turkish government closed more than twenty U.S. military installations in Turkey, permitting NATO activities to continue only at Incirlik near the Syrian border.[37] It is significant in this context that Turkey attributed the closing of the U.S. bases directly to the activities and influence of the Greek lobby on Congress.[38] The strident response of the Turkish government to the perceived Greek-American influence cast the Greek-American community into the role of a transnational actor of considerable import.

Second, the curtailment and later resumption of military aid to Turkey has had a destabilizing effect on political events in the eastern Mediterranean. To date, through the absence of any sanctions and the lifting of the arms embargo, Turkey has retained its territorial gains on Cyprus and thus might be encouraged to undertake further aggression, namely, by making good its threat against the Aegean islands.[39] Turkish warships have been present in the northern and eastern Aegean Sea near the Dodecanese islands and the islands of Lesbos, Khios, and Samos. The major disputes between Greece and Turkey in this area included oil rights in the continental shelf and control of air space.

Third, administration officials claimed that Greek-American political pressure contributed to the breakdown of NATO and Western security in the eastern Mediterranean. The arms embargo precluded any possibility of a negotiated settlement and also provoked Turkey into closing U.S. and NATO surveillance based in Turkey. Consequently, Greek-Americans were held responsible by the Ford administration for weakening the security of Western alliance in the Mediterranean area vis-a-vis the Soviet Union.[40] Similarly, Greece withdrew militarily from NATO in 1974 although remaining a political member of the North Atlantic alliance. Greece's military withdrawal from NATO was a protest against NATO failure to prevent or discourage Turkey's invasion of Cyprus and NATO's acceptance of the 1967 military *coup* in Greece.

The primary concern of the United States was to maintain stability in the southern flank of NATO. American strategic interests are served whether Cyprus is annexed to Greece or Turkey or achieves a stable, independent status.[41] Within this context the putative influence of Greek-Americans once again intruded into the area of interstate relations (NATO) and ultimately may have affected bipolar strategic interests in the eastern Mediterranean resulting in an expanded Soviet presence.

CONCLUSION

The role of Greek-Americans was only one of several factors contributing to the successful passage of the arms-embargo legislation. Greek-Americans staged a well-organized and expeditious response to the Cyprus crisis. The political and emotional repercussions of the invasion of Cyprus were profoundly ethnic and encouraged many factions within the Greek-American community to create an effective grass-roots campaign. Long-standing ethnic institutions such as AHEPA and the Greek Orthodox Church accounted for the early organization and the initial success of the Greek lobby. The involvement of the community was carried on by newly established political groups such as the American Hellenic Institute in Washington, D.C. Over the span of two years, these organizations facilitated the political mobilization of the Greek-American community in the form of telephone and letter-writing campaigns, massive demonstrations in Washington, D.C., and other large cities across the country, and personal contacts with political figures.

The pro-embargo congressional block was the major reason for the successful passage of the arms-embargo legislation, and the Greek lobby would not have been effective without its assistance. Two Greek-American congressmen, primarily Representatives Sarbanes and Brademas, along with Senator Thomas Eagleton and Representative Benjamin Rosenthal, formulated and lobbied for the embargo legislation for a period of two years. These individuals were the core of the pro-embargo forces. Combined with the congressional members who voted for the embargo in protest to the perceived intention of the administration to usurp Congress's decision-making powers, this small group turned the arms-embargo legislation into a major congressional issue.

As this chapter illustrates, the policies of the Ford administration and the anti-embargo forces pushed the Greek-Americans into the arena of world politics and turned them into transnational actors. Aside from the congressional block, Greek-Americans derived their political strength from the degree of political power and influence attributed to them by other international actors: the governments of the United States, Cyprus, Greece, and Turkey. Each of these states perceived Greek-Americans as the primary factor in the formulation and passage of the arms-embargo legislation. Consequently, the Greek-Americans gained transnational influence far outweighing their numbers and previous political importance.

Both the Ford administration and the Turkish government used the Greek lobby to explain why the Congress continued to vote for the embargo. To the Ford administration, the Greek lobby was a scapegoat for the rejection of Ford's and Kissinger's eastern Mediterranean policy. Similarly, the Turkish government found the Greek lobby a convenient scapegoat for the deterioration of Turkish-American relations in the post-Vietnam era, especially following the Turkish invasion of Cyprus. For the political and military elites of Greece and Cyprus, the Greek lobby became a spokesman for the Greek cause and represented the only tangible opposition to the Ford administration's eastern Mediterranean policy. The Greek-American community also apparently represented a potential future lobby of considerable importance for the governments of Greece and Cyprus. All these states played significant roles, whether intentional or not, in turning Greek-Americans into perceived political actors. These states transformed Greek-Americans into transnational actors by attributing to them the political power and influence necessary to define the outcome of the arms-embargo legislation and thus the framework for American foreign policy in the eastern Mediterranean.

Alone, the Greek-Americans could not have successfully influenced the formulation and passage of the arms-embargo legislation in 1974 and 1975. With the support of the pro-embargo congressional block and the strident opposition of the Ford administration and the Turkish government, which completely exaggerated the role played by Greek-Americans, the Greek lobby became one of the most significant factors in the arms-embargo issue, resulting in national and international repercussions. However, Greek-Americans and pro-embargo forces could not sustain their political efforts indefinitely, and, in October 1975, the embargo was partially lifted and finally reversed in July 1978 under the Carter administration.

NOTES

1. *Crisis on Cyprus: 1974*, A Study Mission Report prepared for the use of the Subcommittee to Investigate Problems Connected with Refugees and Escapees of the Committee on the Judiciary, U.S. Senate, 93rd Cong., 2d sess., October 14, 1974, (Washington D.C.: Government Printing Office), p. 14.

2. Ibid., p. 14.

3. Marios L. Evriviades, "The Problem of Cyprus," *Current History*, January 1976, p. 39.

4. United Nations press release of July 19, 1974, in *Crisis on Cyprus: 1974*, p. 15.

5. Evriviades, "The Problem of Cyprus," p. 39.

6. *Crisis on Cyprus: 1974*, p. 16.

7. Evriviades, "The Problem of Cyprus," p. 39.

8. *Crisis on Cyprus: 1974*, p. 15.

9. Evriviades, "The Problem of Cyprus," p. 40.

10. *Crisis on Cyprus: 1974*, p. 16.

11. Ibid.

12. Ibid.

13. John P. Paul, "The Greek Americans and Cyprus: A Study in Ethnic Group Political Behavior," Ph.D. diss., University of Denver, 1979, chap. 5.

14. Ibid.

15. "New Lobby in Town: The Greeks," *Time*, July 14, 1975, pp. 11, 12.

16. Editorial, Howard K. Smith, ABC news commentator, "ABC Evening News," July 9, 1975, as quoted in *Hellenic Times* (New York), July 31, 1975, p. 6.

17. "Victory for America," *Hellenic Chronicle* Boston, Mass. July 31, 1975, p. 10.

18. *AHEPAN*, March–April 1975, p. 10. Rockefeller interview from Taipai, Taiwan, with the *Washington Post*, April 16, 1975.

19. Theodore A. Couloumbis and Sallie M. Hicks, "The Greek Lobby: Illusion or Reality?" p. 93, in Abdul A. Said, ed., *Ethnicity and U.S. Foreign Policy* (New York: Praeger Publishers, 1977).

20. Ibid., p. 88.

21. "Archbishop Iakovos Calls All Greek Orthodox to Join Humanitarian Crusade," *Orthodox Observer* (New York), August 7, 1974, and *Protocol No. 73*, Archbishop Iakovos, Greek Orthodox Archdiocese of North and South America, New York, July 31, 1974.

22. *Orthodox Observer* (New York), August 7, 1974.

23. Statement by Osman Olcay, Turkish ambassador to the United Nations, personal interview, June 27, 1975.

24. R. Novak and R. Evans, "Archbishop Iakovos Meets with President Ford," National Herald (New York), November 10, 1974, pp. 10, 12.

25. *Hellenic Times*, November 14, 1974.

26. "New Lobby in Town: The Greeks," *Time*, July 14, 1975, p. 11.

27. Couloumbis and Hicks, p. 95 in Said, *Ethnicity and U.S. Foreign Policy.*

28. *AHEPAN*, November 1974, p. 9.

29. John P. Paul, "The Greek Americans and Cyprus," pp. 269–83.

30. *Statistical Abstract of the United States*, Department of Commerce, Bureau of the Census, 97th Annual Edition, (Washington D.C.: Government Printing Office), 1976, pp. 19–21.

31. Michael Baronne, *Almanac of American Politics—The Senators, the Representatives, the Governors—Their Records, States, and Districts* (New York: E. P. Dutton & Co., 1976).

32. Paul, "The Greek Americans and Cyprus," pp, 283–84.

33. Roland Evans and Robert Novak, "Blame Turkey on Kissinger," *New York Post*, August 4, 1975, p. 23.

34. Ibid.

35. Mary Russel, "Turkish Aid Terms a Victory for Greek-Americans," *Washington Post*, October 19, 1974, p. 12.

36. "The Power of Unity . . .," *Orthodox Observer*, November 13, 1974, p. 20.

37. Steven V. Roberts, "Turkey Is Halting Most Operations at U.S. Bases," *New York Times*, July 26, 1975, p. 7.

38. Statement by Osman Olcay, Turkish ambassador to the United Nations, personal interview, June 27, 1975.

39. C. L. Sulzberger, "The Truman Doctrine Fades," *New York Times*, May 4, 1975, p. 5.

40. C. L. Sulzberger, "Greece's Sandwich Isles," *New York Times*, October 15, 1975, p. 43.

41. George A. Kourvetaris, "Greece in the Late 1970's: Social-Political Developments," paper presented at the Conference on Greece, organized by the Office of External Research, Bureau of European Affairs, Department of State, Washington, D.C., February 20, 1976, p. 4.

MARTIN SLATER

International Migration and   4
French Foreign Relations

INTRODUCTION

In the summer of 1973, a series of racial attacks in Marseilles left four Algerian workers dead; in retaliation, the Algerian government cut off all further emigration to France. In 1974, the death of several Italian workers in an accident at a Swiss construction site and the lack of adequate compensation for the families of the victims became a political issue in Italy and led to a deterioration in Swiss-Italian relations. More recently, in West Germany, fears of a further massive influx of Turkish workers have apparently been at the root of the West German government's opposition to Turkish entry into the European Economic Community. These events are the more visible evidence of the varied impact that immigration in Western Europe has had on the bilateral relations of certain countries.

That migration should have an impact on relations between labor-sending and labor-receiving nations is perhaps not very surprising. Migrants are, after all, the most highly visible manifestation of the links between two nations. In addition, the transient character of much Western European migration has meant that migrants have remained *foreign* nationals within the immigration countries. It is surprising, then, that the potential impact of migrants is only just beginning to be recognized. Certainly, their rapid increase in numbers in the past fifteen years now makes them difficult to ignore. During the heyday of immigration in the 1960s, for instance, over 1 million migrants each year arrived in the industrial regions of Western Europe. The recession of 1973 put an end to this movement, and, since that time, there has been a stabilization in the immigrant population. By recent estimates, there are at least 13 million foreign migrants in the industrialized nations of Western Europe, representing about 7 percent of the total population and 12 percent of the labor force.[1] The major labor-importing nations are France, West Germany, Britain, Sweden, Switzerland, and the Benelux nations. Migrants are drawn principally from the less-developed regions of the Mediterranean basin in Greece, Italy, Portugal, Spain, Turkey, Yugoslavia, and from the North African nations of Algeria, Morocco, and Tunisia. Only Sweden, with half its migrants from neighboring Finland, and Britain, France, and the Netherlands, with many migrants from former colonies in Asia, the Caribbean, and Africa, have substantial numbers of migrants drawn from other sources.[2]

If it seems clear that migration in Western Europe is likely to have an important impact on relations between the industrialized immigration countries and the nonindustrial emigration countries, it is less clear what the nature of this impact will be. Will it lead to cooperation or to conflict? The examples cited at the beginning of this chapter suggest that migration may be a source of conflict. But conflict and cooperation need not be mutually exclusive. Cooperation, for instance, may take the form of mutual problem solving, in which case it has its basis in conflict. In order to understand some of the linkages between migration, the presence of foreign workers, and the development of conflict or cooperation in international relations, we shall examine the impact of migration on French foreign relations. Our focus will be to consider those domestic issues raised by migration in both labor-importing and labor-exporting countries that are most likely to have an impact on bilateral relations. Broadly speaking, these issues center around two themes: (1) the economic impact of migration in both the sending and the receiving countries; and (2) the sociopolitical integration of foreign workers into the host society. We will show how and under what circumstances these issues may influence, and how perceptions of them have influenced, French foreign relations. Before discussing these issues, let us briefly review the development of French immigration policy.

FRENCH IMMIGRATION IN HISTORICAL PERSPECTIVE

Contrary to common belief, immigration in France, as in many other Western European countries, is not merely a phenomenon of the postwar era. Since the middle of the nineteenth century, France has experienced almost continual immigration. In 1886, the foreign population stood at more than 1,100,000. The majority of migrants came from the neighboring countries of Belgium (43 percent of the total), Italy (23 percent), Germany (9 percent), Spain (7 percent), and Switzerland (7 percent). Many lived and worked in the border regions of France, close to their own regions of origin. Culturally close to the local population, and by all accounts suffering no special job discrimination, migrants were easily integrated. In addition, by 1889, they benefited from a liberal naturalization law.[3]

There were no restrictions on early immigration to France. By the late nineteenth century, however, the government began imposing certain controls.[4] Other changes were also soon to take place. First, facing severe labor shortages after 1900 as a result of increased economic activity and a continued slow rate of population increase,[5] employers began actively recruiting foreign workers in their countries of origin. Second, these new migrants, recruited in Poland and Italy, were no longer drawn from neighboring regions. Third, they were unskilled workers, employed in those agricultural and industrial jobs that had become increasingly unattractive to French workers. These characteristics have set the pattern for later migration.

World War I intensified rather than diminished France's need for foreign labor. To help with the war effort, the government recruited almost five hundred thousand migrants from southern Europe (Italy, Portugal, and Greece) and from French colonies in Indochina and North Africa. North Africa alone supplied 132,000 workers. At the end of the war, in the immediate panic of demobilization, most of these workers were shipped home. Within a couple of years, however, the staggering war losses (1,400,000 Frenchmen dead and 1,500,000 disabled), the continuing effects of a low birth rate, and rapid economic growth caused labor shortages to be felt once again. Employers' associations, independently at first and then through their own organization, the SGI (General Society of Immigration), contracted with foreign governments for the recruit-

ment of labor.[6] Between 1921 and 1931, the number of foreign
migrants in France rose from 1,590,000 to 2,942,000, making up
almost 7 percent of the total population.[7] The main migrant
groups were Italians (30 percent of the total), Poles (19 percent),
Spanish (13 percent), and Belgians (9 percent),[8] contrasting sharply
with the ethnic composition of the foreign population in France
forty-five years earlier. Employed in jobs vacated by the French,
and living in ethnic ghettos, the interwar migrants found
themselves the object of discrimination by the French. With the
government favoring French workers over migrants during the
years of the Great Depression, many migrants returned home. For
a time, in 1937, Spanish Civil War refugees boosted the level of the
foreign population. But soon, World War II further stimulated
homeward flows. By 1945, approximately 1.5 million migrants remained in France.[9]

It was not till the late 1960s that France would once again have
a foreign population as large as it had in 1931. Immediately following
World War II, there were fears that internal labor supplies would
be insufficient to meet the needs of reconstruction. The government's
first five-year plan, therefore, called for the importation of 295,000
foreign workers during 1947.[10] Far fewer came, and, in fact, French
fears of severe labor shortages proved ill founded.[11] Until well
into the 1950s, economic growth was far slower than anticipated.
From 1950 to 1955, if one excludes migration from French colonies,
only 110,000 foreign migrants came to France.[12] By the late 1950s,
however, improved economic growth had begun to swell the ranks
of immigrant workers. The following fifteen years saw a massive
and continuous increase in France's foreign population. From
1,766,100 in 1954, it increased to 2,169,000 in 1962 and to 2,664,060
in 1968.[13] These census figures almost certainly underestimate the
true population. Throughout the 1960s, migrants arrived at the rate
of over one hundred thousand every year, and, by the late 1960s,
this figure was nearer two hundred thousand.[14] Large numbers of
migrants entered clandestinely (as many as 82 percent in 1968),[15]
suggesting that the actual numbers arriving may have been far
higher. By January 1, 1976, according to the reliable statistics of the
Ministry of the Interior, the foreign population of France had increased to 4,196,000. At this time, France had the largest foreign
population of any Western European nation.[16]

The ethnic origin of migrants has changed considerably over the postwar period. In the immediate postwar years, France turned to Italy, her traditional labor supplier. Soon, however, immigration from non-European sources became important. Algerians, granted French citizenship in 1947, began arriving in increasing numbers.[17] Until the late 1950s, the Italian and Algerian migration flows remained dominant. Then, with the massive increase in immigration after 1955, these sources suffered a relative decline in importance. The Algerian War caused a direct decline in Algerian migration, while Italians had begun to migrate internally to their own industrial regions.[18] From the late 1950s until the early 1960s, the Spanish migration flow was dominant and was followed, until the late 1960s and early 1970s, by the Portuguese. More recently, migration from Morocco, Tunisia, Turkey, Yugoslavia, and black Africa has become considerably more important. Table 1 shows that by 1976, non-Europeans as well as *new* European migrant groups from Portugal, Turkey, and Yugoslavia (who had been unrepresented among France's foreign population in 1936) were now the major migrant groups.

Most of the non-European migrants in France come from former French colonies in Africa. Others come from the French Overseas Departments (D.O.M.) of Guyana, Guadeloupe, Martinique, and

Table 1.   Foreign Workers in France by Nationality (at 1/1/76)

North Africans	
Algerians	884,320
Moroccans	322,067
Tunisians	167,463
Europeans	
Portuguese	858,929
Italians	558,205
Spanish	531,384
Yugoslavs	77,810
Turks	59,178

Source: SOPEMI, *Rapport 1976* (Paris: OECD, p. 20).

Réunion.[19] Technically, immigrants from these latter countries are not regarded as foreigners: they are French citizens, enjoying full rights of free circulation, though there are limits to the number that can enter in any one year. During the 1950s, migrants from French colonies in Africa enjoyed these same rights, thus facilitating the large-scale Algerian migration at that time. Since 1962, there has been a separate entry procedure for Algerian migrants, as there has also been since 1963–1964 for migrants from the black African nations of Mali, Mauritius, and Senegal. There are thus three legal regimes of entry for colonials and ex-colonials. Entry requirements have tended to be minimal compared to most other migrants, though entry became increasingly restrictive over the postwar period.[20] Of the other migrants, only those from EEC member nations, nearly all Italians, benefit from liberal entry regulations under the terms of the 1957 Treaty of Rome.[21] Immigrants from all other countries can only enter France after obtaining residence and work permits from the National Office of Immigration (ONI).

The founding of the ONI in 1945 marked a major attempt by the French government to impose its own control on migration. Certainly, and in contrast to the interwar period when employers' associations negotiated recruitment treaties with foreign governments, the government has become much more directly involved in migration. Migration is now a subject for interstate negotiation. The government, however, fell far short in its attempts to control migration. As noted earlier, large numbers of migrants during the 1960s entered clandestinely. Controls were very weakly enforced, and many of the clandestine migrants were able to regularize their status. According to Moulier,[22] with industry in desperate need of migrant labor and yet unable to compete with wages offered migrant workers by German industry, the French government saw a solution to the problem by easing controls on the entry of migrants and their families. The result was a far greater amount of family migration in France compared to West Germany, as well as a more permanent pattern of settlement.

In recent years, the French government has attempted to change the pattern of migration in France to closer conformity with that of West Germany. With the Fontanet and Marcellin circulars of 1972,[23] increased restrictions were imposed on the entry and internal mobility of migrants. These restrictions appeared to be linked to the economic slowdown of the early 1970s. Similarly, the calls for mass repatriation of migrants (in January 1978, for instance, the CNPF, representing French employers, called for the repatriation of 1 million foreign migrants)[24] appear to be linked to the severe recession of 1973 and the lack of adequate recovery. The new French stance suggests a disillusionment with the purported economic benefits of migration and perhaps also some electioneering by the parties involved.[25] Let us, therefore, examine the economic issues raised by French immigration and their effect on bilateral relations.

THE ECONOMIC ISSUES RAISED BY FRENCH IMMIGRATION AND THEIR EFFECT ON BILATERAL RELATIONS

For much of the twentieth century, the migration of foreign workers to France has been regarded as a happy mutuality of interests between labor-importing and labor-exporting nations. Thus, the various French five-year plans of the postwar era all made provision for the importation of foreign labor as a key to the development of the French economy.[26] In 1964, the semiofficial Algerian newspaper, *El Moudjahid*, could also announce that "the departure of our brothers [for France] remains a necessity and serves the reciprocal interests of our two countries."[27]

The labor-exporting countries saw emigration as an immediate solution for their most pressing economic problems. Probably few governments believed that emigration alone would be sufficient to promote economic development. More often, and certainly in the cases of southern Italy and Algeria, the equation was reversed. In other words, it was believed that emigration could only cease once economic development was under way.[28] Emigration thus served as a safety valve, giving labor-exporting countries the chance to set their economies on the road to industrialization.

Specifically, it was hoped that emigration would relieve unemployment, hidden unemployment, and underemployment in the less-developed economies of the labor-exporting nations. These were pressing economic problems, and, in most of France's labor-supplying countries, they had been aggravated by high rates of natural population increase. In Italy, for instance, the rate of unemployment remained above 7 percent for the entire period from 1948 to 1961.[29] In 1960, there were still 1,300,000 unemployed Italians.[30] Most of these unemployed were concentrated in the southern part of the country, which has been the main area of emigration.[31] The majority of migrants came from the agricultural sector. From 1951 to 1961, agricultural employment declined from 42 percent to 29 percent of total employment, revealing the extent of the labor surplus on the land.[32] The extent of hidden unemployment in southern Italy can be judged by the excessively low rates of economic activity in southern regions. Thus, Sicily, in 1959, had an activity rate of 34.7 percent (the lowest in Italy), compared to the high of 52.4 percent for the industrial region of Piedmont.[33] When one also considers that during the decade 1951–1961 the rate of natural population increase in Sicily was 20 percent, it is easy to appreciate the importance of emigration. In the Sicilian case, even a massive emigration of 423,000 persons (10 percent of the total population) could not compensate for the population increase.[34] Population growth was exerting similar pressure in other labor-exporting countries.

By removing surplus population from the land, the governments of the labor-exporting nations hoped that emigration might facilitate economic development. It could certainly raise the productivity of those left behind, thus avoiding, perhaps, the political instability that might arise from land-hungry peasants.[35] With luck, the surplus earned from agriculture would be invested. There were, however, other important advantages to be gained from emigration, particularly in the postwar era.

First, with migration taking place on a temporary basis and usually involving single men, remittances to home countries were expected to help labor-exporting countries with their balance of payments and also increase consumption at home. Remittances have indeed been substantial: in the case of Algerian migrants in France, they stood at 903 million francs and paid for 31 percent of Algeria's imports in 1968. Since 1968, there has been a moderate decline in their importance, though in 1973 they still paid for 18 percent of imports.[36] In other countries, these remittances remain vital even today. Thus, Portugal, with a balance of payments deficit of $1.2 billion in 1977, received over $1 billion from emigrants abroad.

The nine hundred thousand migrants in France alone sent $718.8 million (64.4 percent of the total remittances) home to Portugal.[37]

Second, there was a common belief that migrants, when they eventually returned to their home countries, would be in a position to put to good use the skills they had acquired in an advanced industrial economy. The Algerians, by the early 1970s, were particularly keen to have skilled Algerian migrants return home and play their part in the government's industrialization plans. Besides skills, migrants would also be returning with savings that could be invested in productive enterprises.[38]

If the labor-exporting nations were anxious to have their surplus population migrate to France, French government and industry were no less eager to accept the new migrants. In fact, they actively recruited them. There was widespread acceptance within the government that a flexible labor supply was an important condition for maintaining high rates of economic growth. The best way of achieving this labor flexibility was through the importation of foreign workers. If migration would not lower wages, it could at least be expected to dampen wage increases. Industry would prosper as a result, and more money would be available for investment. For the government, an added bonus of a foreign labor force, as long as the migrants were temporary residents, was that it required very little social infrastructure. Temporary migrants in fit physical condition and without their families were virtually no drain on the state's health, education, and old-age services.[39]

For industry, and particularly the metal, mechanical-engineering, and construction industries, foreign immigration seemed an absolute necessity. In 1961, for instance, when Renault, the state-run automobile firm, urgently needed three thousand low-skilled workers for its Flins and Billancourt plants, its recruiting team found only 193 suitable applicants on the national labor market.[40] French workers no longer wanted the low-skilled jobs in heavy industry. Renault's solution to the problem was to send a team to Abruzzi in central Italy where the necessary number of workers were recruited on short notice. Migrants thus provided the flexibility needed by industry. They also provided a willing and industrious work force for the jobs vacated by French workers—the low- and semi-skilled jobs in industry, where the majority of migrants are now employed.

Thus, the French Ministry of Labor survey of 1971 found that 93.6 percent of salaried foreigners were manual workers, and 66.8 percent were low- or semi-skilled. The same survey shows that 88.2 percent of foreign migrants were employed in the secondary sector of the economy.[41] Linked to the notion that migrants would do work rejected by Frenchmen was the perception of migrants as politically docile. It was thought unlikely that the hard-working migrant would want to engage in industrial action to disrupt production; he was more interested in saving his earnings for the eventual return to his homeland.[42]

Essentially, the perceived mutuality of interests between France and its labor suppliers led to cooperation about migration policy. Dissenting voices were heard, particularly in scholarly circles, which suggested that migration benefited neither labor-importing nor labor-exporting nations. In the case of the latter group, Bohning and others have argued that emigration, because it is selective of young, and able-bodied, and skilled workers, tears holes in the local labor market, removing the very workers most needed in a newly industrializing economy. There were also suggestions that remittances were inflationary because they encouraged consumption rather than investment expenditure and that returning migrants rarely came home with useful skills.[43] There was some concern among the governments of labor-exporting nations that too many skilled migrants were leaving and that too few skilled ones were coming home. But generally, attempts to control the outflow of migrants were unsuccessful, and certainly there was no desire to stop emigration. In fact, the reverse was true.

Within labor-importing countries, doubts were also expressed regarding the benefits of immigration, but they did not come to a head in France until the early 1970s, when increasing controls were imposed on immigration. More important questions in the earlier postwar years had concerned who, in France, was benefiting from migration and who was losing. The obvious "losers" appeared to be indigenous workers in competition with migrant groups. Even though the overall growth rate, to which migration contributed, probably increased their material well-being, they might have been conscious of a relative decline in their position. To their credit, the French trade unions—the CGT (Confédération Générale du Travail), CFDT

(Confédération Française Démocratique du Travail), and FO (Force Ouvrière)—never opposed the policy of immigration. What they did insist upon, however, was that immigration should be closely controlled and that migrants should receive wage parity with indigenous workers.[44] Although these conditions were by no means adhered to, competition between indigenous groups and migrants was minimized by the fact that migrants went overwhelmingly into the low-skilled industrial jobs. French workers, meanwhile, were moving up into skilled and white-collar positions. With full employment in France for much of the postwar era, migrants were hardly a threat. Firms such as Renault simply could not find French applicants for their jobs. Only the racist Right actively campaigned for an end to immigration and the return of migrants. By the 1970s, however, with increasing unemployment among indigenous workers, this view had become respectable among a much wider section of the political community.

The conflicts of interest that developed during the postwar era between France and the emigration countries illustrate the transnational implications of immigration. Basically, conflicts have concerned the flexibility of migrant labor and the skills and training of migrants. As far as most labor-exporting countries are concerned, emigration is still an economic necessity. There are increasing suspicions, however, that emigration has not benefited the underdeveloped areas as much as was anticipated. While there was a decline in emigration to France over the years from certain traditional labor suppliers, this decline was associated more with simple exhaustion of labor resources than with rapid economic development in those areas. Most emigration countries have never been able to cut off unilaterally the supply of foreign labor to France. Some, like Italy, could switch their dependence on France to a dependence on Switzerland, West Germany, and, later, the Americas.[45] Only Algeria, however, has taken a stance of unilaterally banning emigration. The immediate reason in 1973 was the series of racist attacks against Algerians in France, which we shall examine in the next section. But Algeria's willingness to take such a stand no doubt also stemmed from her position as a leading representative of Third World nations, and not least from her own fast-increasing economic wealth resulting from oil and natural-gas revenues. Adler notes that "as migration became less important for Algeria's economy it became more important for Algeria's prestige."[46]

For other emigration countries, and for Algeria during the 1960s, conflict over migration has arisen because of changing French needs. If economic problems are to be sorted out at home, emigration countries need a certain stability and order in their emigration flows. The last thing they need is the sudden and unexpected return of a few hundred thousand workers flooding the local labor market. Thus, a 1971 report by Donat Cattin, the Italian minister of labor, stressed that the presence of two hundred thousand Italians in precarious jobs abroad amounted to their being on the local Italian labor market.[47] In a similar vein, the Algerians during the 1960s were concerned about maintaining fixed quotas of emigrants to France—an issue they pressed for in the French-Algerian migration accords of 1968 and 1971.[48]

While the labor-exporting nations wanted the maximum stability for their migrants, it was something the French government wanted very much to avoid. The advantage of migrant labor was supposed to be its flexibility. In the event of a recession, the government hoped that many migrants would return home. Further, it did not want to commit itself to quotas of immigrants for many years in the future. French immigration had, in fact, been plagued by its inflexibility. During the 1950s, the large amount of colonial immigration meant a more or less permanent addition to the work force. During the 1960s, migration had been relatively uncontrolled. More families had entered France than Europe's other immigration countries. From 1969 to 1972, for instance, family immigration represented 33 percent of total immigration.[49] By 1973–1974, only 47 percent of foreign migrants in France were actively employed, compared to 65 percent in West Germany and 85 percent in Switzerland.[50] The liberal entry procedures for colonials, ex-colonials, and Italians also made control of other sources of French immigration more difficult.

The French government was no doubt aware of the special characteristics of French immigration. In an accord with the Algerian government in 1964, just two years after Algerian independence, the French sought to impose limits on the free circulation of Algerian migrants in France. An annual quota of twelve thousand migrants was established. France clearly hoped to shift further away from any reliance on "favored" ex-colonial migrants and, instead, toward greater reliance on foreign migrants, who were subject to the much stiffer National Office of Immigration (ONI) regulations. The rapid economic growth of the mid- and late 1960s, however, weakened the French migration policy. In the desperate quest for migrants, formal controls were allowed to lapse. Nevertheless, it is significant that throughout the 1960s, in subsequent accords with the Algerian government, the French government was eager to bring the regulations on Algerian workers into line with the restrictive ONI regulations.[51]

For the French, the warning signs about migration policy were visible by the early 1970s. A slowdown in economic growth led to the arrival of fewer migrants, and, by 1972, the government had set out the Marcellin-Fontanet circulars, which were designed to tighten controls on all immigration and, particularly, to prevent the illegal immigration that had been prevalent in the late 1960s. Almost before the effects of these policies could be felt by labor-exporting countries, the recession of 1973 was being felt. In September 1974, the French government placed severe limitations on the number of new work permits to be issued to foreigners.[52] By 1975, with the continued increase in the levels of unemployment, immigration had been reduced almost to a standstill.[53] In that same year, the French government began to offer to unemployed migrants who had been residents in France less than five years inducements to return to their own countries.[54] In September 1977, these inducements were extended to longer-term residents, and, at the same time, the ministry of labor ordered that no new work permits were to be issued to foreigners, nor was family immigration to be permitted for a period of three years.[55] The latter part of this order, which effectively prohibited the reunion of family members, has since been rescinded, but the ban on the import of labor continues. In January 1978, the anti-immigration lobby grew even more vociferous with the call by the Confédération Nationale du Patronat Français (CNPF) for the repatriation of 1 million foreign migrants. When one considers these developoments in the light of President Giscard d'Estaing's policy, expressed in the Seventh Plan formulations of encouraging French workers back into jobs once held by migrants and substituting capital for labor in industry, it seems clear that the French government and industry have decided never again to rely on migrant labor to the extent that they did in the 1960s.[56]

The above developments have had serious implications for traditional labor-exporting countries, which have also been affected by the recession and, in most cases, face severe unemployment. For instance, it is estimated that in Portugal, where there is an active population of 3.2 million, there were five hundred thousand unemployed in June 1976—a rate of unemployment of over 15 percent.[57] We also have the extraordinary situation in Morocco, where, in 1975, there were more immigrants *from* France (French technicians and managers) than there were emigrants *to* France.[58]

As economic conditions in the labor-supply countries have worsened, the new immigration policies have led France into a considerable conflict of interest with its labor suppliers. The French government, though, has ostensibly sought to minimize the blow through other avenues of cooperation. Notably, there has been an attempt to set up programs for the reintegration of migrants into their home economies. In September 1974, the French government announced its intention to finance training programs for returning migrants.[59] The programs were to be run jointly by France and the labor-exporting countries, and, in 1975, talks were held with the Portuguese, Algerian, and Tunisian governments to discuss how the training programs might best fit in with those countries' own development plans.[60]

As noted earlier, the labor-exporting nations had long believed that emigration to France would be an eventual advantage to them because skilled migrants would return who could make a real contribution to industrial development. Since 1971, the Algerian government had been particularly eager to have skilled Algerian workers return. The recession, however, and the real possibility of a mass return revealed how unrealistic those beliefs had been. Immigrants to France, we have already shown, were employed mainly as low- and semi-skilled workers. At the Renault automobile factories, for instance, the sum total of a migrant's training on the assembly line had been a one-half-hour demonstration by another worker. In three weeks, the migrant was expected to do his job proficiently. The labor-exporting countries had understood that migrants would return as skilled technicians and managers. Nothing of the sort took place.

In cooperating with labor-exporting nations on training programs for returning migrants, the French government faced, and still faces, major problems. First is the problem of skills. France is capable of sending home experienced factory workers, but it is a major task to turn these workers into skilled technicians. The second problem is a conflict of numbers. France would like to send home as many workers as possible, however, the labor-exporting nations require a mere handful of skilled technicians, particularly since their own economies are stagnant. In the first full year of its operation, the French training program for returning migrants trained only 270 persons who had been promised jobs in Senegal, Mali, Tunisia, and Algeria.[61] Clearly, this is not the type of mass training program that the French government would like.

It remains to be seen whether the current conflicts about migration policy between France and its labor suppliers can be resolved. The possibility has been raised of replacing immigration to France by direct foreign investment, but there is no guarantee that investment would be made in the labor-exporting nations. Political stability is more often than not the major criterion for foreign investment. And the French government would find it hard to dictate to private companies where that investment should be made.

In discussing the economic impact of migration, the dependent position of France's labor suppliers on the policies of French government and industry is evident. What is not so evident thus far is that while the recent recession gave France the excuse to reverse its policy on migration, the decision was linked as much to the sociopolitical costs of immigration as to the economic costs. It was also concern about the social integration of migrants that led the Algerian government to cut off migration to France. Let us now consider those issues raised by the sociopolitical integration of migrants that have led to bilateral confict.

THE SOCIOPOLITICAL INTEGRATION OF MIGRANTS IN FRANCE AND ITS EFFECT ON BILATERAL RELATIONS

Just before the 1973 recession, France became aware of two major social costs involving migrants. First, the increasing incidence of racial violence, culminating in the racial attacks at Marseilles, made people conscious that the presence of 4 million foreigners in France could create major ethnic divisions and social conflict. Second, the rent strikes in migrant *foyers* (government sponsored immigrant housing) in the late 1960s, and the outbreak of migrant strikes in French factories after 1972, revealed that, despite their being denied political rights, migrants could become a radical political force. At the same time, Algeria, among the labor-exporting nations, began to express concern about the poor treatment and inadequate social and working conditions of migrants. There was particular concern about the increase in racial attacks. All these issues can be seen as reflections of the sociopolitical integration of migrants. There are four major factors relevant to this sociopolitical integration: (1) the cultural and ethnic backgrounds of migrants; (2) the geographical distribution; (3) the urban environment; and (4) the work-place environment. Let us see how each has affected the integration of migrants, eventually bringing about the possibility of conflict in French foreign relations.

THE CULTURAL AND ETHNIC BACKGROUND OF MIGRANTS

An important change in the cultural and ethnic background of migrants in France is, as we noted earlier, the considerable increase in the number of migrants drawn from non-European backgrounds. Though the French-language ability of the non-European migrants is generally of a higher order (because most come from the colonies or ex-colonies) than that of European migrants, there is clear evidence that they arouse more mistrust among the indigenous French population.

The cultural and ethnic background of migrants gives rise, not only to racism on the part of the indigenous population, but also determines, to some extent, the political behavior of migrants. There is little doubt that the cultural isolation of early migrants, their ignorance of or indifference to French politics and society, and their political passivity made them seem unlikely contenders for the role of a revolutionary proletariat.[62] Further, the ethnic diversity of the migrants themselves made collective mass action among migrants seem unlikely. Nevertheless, ethnic solidarity did develop among certain groups of migrants, based, at least in part, on their concentration in similar types of urban and work environments. Before considering these aspects, let us first consider the geographical distribution of migrants.

THE GEOGRAPHICAL DISTRIBUTION OF MIGRANTS

In France, the geographical distribution of migrants has exacerbated racial tensions and risked political instability. Migrants are overwhelmingly concentrated in the major metropolitan areas: fully one-third of France's 4 million migrants live in the Paris region.[63] Other major regions of settlement are Rhone-Alpes and Provence-Cote d'Azur, of which Lyons and Marseilles are, respectively, the major cities. While the proportion of foreigners in France is approximately 7 percent as a whole, in these regions, it is nearer 12 percent. In Paris, for instance, almost 13 percent of the population is foreign. Within these major metropolitan regions, migrants have tended to be concentrated still further in the peripheral or industrial areas of the cities. Thus, in towns such as Gennevilliers, on the outskirts of Paris, the proportion of migrants is reportedly around 30 percent.[64]

The French authorities have been aware of the political consequences of concentrating immigrants in certain zones. In December 1971, a letter from the ministry of the interior to the various prefects read: ". . . we should avoid establishing residential areas for foreign workers in zones where the foreign colony is already at excessive levels."[65]

THE URBAN ENVIRONMENT OF MIGRANTS

Closely linked to the geographical distribution of migrants is their position in the urban environment. During the 1950s and 1960s, many migrants lived in squatter settlements known as *bidonvilles*. These settlements were characterized, not only by slum living conditions, but also by a spatial separation from the residential areas of the indigenous population. Other migrants lived in small cafés and boarding houses or in barracks provided by their employers. These types of accommodations hardly provided security when the loss of a job or an argument with a landlord would most likely mean having to move. The insecure existence of the migrant and the fact that he was usually alone, without his family, meant that he was not an integral part of any local community.

In the 1960s, there was increasing organization of migrant housing by the government. *Bidonvilles*, the only natural community the migrants had, were eliminated and replaced by *foyers*, *cités de transit* (worker housing), and other, more permanent public housing.[66] Conditions in the *foyers* have demoralized many migrants: the migrants have no security; their places often depend on continuing to hold jobs with particular firms; and rent is docked directly from their pay. In return, they receive weekly tickets from their employers entitling them to continued residence in the *foyer*.[67] Inside the *foyers*, discipline is strict: no female visitors are allowed; and male visitors are allowed only for limited periods during the day with the manager's express permission. Finally, all political activity is forbidden. The sanction facing migrants who do not comply is immediate expulsion.[68] Enforcing these rules are French managers, many of whom, according to an employee of SONOCOTRA (the largest organizer of the *foyers* in France), are ex-military personnel whose chief experience for the job is military service in the colonies.[69] Though they are relatively inexpensive, the living conditions in the *foyers* are generally poor, with a lack of private space for residents, the constant noise of returning shift workers, and considerable isolation from normal residential communities.[70] While the *foyers* cater to single men, *cités de transit* were established to cope with families. Here, too, living conditions tend to be extremely poor. I visited one site on the outskirts of Paris that catered to Algerian migrants. It consisted of prefabricated shacks situated in a field of mud surrounded by a wire fence, in an industrial port area. Many of the residents had lived there for ten to twelve years.[71]

Only a small number of migrants have been able to penetrate the public housing market. Formally, they have equal rights with the French population. But there are two problems. First, waiting lists tend to be of several years duration, and, in many cases, migrants are toward the end of the lists because they are the most recent arrivals. Second, to gain access to public housing, a migrant's family must reside in France. The catch is that an entry permit to France is not granted to an immigrant's wife unless the migrant can show, to the satisfaction of the prefecture, that he can provide adequate housing.[72]

The isolation of migrants in the urban environment has emphasized their differences from the indigenous population, thus consolidating ethnic and racial divisions. The housing conditions of migrants have also been a source of irritation and anger for the governments of the labor-exporting nations. They have had the same effect on the migrants and led, in the 1960s, to their first participation in collective political action. The *foyers* have been the center of political action in the urban environment. Mainly, this action has taken the form of rent strikes. While migrants have been supported and encouraged in their strike action by left-wing militants,[73] it was the development of their own ethnic solidarity that formed the basis for their action. A conference of *foyer* managers in 1973 warned that ethnic solidarity was the basis of many rent strikes,[74] and they suggested splitting up the various national groups. Indeed, such policies have now been pursued, particularly following major strikes. Thus, one rent strike by African workers was concluded by splitting them up into three groups and by assigning them to separate houses.[75]

THE WORK-PLACE ENVIRONMENT AND MIGRANTS

The work environment completes the image of migrants' social integration. As noted earlier, the vast majority of migrants are employed as low- and semi-skilled workers in the secondary sector of the economy. They are particularly prominent in the construction, metal, and mechanical-engineering industries, which have a large proportion of the unpleasant jobs that are not attractive to the indigenous population. In the Paris construction industry in 1973, 46.5 percent of construction workers were foreign migrants.[76] In automobile plants and foundries, the figure jumps to 60–70 percent.[77] Within these industries, the high concentration has meant that whole departments or work sites are staffed entirely by migrants. Thus, on many of the large Paris construction sites, over 90 percent of the workers are foreign migrants. In automobile plants such as Renault, Chrysler, and Citroen, over 90 percent of assembly-line workers are foreign migrants.

As I have argued elsewhere,[78] when migrants are concentrated in a stable, large-scale work environment, ethnic solidarity may provide a basis for collective action, as it did in the case of the migrant strike in the heavy presses department at Renault's Billancourt factory in 1973. That migrants have led a number of spectacular and highly radical strikes in the automobile industry is also due to their status as low-skilled production workers in that industry. Such spectacular strikes have not occurred in the construction industry.

Nevertheless, French government and industry could not ignore the growing militancy of migrants in the work place, and they quickly jumped to the conclusion that such behavior could be expected of all migrants, whatever their work conditions. The realization that migrants are not the docile workers they were once thought to be has been a major reason for French industry's current policy of substituting capital for labor. In certain industries, there will always be limits to such a policy. For the moment, however, French employers can demand the repatriation of 1 million immigrants.

For the labor-exporting nations, their concern about migrant employment has focused on three elements: (1) the precarious nature of many migrant jobs; (2) the lack of skills that migrants learn in their jobs; and (3) the demeaning nature of much of the work that migrants do. On the first point, the heavy employment of migrants in the unstable construction industry, for instance, poses the problem that many migrants may be obliged to return home during a slight economic downturn, thus flooding the local labor market in the emigration country. On the second point, the low level of skills of returning migrants makes them of little use for the industrialization plans of the developing countries. Shortly after Algeria cut off emigration to France in 1973, the Algerian government made clear that a condition of future emigration to France would be the training of migrants in useful skills. The third concern—the fact that migrants are employed in the most monotonous, the dirtiest, or the most dangerous jobs, and that these have been rejected by the indigenous population—can hardly be a source of pride to the emigration countries. Reliable statistics show that proportionately far more foreign migrants are killed or injured in work-related accidents than are indigenous workers. The reason has less to do with their abilities than with the type of work they do. Thus, the construction industry, for instance, which has the highest work-accident rate, an average of three workers are killed every day in France.

SOCIAL INTEGRATION OF MIGRANTS AND FOREIGN RELATIONS

While economic issues have often held center stage in bilateral negotiations on migration, the issues that concern the sociocultural integration of migrants are no less important in determining the policy positions of the negotiating parties. For the labor-exporting nations, the poor living and working conditions of their nationals abroad has been a source of concern. For those nations recently emerged from colonialism, such as Algeria, there is surely particular bitterness and humiliation about such treatment. The racist attacks on Algerians in Marseilles were clearly perceived as a national insult. Cutting off Algerian migration to France was a way of asserting economic and political independence.

For the French government, the perceived benefits of migration disappeared, not only with the increasing economic costs of migration, but also with the changing ethnic pattern of migration and the increasing risk of social and political conflict in the work place and in the urban community. It is perhaps important to remember that the French government's perceptions of migrants are largely influenced by its ideological orientation. Should the Left come to power in France, one would expect to see at least an attempt to improve the socioeconomic conditions of migrants as a result of improved social-welfare benefits. At present, however, French concern about the political and social impact of migration has led to a certain intransigence about migration and has brought the government into conflict with the governments of labor-exporting nations.

Finally, the governments of labor-exporting countries have not themselves remained indifferent to the political impact of migration. The Algerian government, for instance, presiding over a centralized socialist state, actively encouraged Algerian migrants in France to join the Communist-led CGT rather than the CFDT with its ideology of decentralized democratic socialism. The Algerian labor unions and the CGT have accordingly issued joint communiques promising cooperation on labor issues. Before 1974, right-wing governments such as Morocco and Portugal were equally concerned that their migrants should *not* indulge in labor-union activity of a radical nature. To enforce this policy, the Portuguese secret police (PIDE) and their Moroccan counterparts have actively spied on the political activities of their nationals in France. The sanctions they hold over migrants include, in the Moroccan case, the government's refusal to grant favorable loans and other benefits to returning migrants.

The position of the French government with regard to the activities of foreign governments in France is not clear. Interviews suggested, however, that the French government has largely ignored the activities of secret police. There is, of course, a French ban on political activity by foreign migrants (which resulted in the expulsion of 150 workers in May 1968), and, to the extent that this rule is enforced, the French authorities lend support to the more reactionary regimes among the labor-exporting nations. There is certainly also concern in France that the support of certain types of union activity by the Algerian government should not impinge on French sovereignty. There has, however, been no public argument about this question to the present time.

CONCLUSION

Interstate conflict about migration issues has increased in the case of French immigration because economic conditions, the pattern of migration, and the nature of migrants have changed. Thus, perceptions of the benefits have also changed, particularly on the part of the French government. From our analysis, it is safe to conclude that the labor-exporting countries would welcome a resumption of emigration to France, though they might wish to obtain certain commitments about the training and work experience of migrants. It is, however, unlikely that a resumption of migration will take place, given the present French government and its concerns about the social and political costs of migration.

What is perhaps most fascinating is that the major conflict over migration stems, not so much from the treatment of foreign migrants in France (though this is an issue of concern), but from the unilateral decision by the French authorities to suspend migration. It seems unlikely that the French will choose to resolve the conflict by resuming migration. The possibility of a Left victory in the March 1978 elections raised many people's hopes of an improvement in the treatment of migrants in France and of a change in the policy of repatriation. However, not even the most optimistic observer expected that such a victory would bring about a return of the policies of mass immigration of the 1960s.

The substantial victory of the government forces in the elections has, as might have been expected, resulted in little change in the migration policy. There can be little prospect, therefore, of France's relations with the labor-exporting nations becoming any less strained in the near future. The passing of the elections has quieted the hysteria of the domestic debate, perhaps easing the way for future discussions with labor-exporting nations about the alternatives to migration.

NOTES

1. Calculated from 1975 national statistics of the following countries: Austria, Belgium, France, Luxembourg, Netherlands, Sweden, Switzerland, United Kingdom, West Germany. For an overview of the migration stocks in Western Europe, see SOPEMI, *Rapport 1976*, OECD, Paris.

2. Ibid., pp. 20, 25 and 28.

3. Bernard Granotier, *Les Travailleurs Immigrés en France* (Paris: Maspero, 1973), p. 41.

4. Ibid., p. 41.

5. Ibid., p. 42.

6. Ibid., p. 43.

7. Yves Tugault, *La Mesure de la Mobilité: Cing Etudes sur les Migrations Internes*, INED, Travaux et Documents, Cahier No. 43 (Presses Universitaires de France, 1964), p. 38.

8. Bernard Granotier, *Les Travailleurs*, p. 43.

9. Stephen Castles and Godula Kosack, *Immigrant Workers and Class Structure in Western Europe* (London: Oxford University Press, 1973), p. 23.

10. See Yann Moulier, "Un Paese d'Immigrazione: la Francia," in Alessandro Serafini, ed., *L'Operaio Multinazionale in Europa* (Milan: Feltrinelli, 1974), p. 43.

11. Between 1946 and 1949, 214,000 foreign migrants entered France through the National Office of Immigration; these figures exclude Algerian migrants. Source: ONI, Paris.

12. ONI statistics.

13. Ministère du Traviail, *Le Dossier de l'Immigration* (Paris, September 1973).

14. In 1969 and 1970, respectively, 195,130 and 212,785 foreign migrants arrived in France. Source: ONI, Paris.

15. Ministère du Travail, *Le Dossier*.

16. West Germany closely followed France with a foreign population of 4,089,000 in 1975. Source: SOPEMI, *Rapport 1976*, p. 14.

17. It was the "Organic Law" of 1947 that redefined Algeria's status as a French colony and gave all Algerians rights of French citizenship. See Stephen Adler, *People in the Pipeline: The Political Economy of Algerian Migration to France, 1962-1974* (Ph.D. diss. MIT, September 1975), p. 72.

18. On the changing direction of the Italian migration flows, see Giovanni Mottura and Enrico Pugliese, "Mercato del Lavoro e Caratteristiche dell' Emigrazione Italiana nell' Ultimo Quindicennio," in P. Leon and M. Marocchi, eds., *Sviluppo Economico Italiano e Forza-Lavoro* (Padova: Marsilio, 1974), pp. 231-56.

19. These departments, similar in status to internal French departments, are administered by a prefect.

20. On the increasing restrictions on Algerian migrants, see, for instance, Stephen Adler, *People in the Pipeline*, ch. 4.

21. The Treaty of Rome provides for the free movement of labor (article 48) among member nations of the EEC.

22. Yann Moulier, "Un Paese d'Immigrazione."

23. The Marcellin Circular of 24 January 1972, issued by the ministry of the interior, and the Fontanet Circular of 23 February 1972, issued by the ministry of labor, both applying to all ONI migrants, provided for the immediate expulsion of illegal migrants after a period of grace ending 16 October 1972. For an analysis, see GISTI, *Dossier sur la Nouvelle Réglementation pour les Travailleurs Immigrés en France*, 10 December 1972.

24. *Le Monde*, 21 January 1978.

25. *New York Times*, 14 February 1978.

26. The one exception is the Seventh Plan, formulated in 1976 after the change in policy toward migrant workers.

27. Quoted in Stephen Adler, *People in the Pipeline*, p. 83, from *El Moudjahid*, no. 165, 1 February 1964.

28. On the Italian case, see Giovanni Mottura and Enrico Pugliese, "Mercato del Lavoro," pp. 255–56.

29. M. M. Postan, *An Economic History of Western Europe* (London: Methuen, 1967), p. 62.

30. M. Paci, *Mercato del Lavoro e Classi Sociali in Italia* (Bologna: Il Mulino, 1973, p. 159.

31. The other principal area of emigration is the northeast.

32. M. Paci, *Mercato del Lavoro*, p. 159.

33. Luca Meldolesi, "Disoccupazione ed Esercito Industriale di Riserva in Italia," in P. Leon and M. Marocchi, eds., *Sviluppo Economico*, p. 142.

34. Claudio Francia, *Il Fenomeno Migratorio in Italia* (Rome: Ente Italiano di Servizio Sociale, 1967), ch. 4.

35. This happened in southern Italy both before and after the fascist period.

36. Stephen Adler, *People in the Pipeline*, p. 235.

37. *New York Times*, 15 February 1978.

38. Stephen Adler, *People in the Pipeline*.

39. On the benefits of migration for the labor-importing nations, an early and influential work was Charles P. Kindleberger, *Europe's Postwar Growth* (Cambridge: Harvard University Press, 1967).

40. *La Croix*, 17 January 1962; *Le Monde*, 12 January 1962; *Le Figaro*, 24 January 1962.

41. Ministère d'Etat chargé des Affaires Sociales, Service des Etudes et Prévisions, *Résultats d'une Enquête sur la Main d'Oeuvre Etrangère, effectuée en juillet 1971* (Paris: 21 March 1973).

42. Scholarly studies, such as that of G. Fofi, *L'Immigrazione Meridionale a Torino* (Milan: Feltrinelli, 1964), characterized the migrant as politically docile.

43. See W. R. Bohning, "Some Thoughts on Emigration from the Mediterranean Basin," *International Labour Review* (Geneva), 3 (no. 3):251–77.

44. See Maryse Tripier, "Concurrence et Différence: les Problèmes Posés au Syndicalisme Ouvrier par les Travailleurs Immigrés," *Sociologie du Travail,* 3 (July–September 1972):331–47.

45. See Giovanni Mottura and Enrico Pugliese, "Mercato del Lavoro."

46. Stephen Adler, *People in the Pipeline,* p. 182.

47. Ministero del Lavoro, *La Politica dell'Impiego nella CEE,* memo presented to Council of Ministers of Social Affairs, 24 June 1971, quoted in G. Mottura and E. Pugliese, "Mercato del Lavoro," p. 232.

48. Stephen Adler, *People in the Pipeline,* ch. 4.

49. Ministère du Travail, *Le Dossier de l'Immigration,* September 1973.

50. My own calculations from SOPEMI, *Rapport 1976,* pp. 14, 18, and 20.

51. Stephen Adler, *People in the Pipeline,* ch. 4.

52. André Lebon, *L'Aide à la Réinsertion des Travailleurs Etrangers dans leur Pays d'Origine,* Ministère du Travail, Direction de la Population et des Migrations, Service de l' Immigration, 1 Place de Fontenoy, Paris, 1977.

53. See SOPEMI, *Rapport 1976,* pp. 20–21; in 1975, only 25,591 migrant workers arrived in France.

54. André Lebon, *L'Aide à la Réinsertion.*

55. Jean Benoît, "Putting the Squeeze on Immigrants," *Manchester Guardian Weekly* 117, no. 16 (1977):11.

56. See André Lebon, *L'Aide à la Réinsertion,* on the formulation of the Seventh Plan with regard to migrant labor.

57. SOPEMI, *Rapport 1976,* p. 52.

58. Ibid., pp. 21 and 52.

59. André Lebon, *L'Aide à la Réinsertion.*

60. *Manchester Guardian,* 22 December 1975.

61. André Lebon, *L'Aide à la Réinsertion.*

62. See Martin Slater, "Migration and Workers' Conflicts in Western Europe," *Studies in Comparative Sociology,* 14 (January 1979):3-4.

63. Ministère du Travail, *Le Dossier de l'Immigration,* September 1973.

64. Estimated by Confédération Générale du Travail (CGT) officials interviewed at Gennevilliers, October 1974.

65. Letter from ministry of the interior addressed to prefects, dated 16 December 1971, Paris.

66. For a full description of migrant housing, see SCOOPER, *Eléments d'Information sur l'Offre Publique de Logements pour les Travailleurs Immgrés et leurs Familles,* IAURP, February 1973.

67. Article 3 of ADEF *foyer* regulations.

68. CIMADE, *Etude du GISTI sur les Foyers pour les Travailleurs Immigrés,* Paris, July 1973.

69. Interview, Paris, October 1974 with *foyer* employee.

70. Ibid.

71. Visited in company of CGT official at Gennevilliers, 14 November 1974.

72. SCOOPER, *Eléments d'Information.*

73. This is true, particularly by the small political groups to the left of the Communist party, for example, Rouge.

74. *Compte Rendu*, article 3 of ADEF *foyer* regulations.

75. *Le Monde*, 27–28 January 1974.

76. Federation National du Bâtiment, Paris.

77. See F. Rerat et al., "Les Emplois Tenus par la Main d'Oeuvre Etrangère," in *Trois Approches des Problèmes d'Emploi* (Presses Universitaires de France, 1974), table 8, p. 45.

78. Martin Slater, "Migration and Workers' Conflicts."

JAMES P. PISCATORI*

The Formation of the Saʿūdī Identity: A Case Study of the Utility of Transnationalism

5

Saʿūdī Arabia[1] is interesting, not only for its uncommon customs and wealth, but also because it is a country whose name derives from that of the royal family, the legitimacy of which is tied to transnational forces. It is certainly not the only country that has been affected and even shaped by transnationalism, but it is unique in the pronounced impact that the dynasty has had in defining the national identity. Unlike the way the nationals of Hāshimite Jordan and ʿAlawī Morocco think of themselves, the subjects of the Saʿūdī monarchy refer to themselves by the very name of the royal family. The dominance of the dynasty and its successful use of Islam to enhance its rule largely explain the development of the Saʿūdī identity among a people that previously lacked a national consciousness.

I shall argue that identity links with transnationalism in the Saʿūdī case in the following ways: the effort to structure a transnational force, Islam, helped to integrate the tribes and to encourage a transtribal identity; transnational values were helpful in legitimating the control of the Saʿūdī elite over a disunited territory; and the Saʿūds used one transnational force, Islam, to combat the delegitimating effects of another transnational force, pan-Arabism, and thereby augmented the desirability of popular association with themselves. For these reasons, over time, identification with the crown

*I am grateful to Dr. Shafqat Shah and to Brian Klunk for their assistance in the preparation of this chapter. I particularly wish to express my appreciation to William Sands for his careful reading of a draft and for his appropriate suggestions and corrections.

leads to Sa ʿūdī nationalism,[2] but I employ the broader term of "identity" here to refer to a state of mind that both precedes and includes the notion of allegiance to a nation-state.

EMERGENCE OF AN EARLY SA ʿŪDĪ IDENTITY

It is, of course, an error to assume that the present-day kingdom of Sa ʿūdī Arabia originated in a cultural, historical, or political vacuum. On the contrary, in the pre-Islamic era, the peninsula became increasingly Arab, with Arabic emerging as the universal language. In addition, the revolution of Muḥammad began a new era in which religious solidarity added to ethnic commonalty, even inspiring the new believers, over time, to eliminate the Christian and Jewish enclaves from the area. The compacts with the non-Muslim communities of Najrān and al-ʿAqaba must be seen, on the level of historical effect, as interim arrangements that did not halt the process by which the region became religiously homogeneous. With political control facilitated by the homogeneity, the mid-seventh-century community, or *umma*, of the Prophet and his four immediate successors emerges as the precedent for political unification of the peninsula.

Yet Muḥammad's new order, while brilliantly synthesizing religion and politics, was not able to transcend either the traditional notion of obedience to a particular leader or the bonds of tribal loyalties themselves. The identification of apostasy with treason, though productive of a regime greater than those of the individual tribes and towns, was not sufficient to break down basic identities and, in so doing, create a new and enduring communal identity. Muḥammad's death, therefore, precipitated the wars of *ridda*, or apostasy, in which the tribes revolted and the *khalīfa* reasserted control over them. As the political center gradually shifted from al-Madīna to Damascus, Baghdad, Cairo, and Istanbul, peninsular unity dissipated again, and the local inhabitants concentrated their loyalties primarily on tribe or town and marginally on province.[3] The Ottomans were able to assert some direction over al-Ḥijāz and its holy places and over the al-Aḥsāʾ province on the Persian Gulf coast, yet the position of the Sublime Porte was generally weak. (Map 1 shows the principal cities and regions referred to in the text.) Despite the fragmentation, a certain pride of place remained through-

SAʿŪDĪ ARABIA

IRAN

IRAQ

JORDAN

Sinai

al-ʿAqaba

PERSIAN GULF

KUWAYT

al-Buṣayya

JABAL SHAMMAR

Ḥāʾil

al-Ajfar

NAJD

al-Arṭāwiyya

al-Sabala

SUDAYR

Dukhna

QAṢĪM

WASHM

Dirʿiyya

al-Zahrān

al-Riyāḍ

al-Ghaṭghaṭ

BAHRAYN

QATAR

AL-AḤSĀʾ

UNITED ARAB AMIRATES

OMAN

AL-RUBʿ AL-KHĀLĪ

SOUTH YAMAN

al-Khurma

al-Madina

ʿASĪR

Najrān

NORTH YAMAN

Makka

al-Ṭāʾif

Jidda

AL-ḤIJĀZ

RED SEA

SUDAN

ETHIOPIA

out the peninsula because of its incorporation of the two holiest cities of Islam, and at least some Muslim scholars have argued that the entire region partakes of a special juridical status because it was the setting of the Prophet.[4]

Consciousness of the immediate relevance of Muḥammad's golden era reached its fullest expression in the eighteenth century in the Najd, the central area of the peninsula that regularly escaped external control because of its distance from the coasts, its inhospitable environment, and its relative economic unimportance. There, in 1744, Muḥammad ibn Saʿūd and Muḥammad ibn ʿAbd al-Wahhāb concluded an extraordinary alliance; the former was a local *amīr* and the latter, a reformer without honor in the Prophet's own country. No honor was given because of the harshness of the message: the absolute unity of God prohibits worship of and reliance on saints (followers called themselves *muwaḥḥidūn*—believers in God's unity); prayer is mandatory; and the *lex talionis* of the Qurʾān is to be strictly applied. Muḥammad ibn ʿAbd al-Wahhāb not only preached against the deviations of folk Islam, but he also took action by destroying trees that had been worshipped and tombs that had been built for the glory of men and, on at least one occasion, by stoning to death a woman adulterer.[5]

Following his reputation and being peripatetic because of it, Muḥammad ibn ʿAbd al-Wahhāb entered the territory of the Āl Saʿūd, where the *amīr* received him warmly because of the intercession by influential townspeople who were convinced of the importance of his teachings. There was also, no doubt, the hope that this singular crusader might provide some of the early Islamic fervor that would be useful to the *amīr* in regional politics. Political promise was implicit in ʿAbd al-Wahhāb's response to his greeting: "Be you too assured of honour and power, for who so believeth in the One God and worketh His will, he shall have the kingdom of the country and its people."[6] The alliance of the two families did indeed lead to the establishment of the first Saʿūdī state, which dates from 1773, when al-Riyāḍ fell to their control, until 1819, when it was defeated at the hands of the Ottoman pasha of Egypt. Their empire united, for the first time since the days of the Prophet, the greatest portion of the lands of the current kingdom—the Najad, al-Aḥsāʾ, Asīr, and part of al-Ḥijāz, including the holy cities. The Saʿūdī-*muwaḥḥidūn* possession of Makka and al-Madīna, their destruction of local temples, their interruption of the *ḥajj*, or pilgrimage, and their expansion into Iraq and to the neighborhood of Damascus prompted the Ottomans to curtail their power. The shifting of allegiance by such key tribes as the Muṭavr, the ʿUtavba, and the Ḥarb facilitated their defeat.[7]

It was not long after the forces of Ibrāhīm Pasha razed Dirʿīyya, the traditional Saʿūdī capital, that a second Saʿūdī state began to emerge. It reached its strongest position in the 1860s under Fayṣal, a direct descendant of Muḥammad ibn Saʿūd. Soon thereafter, rivalry within the family left the state vulnerable to attack in the east and west by the Ottomans or their representatives and in the Najd by another important family, the Rashīds. Muḥammad ibn Rashīd ended Saʿūdī control in 1891, when he drove ʿAbd al-Raḥmān, father of the first king of Saʿūdī Arabia, into exile in Kuwayt.[8]

The establishment of Saʿūdī control during these two periods was due to a combination of military prowess by the successive rulers and religious zeal by both the rulers and the ruled. Islam, making no analytical destinction between the *regnum* and the *sacerdotium*, generated a vigorous political movement in the Arabia of the eighteenth and nineteenth centuries. The relationship was mutually beneficial: fighting for a great cause—purging the land of the Prophet of unworthy innovations—easily lured Badawīn soldiers, especially when the Saʿūdī ruler proclaimed a *jihād* in adverse times. And one of the first acts after victory was the instruction of the newly conquered in the fundamental principles of the faith, freed from the encrustations of the centuries. Moreover, an Islamic association that allowed the Saʿūdī rulers to claim the title of *imān*, or leader of the faithful, unquestionably enhanced their political acceptability,

The *muwaḥḥidūn* spirit, though of inestimable value in extending and, to a degree, maintaining Saʿūdī control, did not induce complete loyalty to the state. Rather, there was a constant need to reassert central control by punitive raids on tribes and towns; even the most cursory reader of Philby's accounts gains the impression that Saʿūdī history is a series of raids and counter raids. Perhaps the most important reasons central direction was minimal are the independent nature of the Badawīn, the countervailing impact of outside forces such as the Ottomans and the *sharīf of* al-Ḥijāz, and the expectation by the governors themselves that regular tax payments and prayer were sufficient acts of obedience. The assuring of loyalties and the creating of a nation-state had to wait for the twentieth century, when a Saʿūdī identity emerges from and adds to Saʿūdī control. The process has had five stages that illustrate the utility of transnational values.

INITIAL SUCCESS OF ʿABD AL-ʿAZĪZ

The oldest son of ʿAbd al-Raḥmān chafed under the ignominy of exile in Kuwayt and soon forayed into Rashīdī-held territory. After first experiencing defeat, ʿAbd al-ʿAzīz (commonly known in the West as Ibn Saʿūd) had a remarkable number of victories in both frontal assaults and covert operations. The most famous of the latter type was the capture of al-Riyāḍ in 1901–1902, when he and a small group scaled the walls of the city at night and killed the governor, Ajlān. Reinforcing his position in the area of the capital, ʿAbd al-ʿAzīz was able, during the years 1902 to 1912, to reestablish Saʿūdī hegemony over Qaṣīm, Washm, and Sudayr—in short, over the Najd. A decisive battle occurred in 1904, when the Rashīds called upon the two pillars of their rule, tribesmen from the Jabal Shammar and the Ottoman Turks, to stop the Saʿūdī advance. The failure of the effort guaranteed the long-range success of ʿAbd al-ʿAzīz, although the task was not easy mainly because of the unpredictability of the tribes under his control. In 1908, for example, a rebellion by parts of the ʿAjmān and Hazzānī tribes supposedly under Saʿūdī control forced ʿAbd al-ʿAzīz to turn his attention away from the battle with sharīf Ḥusayn of Makka.[9]

Two factors account for the light accent on Islam in this period. First, ʿAbd al-ʿAzīz was more interested in regaining a territorial base than in advancing the muwaḥḥidūn ideals. Second, the invocation of Islam would have been somewhat inappropriate then because the Rashīds themselves were followers of shaykh ʿAbd al-Wahhāb. Questions of Islamic orthodoxy were not relevant in this clash of local dynasties, particularly when the Saʿūds viewed the Rashīds, originally their own appointees as governors of Ḥāʾil, as usurpers. Their denunciation as errant believers would come during the next period.

EXTENSION OF SAʿ ŪDĪ CONTROL

The second period, ranging from 1912 to 1927, was one of expanding Saʿūdī control into the Turkish-influenced areas of al-Ḥijāz, ʿAsīr, and al-Aḥsāʾ. The prime source of support became the *ikhwān* movement that ʿAbd al-ʿAzīz established in 1912. It was a radical idea for the Arabian peninsula and involved the settling of the Badawīn in agricultural communities in which the strict, rather puritanical injunctions of Muḥammad ibn ʿAbd al-Wahhāb governed daily life. Both ʿAbd al-ʿAzīz and the nomads derived benefits from the translation of the concept into action. The former, weary of the difficulties of raising and maintaining a regular army of diverse and mobile tribesmen, gained a ready source of more dependable fighters. The latter had the opportunity, when not fighting, to learn farming skills and, when fighting, to acquire booty, rigorously distributed according to Qurʾānic law whereby the warriors get four-fifths and the "state," one-fifth of the total.[10]

More importantly, the movement was attractive to the Badawīn since it provided an opportunity for them to participate in what seemed to be a microcosm of the golden *umma* of the Prophet and the rightly guided caliphs. As T. E. Lawrence wrote, "The ascetic tribes of the desert are always looking for a new creed, and the stern puritanism with which the Wahabi name was associated appealed to the most energetic of them."[11] The terminology of the movement was unmistakably symbolic: it was a movement of brothers (*ikhwān*), and an individual settlement was a *hijra*, the term generally used to denote the Prophet's flight from Makka to al-Madīna, where he established the archetypical religiopolitical community. Because the demands of communal life were strange to the independent nomads, especially when set by the precepts of ʿAbd al-Wahhāb, ʿAbd al-ʿAzīz undoubtedly exercised force to induce some to settle and remain. Amīn al-Riḥānī has testified that the Saʿūdī leader reminded the *ikhwān* that "it was by the sword that we have conquered you," and a British official thought it noteworthy that the brothers were reduced to a state of absolute dependence on ʿAbd al-ʿAzīz.[12] There is no question, however, that the attraction of the *hijra* was substantial: the "flight" from desert to town was only part of the larger "flight" from the mundane to the paradisal.

ᶜAbd al-ᶜAzīz established the first camp at al-Arṭāwiyya in the Najd in 1912, and it settled sections of the Muṭayr.[13] Other major *hijar* were at al-Ghaṭghaṭ, settled by part of the ᶜUtayba; Dukhna, by the Ḥarb; and al-Ajfar, by the Shammar. Each settlement was organized into three fighting groups: those ever ready to do battle; those who normally engaged in herding but who were prepared to be mobilized; and those dedicated to agriculture and commerce who could be called on to fight only when the *ᶜulamāʾ*, or religious scholars, thought it necessary. By 1930, there were about two hundred sites from which ᶜAbd al-ᶜAzīz was able to draw between twenty-five and thirty thousand men for the vanguard of his fighting forces.[14] These men shared with the Muslim warriors of the seventh century a concentrated devotion to the cause of Islam, which, in the case of the *ikhwān*, has been nearly universally labelled "fanatical" and "ferocious." They occasionally engaged in excess, as when they killed more than two hundred Ḥijāzī troops at al-Khurma in 1919 and when they laid brutal siege to al-Ṭāʾif in 1924. Fiery devotion is also seen in their unrealized desire to destroy the Prophet's tomb for its blasphemy.

As a whole, the brotherhood movement served ᶜAbd al-ᶜAzīz well in three short-term ways. First, it harnessed the energy of several major tribes, including portions of the Muṭayr, ᶜUtayba, ᶜAnayza, Qaḥṭān, Ḥarb, ᶜAjmān, Shammar, and ᶜAwāzim tribes. Filling the "unpledged allegiance of their minds,"[15] the movement prohibited intertribal warfare, offered a loyalty to a cause greater than that of the tribe, and inspired a readiness to fight on behalf of that loyalty. Members of the *ikhwān* viewed themselves as righteous Muslims, and the conviction strengthened their devotion to both the *muwaḥḥidūn* ideals and the Saᶜūdī guardians of the faith. ᶜAbd al-ᶜAzīz emerged as the acknowledged leader of this "unnatural harmony of the tribal forces,"[16] not only for his cunning, but also because he was the direct descendant of the Saᶜūdī who allied with ᶜAbd al-Wahhāb;he was the dispenser of loot gained from just battle with the errant believer; and he was the son of the *imām*. ᶜAbd al-ᶜAzīz thus gained relative stability among the Badawīn, as well as vigorous fighters from their number and a measure of legitimacy as their supratribal leader.

Second, the movement served as a way to crystallize the dispute with the Rashīds in the Najd. The *ikhwān* followers pronounced themselves the true followers of ʿAbd al-Wahhāb, and, by extension, they considered the Rashīds deviants. Unlike the earlier period, these political rivals could now be attacked as unfaithful students of the Wahhābī teachings because of the existence of the structured movement. The delegitimation of the Rashīds' orthodoxy, coupled with the harshness of their rule, hastened the demise of their control of central Arabia. Whether or not the ideological argument had the paramount impact, the *ikhwān* militia was instrumental in the 1921 capture of Ḥāʾil, the Rashīdī center.

Finally, the *ikhwān* operated as an organized opposition, complete with its own propaganda, to the Ottoman Turks and their Arab, Hāshimite proconsuls in al-Ḥijāz against whom the Sa ʿūdī-Wahhābī forces finally prevailed in late 1925 and early 1926. The Ottomans and the Hāshimites were a threat to the Sa ʿūdī dynasty in more than the military sense, for they claimed to represent Sunnī orthodoxy, and hence many accepted them as the natural guardians of the holy places. ʿAbd al-ʿAzīz countered the claim with a reassertion of the *muwaḥ-ḥidūn* indictment: the rulers of the holy land had been unfaithful to Muḥammad's teaching by allowing the growth of saint cults and temples, by failing to halt the veneration of the Prophet himself despite the fact that he was not God but only the messenger of God, and by acquiescing in lax moral standards.

With ʿAbd al-ʿAziz regularly and colorfully denouncing Ḥusayn and his allies as infidels,[17] the restoration of the holy land to unadorned Islam became the goal. The fervor to accomplish it increased under the impact of two events: after World War I, the British placed Fayṣal and ʿAbd Allāh, the sons of *sharīf Ḥusayn* of Makka, on the thrones of Iraq and Transjordan; and, in 1924, after Atatürk abolished the caliphate, the *sharīf* assumed the title of the leader of Islam.[18] ʿAbd al-ʿAzīz was doubly outraged since his Hāshimite rivals were now entrenched in the lands to the north and since they had proved their improbity once again by seizing the caliphal mantle. By this latter audacity, the Hāshimites further inflamed the members of the *ikhwān*. Feelings were so high that, when the *ikhwān* warriors attacked the first major city of al-Ḥijāz, they began without the permission of ʿAbd al-ʿAzīz and ended with hundreds massacred.

Incidents of such a dramatic kind attracted world concern, but there was little agreement, even among "Arabists," as to the long-term significance of the events. At a meeting of the Central Asian Society in London in 1926, for example, H. St. J. Philby and D. G. Hogarth expressed opposite perspectives on the likely durability of the *muwaḥḥidūn* "triumph." Philby thought that ʿAbd al-ʿAzīz's success was so firm that Yaman would soon fall to his control, and that he would be acclaimed as *khalīfa*. Hogarth thought that, since neither the religious fervor could be sustained nor intertribal raiding stopped, the movement was unlikely to endure. Both were wrong. Philby, always the devoted admirer of the Saʿūdī leader, overestimated the ease with which Saʿūdī-*muwaḥḥidūn* success was attained. And Hogarth underestimated the ability of a forceful leader to change the status quo: "[i]t is all very well to try and settle the Bedouin on the land, but in so trying you run counter to the tradition of countless generations, and deprive him of what has always been his chief interest in life [that is, raiding]."[19]

The *ikhwān* movement advanced ʿAbd al-ʿAzīz's long-term interest precisely by helping to overcome this traditional pattern in laying the groundwork for a national identity. Three new, mutually reinforcing factors emerged to help shape this identity: a sense of transtribal solidarity; attachment to the land; and acceptance of Saʿūdī authority. The idea that a great and holy cause united diverse tribesmen strengthened the political position of the Saʿūds who initiated the cause; settled communities helped to bring previously nomadic individuals into contact with each other; and the elite's general acceptance empowered it to enforce, if necessary, the prohibition on intertribal fighting and the requirement of support for the *hijra*. Though these factors were in a rudimentary form in this period, they are early versions of the indispensable conditions of nation-statehood: peoplehood, territoriality, and effective government.[20]

The *ikhwān*, therefore, effectively advanced, in the short and the long run, ʿAbd al-ʿAzīz's religious, sociological, and political goals —all virtually indistinguishable in his mind as it would be in the mind of every good Muslim. As an anonymous contemporary observer wrote:

Ibn Saʾud has reverted to the time-honored practice of using the religious beliefs of his subjects to help him forge a weapon with which to push forward his political dynastic ambitions; finding the social structure of his State unsuitable for his ambitions, he has created a military class, and it is thus, when we hear the panic-stricken Bedwin shouting "Ikhwàn! Ikhwàn!" they are not thinking of an attack from the tribes or fellaheen of Najd, but from the Ikhwan colonists—that terrible weapon born in the brain of a king among men, and forged by the hand of a master of statecraft.[21]

The instrumentality of Islam was not only obvious to ʿAbd al-ʿAzīz, it was also preferable if the usage of another transnational force, pan-Arabism, was the alternative. The search for legitimacy based on a reformist vision of Islam, surely, could only have been fruitful when conducted at the expense of other Muslims—in this case, both the Ottoman Turks and the Arab Hāshimites. The Saʿūds could direct an institutionalized Islamic movement at two rivals, which they could not have done if they had invoked only pan-Arab sentiments. ʿAbd al-ʿAzīz's distrust of the "Arab awakening" is seen in his suggestion to the Turks that either unification of all Arabs under one ruler, presumably himself, or independence of individual states within a loose Ottoman confederation was the answer to growing demands for change within the empire.[22] The fact that he mentioned the second possibility at a time when Arab nationalism was definitely growing indicates his suspicion of Hāshimite power, and implies his preference for Islam as a way of legitimating himself and of forging a larger identity by using it to oppose the unfaithful among the believers.

CONSOLIDATION OF SA ʿŪDĪ CONTROL

During the third stage, from 1927 to 1953, the Saʿūds solidified their control over the present kingdom, and the growth in national awareness enhanced their legitimacy. Consolidation, however, was not possible until ʿAbd al-ʿAzīz eliminated the one remaining threat to his authority that, ironically, came from members of the *ikhwān.* ʿAbd al-ʿAzīz's use of an institutionalized transnational force reached its logical, transnational conclusion in 1928–1929, when members of the movement attempted to spread the word in the British-mandated territories to the north and against fellow believers.

The movement across established frontiers had begun as early as 1920–1922, when there were raids into Kuwayt and Iraq. At first, some tribesmen were probably following the normal pastoral cycle that did not respect newly defined state boundaries. But eventually, members of the *ikhwān* joined in the fighting, prompted by a zealous pursuit of *muwaḥḥidūn* reformation and by the wish to retaliate against attacks from those areas by members of the Shammar tribe who had supported the Rashīdī rivals. One of the most active *ikhwān* leaders was the *shaykh* of the Muṭayr, Fayṣal al-Dawīsh, over whom ʿAbd al-ʿAzīz exercised tenuous authority at best. At the time of the Kuwayt Conference in 1923, designed to reconcile Najdī and Hāshimite differences, al-Dawīsh led an unauthorized raid against the Hāshimites in the northern Ḥijāz. Although the British were never convinced that such raids were not approved by ʿAbd al- ʿAzīz, it is clear that al-Dawīsh was increasingly upset with Saʿūd's manner of governing and able to defy his authority.

A particular point of contention was the nature of the relationship with Great Britain. In February 1924, for example, the *imām* ʿAbd al-Raḥmān warned his son of the anger among his people at the policy that relied on the British to restrain would-be raiders and that obligated him to refrain from redressing the injuries directly. Fayṣal al-Dawīsh himself wrote to demand action from ʿAbd al-ʿAzīz to prevent further raids from neighboring areas and ominously added that "we cannot stand it any longer."[23] One month later, al-Dawīsh took matters into his own hands when he attacked shepherds in Iraq.

The defeat of the Hāshimites in 1927–1928 prompted a direct confrontation by stimulating the unrest of *ikhwān* members. The victory deprived them of an outlet for their energies and a source of booty, but it allowed ʿAbd al-ʿAzīz to attend to the renegades within his own camp. In 1928, al-Dawīsh led a Badawīn attack on the al-Buṣayya fort in Iraq that had become the detested symbol of encroachments on Badawīn maneuverability. When he turned, in the Najd, against portions of the Shammar and ʿAnayza faithful to ʿAbd al-ʿAzīz, the threat to Saʿūdī hegemony was clear. Resorting to aerial bombings of *ikhwān* settlements whose members had crossed into mandate territories, the British exacerbated the situation by rendering ʿAbd al-ʿAzīz vulnerable to the charge that he was not protecting his subjects. More importantly, the rebels launched an ideological offensive, denouncing ʿAbd al-ʿAzīz's tergiversation of the *ikhwān* cause because of his dealing with the infidel British and his introduction of such objectionable Western devices as the automobile, radio, and telegraph. At a major tribal convocation in late 1928, the *ʿulamāʾ* ruled that the telegraph was at least not unlawful,[24] but they more clearly expressed their resentment of ʿAbd al-ʿAzīz's preventing them from *jihād* against the British-protected tribes of Iraq and Transjordan. The frontier post, constructed to stop traditional raiding and counterraiding, prompted this claim: "Our sacred rights are being disgraced before our eyes."[25]

Because ʿAbd al-ʿAzīz could hardly have claimed to rule on behalf of the *muwaḥḥidūn* vision of Islam if followers of *shaykh* ʿAbd al-Wahhāb denounced the king's deviationism,[26] the only solution was the reassertion of control through military defeat of the brotherhood rebels. He accomplished the objective by decisively routing them in the battle of al-Sabala in March 1929, and by eliminating the remaining opposition among the Muṭayr and ʿAjmān in early 1930. With these confrontations, the *ikhwān* movement had come full circle: created to advance a reformist world view of Islam, it flourished while legitimating the Saʿūdī leadership and then took its final, fatal turn by rejecting that leadership for unfaithful adherence to the world view. The institutionalization of Islam in the *ikhwān*, which had been unquestionably useful in the promotion of an identity above that of the tribe, became dysfunctional when it sought to disentangle that remarkable Saʿūdī-*muwaḥḥidūn* alliance and so dissociate the larger identity from the dynasty. As Philby, in his characteristically dramatic way, wrote of the *ikhwān* and ʿAbd al-ʿAzīz: "The Frankenstein of his own creation would surely have destroyed him, if he had not taken the initiative of destroying it himself."[27]

With the brotherhood curbed, ʿAbd al-ʿAzīz was soon in undisputed control of his territory—a fact that was accepted by the major powers of the world. The country, officially proclaimed as the Kingdom of Saʿūdī Arabia in 1932, was becoming a nation-state not merely because of the recognition of other states. It was increasingly able to give substance to the legal illusion because the fundamental elements of territoriality, effective government, and peoplehood were solidifying. Although statesmen had not, and in some instances still have not, delimited exact frontier lines, the capture of the ʿAsīr from the Yaman in 1934 settled the general physical dimensions of the kingdom. Additionally, although ʿAbd al-ʿAzīz is a prime example of the patrimonial leader,[28] he did initiate an amount of institutionalization, particularly in the later years of his reign. He and his counselors established schools, developed a bureaucracy, and created a regular army and a paramilitary guard. The result was a government able to satisfy, albeit minimally, basic domestic needs and to enter into foreign relations.

Lastly, consciousness of a common identity was on the rise as ʿAbd al-ʿAzīz's diverse subjects were reminded of their common allegiance to his regime. Three factors furthered the sense of community. First, people submitted to a common government that proved to be functional and whose legitimacy was enhanced because of the functionalism. In addition to summoning a common obedience from a variety of tribes, villages, and towns, the government, through such institutions as the schools and the army, functioned, in the absence of long-standing traditions, as a concrete reminder of common interests. Second, ʿAbd al-ʿAzīz was skillful in demonstrating that strange bedfellows make good politics: by marrying members of defeated or distant tribes, he contributed mightily toward making real the notion that the Āl Saʿūd is the national tribe.

Finally, although the boisterous days of the *ikhwān* were over, the government relied on more subtle ways to reinforce the image of its intimate linkage with Islam. Qurʾānic law was the law of the land, and responsibility for protection of the holy places and for the pilgrims going there was willingly accepted by the ruling family. The leadership further strengthenend its position by promoting as proper dogma the tenets of the Ḥanbalī school with which it had been historically associated. The government particularly enforced its standards of *imām* appointments and mosque education in al-Ḥijāz, where there had been improper practices under the Hāshimites, and, in al-Aḥsāʾ, the Shīʿītes were the objects of discrimination, if not of persecution as they charged.[29]

Force undeniably played a major role in the consolidation of Saʿūdī rule. I want to stress that the association of the Saʿūds with the guardians of the law and land of the Scriptures and with orthodox doctrine also helped to validate the regime. That validation, in turn, helped to instill a sense of common allegiance to it among diverse and hitherto unrelated subjects.

CHALLENGE TO SAʿŪDĪ LEGITIMACY AND IDENTITY

In the period between 1953 and 1967, threats to the Saʿūdī rule reappeared. A strike by Arab oil workers, which occurred just prior to Saʿūd's accession to the throne, was an omen for his reign. It was indeed a troubled period that followed the transition from the rule of the father, who died in November 1953, to that of the son. The difficulties were due to several reasons: (1) Saʿūd clearly lacked the skill of administration and the interest in governing that ʿAbd al-ʿAzīz had; (2) oil wealth, which had grown dramatically since the early meager returns but soon to level off, allowed Saʿūd to indulge his lavish taste, with the Nāṣiriyya palace complex as the egregious example of the new king's ostentation; (3) the increasing contact with Westerners inspired skeptics to doubt the ability of a monarchical regime, especially one headed by so lamentable a monarch, to steer Saʿūdī Arabia toward modernization; and (4) the Arab defeat in the first Arab-Israeli War, the resultant crisis of self-examination in the Arab world, and the Egyptian revolution prompted an identification with pan-Arabism that had previously been latent in the peninsula.

The last factor proved to be especially nettlesome, as it took the shape of Nāṣirism, a vibrant, transnational ideology urging Arabs to rid themselves of both imperialists and reactionaries.[30] Nāṣir was uncommonly adept at combining a personal attractiveness with seeming success at defending Arab dignity, as at Suez. For his efforts, the Arabs throughout the region revered his person and his message. When the people of Saʿūdī Arabia affirmed his popularity during a 1956 state visit, the Saʿūds could not have missed the implications. In fact, they perceived that Nāṣirism was so significant a force to contend with that they framed several policies in response to it. At first they deferred to the Nāṣirist appeal, as seen in the 1956 decision to postpone consideration of extending the American lease to the al-Ẓahrān air base. Soon thereafter, however, Nāṣir's pronounced revolutionary rhetoric and, more importantly, the direction in which it was addressed influenced the decision to improve relations with the United States. For whatever reason, King Saʿūd then encouraged an assassination attempt against Nāṣir, which, when set against the "radicals'" union of Egypt and Syria, combined to cause a full-fledged cold war between Cairo and al-Riyāḍ.[31] The crisis, precipitated by Nāṣir's anti-Saʿūdī position and by his popularity, and confirmed by the king's ineptitude, persuaded the royal family that Saʿūd must concede power to the crown prince if the dynasty were to survive.

The royal brothers quarreled, however, as King Saʿūd fell under the influence of members of the royal family who had succumbed to Nāṣir's influence. Prince Ṭalāl, a minister of finance, and *shaykh* ʿAbd Allāh al-Ṭāriqī, minister of petroleum, led the small coterie. They advocated major reforms that would have circumscribed the religious law and introduced liberal political institutions. Fayṣal, interposing himself between a weak brother and impatient reformers, succeeded in heightening the humiliation of the former and the impatience of the latter. Nāṣir was disturbed by the cabinet reshuffle in September 1961 that removed Ṭalāl from an official post and, accordingly, he accelerated his opposition to the government in al-Riyāḍ. A particularly piercing manner of criticism was to use the *shaykh* of al-Azhar, the premier center of learning in the Islamic world, to criticize the Saʿūds. In March 1962, for example, the religious leader denounced the "immoral living of the Arabian peninsula." As the king increasingly lost power to the crown prince and as the attacks from Egypt mounted, Fayṣal was able to solidify his position further by removing Prince Nawwaf, Ṭalāl's replacement at the finance ministry, and al-Ṭāriqī from the cabinet.[32]

In the propaganda war with Egypt that ensued, though the Saʿūds could not compete in pan-Arab sentiment, they could, and did, use Islam as an ideological weapon. At *ḥajj* time in 1962, for instance, the Saʿūdī government refused to accept the *kiswa*, the covering of the *Kaʿba*, which is traditionally made by the Egyptians. The government also used the occasion of the annual pilgrimage to convene leading *ʿulamāʾ* for the purpose of denouncing socialism and for establishing a conservative League of the Islamic World.[33] The dispute crystallized in August 1963, when Prince Ṭalāl, announcing his intention to visit Nāṣir, proclaimed that, if a "welfare state" was to be established in Saʿūdī Arabia, then reliance must be made on the "liberated [Arab] countries which work for the welfare of my country in the first place." The Nāṣirist threat to the Saʿūds' legitimacy, and perhaps survival, became ever more manifest when Princes Nawwāf, Badr, Fawwāz, and ʿAbd al-Muḥsin and their cousin Saʿd bin Fahd joined Ṭalāl in inevitable exile, where they denounced the royal family and tribal leaders and established the Arab Nationalist Front for the purpose of creating a democratic order in a "free Saudi Arabia."[34]

If the propaganda blasts from Cairo made the Saʿūdī rulers uncomfortable and even unnerved them, the Egyptian intervention in the Yaman in September 1962 on the side of the "republican" forces alarmed them. Although there was no great sympathy for the deposed Zaydī *imām*, the Saʿūdī government felt obligated to give support to the "royalist" side. In so doing, the progressive-conservative confrontation that Nāṣir discussed so often seemed to take apocalyptic form. More redoubtable than the proximity of Egyptian soldiers and airplanes was the expectation of the "domino effect" on Saʿūdī Arabia. There was cause for concern as evidenced by the memorandum, signed by six former members of the Saʿūdī government, that called for the recognition of the new Yamanī regime. The ruling family did not ignore the impact of these events: Fayṣal received all executive power, and he announced a far-reaching program of internal reform, including commitments to establish national and regional consultative councils, to revise the religious-based legal system, and to promulgate labor and social-welfare regulations.[35]

As the Yamanī conflict continued, Fayṣal's steady hands were able to fashion relative domestic harmony. He was successful largely because Nāṣir's revolutionary vision began to appear less prepossessing to the dissatisfied element as the Egyptians were progressively mired in the complexities of Yamanī tribal politics. Moreover, the dissident *amīrs* in exile fell to quarrelling with their Cairene host, partly because they conceded that Fayṣal was indeed introducing reforms and partly because Nāṣir flirted with the hopelessly unfit Saʿūd at their summit in January 1964. The result was recantation by the princes *qua* Jacobins and the admission, long-awaited in al-Riyāḍ, that "lustrous slogans and promises" had gulled them.[36]

Although the family soon deposed Saʿūd and made Fayṣal the king he had long effectively been, the problem of Nāṣir did not go away, no matter how less urgent a problem it was. With his control of internal politics secure and Nāṣir's ideological offensive now blunted, Fayṣal launched a counteroffensive stressing Islamic, rather than Arab, unity. In December 1965, the king and the shah of Iran appealed for an Islamic summit meeting, and a month later in Jordan, Fayṣal denounced those opposed to an alliance of Muslims as enemies of Islam. Though the new Saʿūdī ruler cleverly stressed that there would be no conflict between an Islamic organization and an Arab one since both ought to foster "Islamic brotherhood," there is no question that the king was attempting to create a cohesive, traditionalist bloc in the ongoing Arab cold war.[37] Such was at least the perception of the Algerians, who found the idea incompatible with contemporary international relations, and the Egyptians, who denounced the alliance as the handiwork of the imperialists.[38]

The plan was singularly ineffective in foreign relations, but it may have had an important domestic impact: it bolstered the legitimacy of the regime by reconfirming its identification with Islam. Nāṣir huffed and puffed, though to little success by late 1966; yet, the Saʿūdī leadership could not have afforded to disregard the potential impact on its people. It could not have done so especially when the newspaper al-Ahrām was carrying on the same front page a picture of Nāṣir greeting Saʿūd in his new home-in-exile in Cairo and a headline announcing that the Tapline had been blown up. [39] It is true that Saʿūd's presence in Nāṣir's capital was cause more for pity than for alarm: "Saud's principal activity during his stay in Cairo was his nightly tieup of the Hotel Semiramis switchboard with telephone calls to his aged mother in Riyadh."[40] But the image of a divided royal family did not portend well for the regime's acceptability while reports were emanating from Beirut and Cairo that the Union of the People of the Arabian Peninsula (tanẓīm ittiḥād shaʿb al-jazīra al-ʿarabiyya) was claiming responsibility for several acts of terrorism within the country.

In denouncing ten Yamanīs as agents of Nāṣir and in holding them responsible for explosions in al-Riyāḍ, the Ministry of Interior warned, in March 1967: "We have been patient, but we shall use a mailed fist against anyone who tries to attack us or transgress against the sanctities of Islam."[41] Linking the security of the kingdom with the sanctity of Islam was effective in bolstering the position of Fayṣal and his government. If for no other reason, they could attack Nāṣir as the proponent of a socialist creed hostile to Islam, and they could associate Saʿūd, who had denounced Fayṣal as a traitor and who been hailed in Egypt and the Yaman as the legitimate king of Saʿūdī Arabia,[42] with the enemies of Islam.

If the period between 1953 and 1967 is notable for the rising volume of attacks on Saʿūdī Arabia, it is also notable for the kind of response made to them. Since part of the ideological baggage of the "progressive" forces was pan-Arabism, then pan-Islam was a natural counterpoise for the Saʿūdīs in the dynamic of interaction. Fayṣal's strong emphasis on Islamic solidarity helped to repair the damage to Saʿūdī Arabia's prestige caused by Nāṣir's attacks, and it was also useful in terms of the Saʿūdī identity. Because of the absence of a prior national consciousness, the dynasty-connected identity of Saʿūdī Arabia is intimately tied to the legitimacy of the dynasty itself. Intra-elite divisions, whether due to Ṭalāl's reforms or to Saʿūd's deposition by Fayṣal, called into question that legitimacy. The fact that a number of citizens found Nāṣirist ideology attractive at a time when their awareness of the external world, and presumably of political alternatives, had increased also helped to put the regime on the defensive. The rise in levels of education, in the number of students studying abroad, and in the audience of the "Voice of the Arabs" from Cairo had political implications the government could not ignore. Pan-Islam, though proposed sincerely by the devout Fayṣal, also had an instrumental effect: it strengthened the regime's standing at home by reinforcing the point that the national identity is tied to a force greater than Arab *qawmiyya*, or nationalism. As pan-Arabism was an adjunct of Egyptian nationalism under Nāṣir, the Saʿūdī leadership was not oblivious to the utility of pan-Islam to combat the pull of a rival, attractive transnational value.

STRENGTHENING THE SAʿŪDĪ LEGITIMACY AND IDENTITY

The period after the 1967 Arab-Israeli War engendered new confidence in the Saʿūds that the rivalry and threats to their rule were decreasing. The primary reason for this self-assurance was the weakening of Nāṣir after the June debacle. Fayṣal found himself in the agreeable position of vouchsafing to a humbled rival more than $100 million in aid.[43] He also extracted a concession from Nāṣir to remove Egyptian troops from the Yaman by December 1967. As a result, Fayṣal thought that the regime was sufficiently stable in early 1968 to appoint two erstwhile dissidents, Princes Badr and Nawwaf, to important political posts.[44]

Yet, there was to be more turmoil before the relative placidity of the 1970s. Although there was unanimous outrage throughout the Arab-Islamic world at the burning of the al-Aqṣā mosque in Jerusalem in August 1969, Nāṣir and Fayṣal disagreed in the attempt to formulate a common sense. The Egyptian leader had endorsed the idea of an Islamic summit in order to express the general resentment, but had also insisted on the need for an Arab summit to deal with practical measures for the liberation of the occupied territories. Fayṣal objected to the proposed summit of Arab leaders, partly because of the recent memory of Nāṣir's use of Arabism to isolate Saʿūdī Arabia and partly because of the suspicion that the summit would reduce Egypt's burden in the Arab-Israeli conflict and thereby encourage a return to its policy of meddling in Arab affairs. Perhaps more importantly, the promotion of an Arab summit could only have been viewed as a vapid response to Fayṣal's call for a *jihād* against Israel.[45]

At virtually the same time, the government uncovered a plot by the air force to stage a coup, and, with the lesson of the days-old Libyan "revolution" clearly in mind, it led to the arrest of hundreds. Border clashes with South Yaman soon accompanied the reappearance of antiregime subversion, but superior force met the internal and external challenges.[46] The National Guard controlled the dissident air force elements, greater numbers and better equipment outmatched the South Yamanīs, and both successes confirmed the prudence of a policy designed to strengthen the Saʿūdī military.

As disturbing as these events were, they were fundamentally different from earlier problems: though Nāṣirism persisted, it was with diminished verve now that Nāṣir was financially dependent on Fayṣal. There was still resentment at the king's refusal to grant every Egyptian financial wish at the Rabāṭ meeting in late 1969, but, according to Muḥammad Haykal, Nāṣir also took pains to certify that Egypt had not been involved in anti-Saʿūdī activity since 1967.[47] Opposition surfaced from time to time, but the threat to the regime in Saʿūdī Arabia lessened as the Egyptians, Syrians, and Palestinians became financially dependent on it.

This environment provided an opportunity for the Saʿūds to advance their legitimacy and, in so doing, to contribute to the solidification of the national identity. Before 1967, pan-Islam was the cachet of the royal family, and, after 1969, it was two transnational forces, now indissolubly linked—Arabism and Islam. When Fayṣal denounced the local agents of communism in 1971, the target was no longer the Nāṣirists but rather the Zionists. The burning of the al-Aqṣā mosque symbolizes the welding of the interests of the pan-Arabists and the pan-Muslims into the common goal of opposing Israel; and the imposition of the 1973 oil embargo symbolizes the emergence of the Saʿūdīs among the undisputed leaders of the Arab world. The death of Nāṣir and the active cooperation in the October war with his more trustworthy successor certainly enhanced the Arab content of Fayṣal's policy. In September 1974, for example, the king issued a reminder that, when the Arabs were unified in the first centuries of the Islamic era, they had been capable of great things. He suggested at another point that the present cohesion among Muslims, presumably stimulated by his steadfast exhortations, provides an example for those wishing to advance Arab unity.[48]

One of his closest advisers explained the king's position in the following way:

King Faisal realized early and with conviction that Islam was the framework, the only sure one in fact, which would unify the Arabs and regain for them their lost prestige and power. It was necessary, he thought, that the Arabs should return to the right path of Islam. He organized the movement of Islamic fundamentalism, not as an alternative to Arab nationalism as some may have mistakenly believed, but as the overall canopy under which all Arabs would rally.[49]

While the thesis is arguable, I cannot disagree that currently the Sa ᶜūdī leadership is committed to a policy that encourages Arabism within an Islamic framework. The Sa ᶜūds advance Arabism as sometimes secondary to, sometimes coterminous with, but never superior to, Islam. Upon succeeding to the throne, Khālid affirmed that Islam would be the first pillar of his rule, with Arab cooperation the second.[50] He expressed his government's policy most clearly when he spoke of the connection in solidarity (taḍāmun) between Islam and Arabdom: "The Kingdom is in duty bound by the Qurʾānic policy of Islamic solidarity. It is a complement [makamal] to the policy of Arab solidarity that we seek to have established."[51] Even rapprochement [taqārub] among the Arabs, Prince Fahd warns, is dependent on the principles of both Islam and Arabism [ᶜurūba].[52]

Though the relative increase in emphasis on Arab cohesion does not entail a diminution of Islam as the primary symbol of legitimacy, it does reflect the fact that Sa ᶜūdī Arabia has become "the pole" of Arab politics.[53] Because of its special ties with the United States and its great oil wealth, the kingdom is able to play an active role in the search for an Arab-Israeli settlement, a resolution of the Lebanese crisis, and stability in the Red Sea-Horn of Africa region. There could be no more succinct confirmation of the dramatic change in position than the Gallic maxim on the particular relationship (at least for awhile) with Egypt: "Ryad finances, Cairo acts."54

The congeniality of the international environment may allow the Saʿūdī leadership to interlace pan-Arab with Islamic sentiments, but there is also utility in invoking both these transnational forces, for they assist in broadening the base of the regime's legitimacy and thereby the grounds for identification with the Saʿūds. The staggeringly high oil revenue has provided the means by which many potential dissidents are co-opted into the prevailing system, while, at the same time, it is creating the most demanding trial of the system. As modernization stimulates the broadening of the technocratic elite into a middle class, the absorptive capacity of the Saʿūdī establishment will decline, while the demands made on it are likely to increase.

Although there are no reliable figures in a country whose one official census has yet to be made public, William Rugh refers to a "New Middle Class"55 that, if defined by recipients of a non-Qurʾānic university education, would now number in the thousands. Bound together by common exposure to secular education, by a shared modernist perspective, and perhaps also by congruent foreign experiences, members of this "class" form *shilal*, or transtribal and transfamilial groups. Once supportive of the government's policies to restrict the power of the *muṭṭawwiʿyyīn*, or religious gendarmes, and to advance the social condition of women, these groups may not always be committed to the royal family's perception of the desirable rate of change. The presence of over 1 million foreigners, among whom are thirty thousand Americans, contributes to the demands of these groups for quicker modernization because of the first-hand knowledge thereby gained of other, some better, ways of life. Many hope to replace the outsiders in economic status whether or not they also wish to assume the burdens of the work needed to be done.

Judith Miller quotes a government official unperturbed by the rapid changes within Saʿūdī Arabia: " . . . you do not see soldiers with machine guns on our streets to maintain order. We are a very cohesive society, and we shall survive it all—the foreigners, the military growth, the rapid development. Wait and see."56 Perhaps unalarmed, the Saʿūdī governors would unlikely be complacent if they reflected on the fact that it was the members of the "New Middle Class" whose "class consciousness" was so easily and so recently raised by the Egyptian media. There is, thus, an obvious utility in the ideological commitment to an Islamic Arabism, witnessed so well in the joint demands for the liberation of Jerusalem and for the creation of a Palestinian state. The connected values make the modern-educated and the technocrats feel that, no matter how securely their identity is tied to the Islamic past, it is also firmly linked with the progress of the Arab future.

There is a second utility to be derived from reliance on these conjoint transnational forces. Because Arabian unity has been confined to two periods—the classical and the contemporary—provincial identities have been an enduring reality. Though people have always directed primary loyalty to tribe or town, there has also been a long-standing, inchoate identification with geographical areas conventionally, yet roughly, delimited by mountains, plateaus, and tribal dominions. Over time, the regions have become distinct. Al-Ḥijāz has borne the mark of cosmopolitanism stimulated by the blending of the races, customs, and cuisines of the pilgrims; ʿAsīr has been architecturally and topographically Yamanī; al-Aḥsāʾ has had large numbers of Shīʿite and South Asian residents; and the Najd has been denoted by the simplicity of the Badawīn life and the starkness of the *muwaḥḥidūn* way. Recognized as units, these areas were distinguished further by becoming administratively separate, even to the extent that interregional travelers in the 1940s and 1950s were required to have visas.[57]

The Najdī and Ḥijāzī are as recognizable stereotypes today as they were to Blunt, Burkhart, and Lawrence. Levon Melikian gives evidence that regional perceptions are strong, at least among Saʿūdī students:

Saudis from Al-Hasa [eastern province] were described by Saudis from the other three provinces as revolutionaries, down-trodden, industrious, nationalist, practical, and sectarian. Those from Hijaz [western province] were identified as mercantile, nervous, hospitable, artistic, sociable, and progressive. Saudis from Najd [central province] were described as reactionary, conservative, religious, hospitable, sectarian, and miserly; whereas those from Asir [southern province] were labeled as being poor, simple, ignorant, patient, generous, and backward.[58]

While the persistence of provincial stereotypes attests to the existence of provincial identities, it does not, of course, automatically suggest that identification with region is done at the expense of identification with nation. That potential exists, however, especially in a country lacking a well-defined national tradition. The Saᶜūdī government has long been concerned with the strength of regional sentiments and has specifically reacted to it. ᶜAbd al-ᶜAzīz himself, for example, was mindful not to infringe on the independent spirit of ᶜAbd Allāh ibn Jilūwī, the governor of al-Aḥsāʾ. Fayṣal also pledged a reform that would allow advisory bodies to assist the work of provincial officials. The government has occasionally adopted less conciliatory measures. For example, it arrested approximately thirty persons in the eastern province in May 1970 for their political views.[59] The reliability of this region's loyalty is particularly worrisome to the Saᶜūdī leadership in light of the fact that one-quarter of the world's oil reserves lies there, accounting for 95 percent of Saᶜūdī Arabia's national income. In this at times subdued and at times pronounced concern over provincial loyalties, the Saᶜūd family is assisted by the simultaneous appeal to Islam and to Arabism, for they are the two unquestioned common bonds shared by the provincials.[60]

These transnational values, finally, have utility for the advancement of a national consciousness among the nomads, who constitute roughly 20 percent of the population. The Badawīn define loyalties by the tribe (qabīla), while they make immediate identification with the tribal subdivisions of the lineage (fakhdh) and the household (bayt). The tribe has always been the fundamental unit by which the Badū shapes his world view and the political organization to which he automatically gives allegiance. As modern Saᶜūdī Arabia has developed, there has been recognition of the delicate relationship between the royal rulers and the major tribes.[61] The government makes every effort to satisfy tribal grievances by encouraging direct contacts with the royal family in audience; it diverts sizable funds both for facilitating nomadic pastoralism and for promoting sedentarization, as in the King Fayṣal Settlement Project; and the National Guard (al-ḥaras al-waṭanī) recruits the robust Badawīn, thereby assuring that their enthusiasm infuses the force and that they feel a connection with the royal family whom they are paid to defend.

Still, as Donald Cole points out, "the tribe continues to be a primary unit of political identification, and people relate to the state as members of a tribe rather than as individual citzens."[62] The Saʿūd family undoubtedly is not yet prepared to reject as entirely irrelevant Palgrave's conclusion that the nomads do not fight for home and country, which they lack, but for petty possessions.[63] In the search to integrate the tribes into a Saʿūdī Arabian nation, however, there is a fortuitous coincidence in their values and in those currently espoused by the government. The Badawīn of the Arabian peninsula have always considered themselves to be the prototypical Arabs, as Ibn Khaldūn deemed proper and as any present-day visitor to the area will be quickly and gratuitously informed. Tribesmen could hardly look with disfavor upon the Saʿūds from whose ranks they emerged to remind the Arabs generally of the values of authentic Arabism. The most significant of those values is Islam, and, now, memories of the tribally based *ikhwān* mingle with renewed emphasis on the king as leader of the faith to produce a sense of identification with the Saʿūds. To cite one example, the Āl Murra tribesmen of al-Rub al-Khālī, the infamous Empty Quarter, tender allegiance to the Saʿūdī state in spite of the bureaucracy and because of the royal family with its special Islamic mission.[64]

Tribal society, Louise Sweet reminds us, is characterized by the "ideological superstructure of the tribal genealogies," which distinguishes and often hierarchizes the tribes.[65] The same instinct that allows the noble to be set apart from the common tribe perhaps motivates the emergence of a symbolic, superior Saʿūdī "tribe."[66] Over time, ʿAbd al-ʿAzīz becomes the eponymous founder of the national tribe, and the nation gives palpable form to the Arab and Islamic *umma*, hitherto only a remote abstraction to the Badawīn. It is a curious blending of tribal and universal perspectives, of the nonnational and transnational, which I believe is conducive to the building and the supporting of a national consciousness.

The current emphasis on Arabism and Islam, in sum, redounds mostly to the benefit of the Saʿūdī rulers as they attempt to solidify the national identity. Whether the individual's perspective is affected by socioeconomic position, by province, or by tribe, these transnational forces remind him that he is part of greater worlds; their invocation enhances the legitimacy of the elite by tying it to ancient symbols reaffirmed; and both effects contribute to the concretizing of an identity that is Saʿūdī and national. The long-range desire of the kings and princes of Saᶜūdī Arabia may be for the unity of Arabs and Muslims, but there is also an interim usefulness in fastening the Saᶜūdī identity to the combined Arab-Muslim heritage. In a period when control is relatively firm and when the oil revenues have magnified the government's impact internally and externally, the national identity is likely to be further enhanced by the belief among Saᶜūdīs that their overlords—and by extension, they themselves—are the premier Muslims and premier Arabs.

But in the aftermath of the Iranian revolution, there is evidence that Saᶜūdī Arabia faces challenges from yet another transnational force—this time, ironically, from fundamentalist Islam. It seems odd to think of the Islamic "Right" putting on the defensive a regime that prides itself on its orthodoxy. It is, however, precisely because of Islam's importance to its legitimacy that the royal family is vulnerable to charges that it is not Islamic enough. It is open to the particular and, I believe, valid criticisms that the monarchy is not sanctioned by classical political theory, that it is introducing innovations, through the fabulous five year plans, which are eroding traditional values, and that it is immoderately corrupt. The parallel with Fayṣal al-Dawīsh's attacks of the 1920s must seem uncomfortable to the sons of ᶜAbd al-ᶜAzīz.

The stunning occupation of the Holy Mosque of Makka by several hundred people in late November 1979 is evidence that, today, there is some religious-based opposition to the regime. The government's bitter denunciation of the attackers as modern-day Carmathians, its care to secure a *fatwā* before ordering the military recapture of the mosque, and the extensive press coverage of the nearly universal Muslim outrage at the occupation and praise for the counteraction[67] indicate the seriousness with which the Saᶜūdī rulers took this ideological and thus political challenge. It seems unlikely that they will face a revival of the *ikhwān*, but as they proclaim themselves to be both good Arabs and good Muslims, they will need, perhaps, to stress again the latter's primacy, as they did in earlier periods. While *āyatullāh* Khumaynī exercises some influence over the Shīʿa of the eastern province, I doubt that their unrest is as dangerous as would be the rise of a contemporary ᶜAbd al-Wahhāb encouraged by the great belief now in an "Islamic revival."[68] The events of 1979 are a reminder of the inherent precariousness of tying political legitimacy to a transnational value and of the possible, ensuing difficulty of maintaining the national identity.

CONCLUSION

In the seven decades of this century, Saʿūdī Arabia has been undergoing the process of becoming a nation-state complete with its own identity. It has been an irregular experience for many reasons: there was neither a preexisting historical identity to call upon nor a colonial presence to react to; there was neither a territorial unity to rely on nor a general political authority to replace; there was neither a nationalist party to lead nor even a bourgeoisie to organize. Though irregular, the process does not seem unique if we remember the histories of the Hohenzollern and Savoy dynasties in Germany and Italy. The Saʿūds similarly created their domain by the hearty application of force, but, in the process by which an intermittently unified peninsula gained a unified identity, there, perhaps, has been a rare utility in invoking key transnational values. This utility has manifested itself in two major ways.

First, Islam proved useful by providing the framework within which the Saʿūds could establish a new form of political control and, because of it, create an elementary identity. ʿAbd al-ʿAzīz realized early that repeated battles with the tribes and sieges of the towns would continue to characterize Saʿūdī rule, unless he created a greater authority. In Islam, he found both an alternative, automatic loyalty and a model for the revolutionary transformation of society. The *muwaḥḥidūn* version of the model was particularly appropriate because of its uncompromising demand of fidelity to Islam and its militant commitment to reform men's lives. In this sense, the *ikhwān* represents an institutionalization of Islamic vitality for the purpose of superseding, not destroying, tribal-town loyalties. Precisely because Islam provided the milieu within which the Saʿūds structured a different kind of authority, it helped them to fashion a rudimentary "national" identity. As members of the brotherhood thought of themselves as the true believers, a we-they dichotomization, basic to the process of self-identification, developed. The oppositional element, indeed, appears central to the emergence of what Crawford Young calls "political identity."[69] Islam, in short, provided the context within which was designed a radically different authority that, in turn, because of its intimate association with the Sa'ūds, prompted an elementary identification with them.

Second, the Sa'ūds have used transnational forces to legitimate their rule and thereby to enhance the process of identity-building. If, in the first instance, they used Islam to help generate an authoritative structure, in the second, they used it to help in rendering the regime ever more acceptable. In a continuing process, the royal family associates itself with Arabism and Islam, which are particularly well-suited for a legitimating role because of the traditionally Badawīn and Islamic demand that rulers ought to be validated by their ortho-doxy. Scholars write that Arabian mores require examination and approbation of the qualities of each new *shaykh*, and that classical thinkers in Islam held that "the people owe him [the caliph] obedience, from which they can be released if he is immoral, holds unorthodox opinions or has physical infirmities which make it impossible for him to perform his functions."[70] In addition, the leadership could manipulate these values easily because of the cultural homogeneity of the people. The uniformity of ethnic stock and language, as well as the absence of minorities and rigidly defined class divisions, indicate that, at least until now, there has been little depreciation of the values as primary symbols. Indeed, they might become more im-portant than ever as modernization stimulates nostalgia for a simpler era.

While rulers can use transnational forces to advance the legitimacy of their regime, they can also set value against value, symbol against symbol, to preclude delegitimation. For example, the Sa'ūds defended themselves against the criticisms of the Ḥijāzīs by relying on the teachings of 'Abd al-Wahhāb to countercharge the *sharīf* with moral corruption. They also used pan-Islam to offset Nāṣir's pan-Arabism with its anti-Sa'ūdī allusions. This pattern suggests an addition to Majid Khadduri's two generalizations on Islam and nationalism. He argues, first, that the eastern states of the Arab world rejected Islam as an aid to their nationalist movements because independence was sought from their fellow Muslims—the Ottomans; and, second, that the Maghribī Arab states, not under strong Ottoman control, called on Islam as a means to fuel independence movements against their colonialists—the Western powers.[71] In the first instance, nationalists rejected Islam as a potential support of nationalism because it would have led to conflict with the goals of other Muslims, and, in the second instance, they relied on Islam precisely because it did not conflict. Rather, Saᶜūdī Arabia represents the case where "nationalists" used Islam against other Muslims—the Hāshimites and Nāṣirists—in order simultaneously to legitimate the Saᶜūdī regime and to encourage the development of a Saᶜūdī identity.

The relationship between legitimacy and identity is an intimate one in the example of Saᶜūdī Arabia. Allegiance to the Saᶜūd family provided the common tie that was necessary if the peninsula were to become a corporate unit and if a "political identity" based on the idea of distinctiveness were to develop into a "social" one with the implicit notion of communality. The family's masterful extension of its power made it unique in the area's fractious history, and its claim to rectitude as well as power further infused it with monarchical qualities and made it the focus for political and social planning. This case points to a corollary to Michael Hudson's postulate on legitimacy: "In the Arab world those leaders who successfully associate themselves with the fulfillment of abstract but highly valued goals pertaining to sacred obligations, corporate identity, or deeply valued principles are likely to last longer and perform better than those who can induce compliance only on the basis of fear or expediency."[72] While invocation of the Arab and Islamic identities certainly enhances the legitimacy of an Arab regime, in the instance of Saᶜūdī Arabia, where a local identity was lacking, the legitimacy of the state, in its turn, also directly inspires a national consciousness.

Richard Nolte, presenting a different perspective, argued, in the early 1960s, that nationalism in Saᶜūdī Arabia would develop in spite of, rather than because of, the king. "Treason," he wrote, "is not defined by the nationalists with reference to the Saudi state, but rather according to the canons of Arab nationalism." Though he also referred to a "separate identity," it is "the great Arab caravan" that he saw as central to a Saᶜūdī identity.[73] By way of contrast, I believe that time has shown the Saᶜūd family capable of informing a national identity primarily because it is legitimated by an Islam that countered the potential delegitimating impact of a larger Arab identity advanced by Nāṣir. The Saᶜūdī identity, therefore, is not so much a subunit of Arab nationalism as it is a reaction to it. While I accept that there is a close relationship between *qawmiyya* and *waṭaniyya*, the general and local varieties of nationalism, I wish to emphasize that Saʿūdī nationalism is not merely Arab nationalism writ small, but it is also an identity unavoidably predicated on loyalty to a particular dynasty.

The future of the Saʿūdī identity is naturally tied to the future of the Saʿūdī monarchy, which until the mosque seizure, experts had assumed would survive, at least in the short term. Halliday thought that the "vicious regime" has been strengthened by petroleum riches;[74] Hudson, that governmental capabilities have been solidified before the complicating disappearance of traditional ties;[75] and and Malone, that the royalist National Guard, trained by Jordanian army "experts in repression," deters the would-be revolutionaries for the present.[76] Since late 1979, the perspectives have become more pessimistic.[77] The durability of the Saʿūdī identity, however, does not so much depend on the brute force of the regime as on its legitimacy. And the evidence by and large indicates that, far from widening the gap as Nye and Keohane suggest, transnational forces may be useful in shortening the distance between the Saʿūdī elite and the masses. The highly permeable nature of Arab societies and the noncolonial and tribal characteristics of Saʿūdī Arabia suggest the opposite of the conclusion that " [p]olitics often revolves around nationalists' efforts to diminish transnational ties."[78] Insofar as the members of the royal family, viewed here as the archetypical Saʿūdī nationalists, are able to continue to manipulate those ties, then their legitimacy is augmented. It is not, however, also assured, and an Arabia without Sulṭān, or even Khālid and Fahd, is conceivable. But we ought not underestimate the example of almost fifty years of relative unity and the impact of socialization. Even should republicans displace them, the Saʿūds will likely retain their role as progenitors of a national heritage.

NOTES

1. I have tried to be precise in the transliteration of Arabic names, but the effort has not been entirely successful. With place names whose transliterations would render the words unfamiliar, the conventional spellings have been followed. "Saʿūdī Arabia" is obviously a compromise that seeks to make clear the connection with the Saʿūd family.

2. Hans Kohn defines nationalism as "a state of mind in which the supreme loyalty of the individual is felt to be due to the nation state." See his "Hebrew and Greek Routes of Modern Nationalism" in Ivo Duchacek, ed., *Conflict and Cooperation Among Nations* (New York: Holt, Rinehart and Winston, 1960), p. 39.

3. See, generally, Bernard Lewis, *The Arabs in History*, rev. ed. (New York: Harper Torch Books, 1966).

4. Muhammad Hamidullah, *The Muslim Conduct of State*, 4th ed. rev. (Lahore, Pakistan: Sh. Muhammad Ashraf, 1961), § 202, p. 109; § 324, p. 169; § 504, p. 245; and § 669, p. 325. Also see Mahid Khadduri, *War and Peace in the Law of Islam* (Baltimore: Johns Hopkins Press, 1955), pp. 158–60.

5. The authoritative exposition on "Unitarianism" or the beliefs of Muḥammad ibn ʿAbd al Wahhāb is found in George S. Rentz, "Muḥammad ibn ʿAbd al-Wahhāb (1703/04–1792) and the Beginnings of Unitarian Empire in Arabia" (Ph.D. diss., University of California at Berkeley, 1948). Also see H. St. John Philby, *Saʿūdī Arabia* (Beirut: Librairie du Liban, 1968), pp. 33–38.

6. Philby, *Saʿūdī Arabia*, p. 39.

7. Phoenix, "A Brief Outline of the Wahhabi Movement," *Journal of the Central Asian Society* 17, part 4 (October 1930):404.

8. For a succinct review of this history, see Joseph J. Malone, *The Arab Lands of Western Asia* (Englewood Cliffs, N.J.: Prentice-Hall, 1973), pp. 146–50. Also see, generally, Amīn al-Riḥānī, *Tārīkh Najd al-Ḥadīth wa Mulḥaqāt* (Beirut: Al-Maṭbaʿa al-ʿAlamiyya li-Yūsuf Sadr, 1928).

9. K. S. Twitchell, *Saudi Arabia* (Princeton: Princeton University Press, 1958), p. 155.

10. Qurʾān, Sūra VIII:1, 41. Also see Khadduri, *War and Peace in the Law of Islam*, pp. 120–25.

11. Col. T. E. Lawrence, "Secrets of the War on Mecca," *Daily Express* (London) May 28, 1920, p. 1.

12. Ameen Rihani, *Ibn Saʾoud of Arabia: His People and His Land* (London: Constable & Co., 1928), p. 214; also see pp. 191–92. Additionally, see Phoenix, "A Brief Outline," p. 412. As a general reference, see Amīn al-Riḥānī, *Mulūk al-ʿArab* (Beirut: Al-Maṭbaʿa al-ʿAlamiyya li-Yūsuf Sadr, 1925). The British official was the political resident at Bahrayn who passed on his comments to the secretary of state for the colonies in telegram (P) No. 59-T of 20 March 1928. India Office Records, R/15/5/30.

13. The date has sometimes been given as 1911, as, for instance, in Ḥafiẓ Wahba, *Jazīrat al-ʿArab Fī al-Qarun al-ʿIshrīn* 4th ed. (Cairo: Maktabat al-Nahḍa al-Misriyya, 1961), p. 293. But the overwhelming majority of writers give the equivalent of the Islamic year 1330 as 1912. Even *shaykh* Wahba used the year 1912 in his *Arabian Days* (London: Arthur Barker Limited, 1964), p. 126. It should also be noted that Wahba stressed that the original settlement was a mixture (*khalīṭ*) of Ḥarb and Muṭayr tribesmen. It is a point repeated in *Arabian Days*, but most references suggest that the first settlement was predominantly, if not exclusively, of Muṭayr elements. This interpretation, however, does not negate the fact that the members of one tribe were not exclusively settled in one *hijra* but were rather spread among a number of

different communities. See *al-Akbār*, 10 August 1924. Whatever the composition of al-Arṭāwiyya and others, it is clear that the *hijar* were generally preoccupied with one experiment—sedentarization—and largely shied away from a second experiment —cross-tribal settlement.

14. For information on the *ikhwān*, see George Rentz, "al-Ikhwān," *The Encyclopedia of Islam*, pp. 1064–68; John S. Habib, *Ibn Saʾudʾs Warriors of Islam: The Ikhwan of Najd and Their Role in the Creation of the Saʾudi Kingdom* (Leiden, Netherlands: E. J. Brill, 1978); Philby, *Saʿudi Arabia*, pp. 261–64; Rihani, *Ibn Saʾoud*, pp. 191–99, pp. 207–14; Wahba, *Jazīrat*, pp. 293–312; Wahba, *Arabian Days*, pp. 125–45; Phoenix, "A Brief Outline" pp. 413–16; David G. Edens, "The Anatomy of the Saudi Revolution," *International Journal of Middle Eastern Studies*, 5 (1974): 57–59.

15. T. E. Lawrence, *Seven Pillars of Wisdom* (New York: Garden City Publishing, 1938), p. 42.

16. H. St. J. B. Philby, "The Triumph of the Wahhabis," *Journal of the Central Asian Society* 13, part 4 (October 1926):296.

17. For example, in a letter of 15 Dhu al-Ḥijja 1338 (30 August 1920) to the British political agent Bahrayn, ʿAbd al-ʿAzīz called them the "tip of infidelity's teat" (*raʾs al-kafr al-ḍarʿ*). India Office Records, file R/15/2/37.

18. Philby, *Saʿudi Arabia*, pp. 279–88.

19. Philby, "The Triumph," pp. 312–13, 314–16, quote at p. 315.

20. These, along with the capacity to enter into foreign relations, are the essential factors of statehood recognized in international law, as seen in article 1 of the Montevideo Convention on Rights and Duties of States (1933) and in section 4 of the Foreign Relations Law of the United States (second restatement, 1965).

21. Phoenix, "A Brief Outline," p. 414.

22. Philby, *Saʿudi Arabia*, pp. 259–60.

23. Letter of ʿAbd al-Raḥmān to ʿAbd al-ʿAzīz,3 Rajab 1342 (8 February 1924); quote in letter of Fayṣal al-Dawīsh to ʿAbd al-ʿAzīz, 4 Rajab 1342 (9 February 1924). India Office Records, file R/15/5/70. For an overview of these events, see Gary Troeller, *The Birth of Saudi Arabia: Britain and the Rise of the House of Saʿud* (London: Frank Cass, 1976).

24. For the position of the *ʿulamāʾ*, see George Rentz, "Wahhabism and Saudi Arabia," in Derek Hopwood, ed., *The Arabian Peninsula: Society and Politics* (London: George Allen and Unwin, 1972), pp. 64–65. For the argument that the tribes feared an increase of central control and for a good discussion of the revolt in general, see "The Iraq-Najd Frontier," *Journal of the Central Asian Society* 17, part 1 (January 1930):85–90, especially p. 86.

25. Quote in "Statement of the Men of the Conference," enclosed in a letter from Mr. Jakins to Austen Chamberlain, no. 231 of 31 December 1928 in British Foreign Office Records, FO 371/13713, E 387/3/91. Compare with the quote in "The Iraq-Najd Frontier," p. 87: "Let him [ʿAbd al-ʿAzīz] join us in a jihad against the infidels. If he does not do so, it will be proof that he is himself in secret relations to bring them into Najd."

26. ʿAbd al-ʿAzīz assumed the title of king in 1926, when he was acclaimed as the "King of the Ḥijāz and Sultan of Najd and its Dependencies" by the Ḥijāzīs after his victory there.

27. Philby, Saʿudi Arabia, p. 313. Also see H. R. P. Dickson, Kuwait and Her Neighbors (London: George Allen and Unwin, 1956), pp. 300–32.

28. James A. Bill and Carl Leiden, The Middle East: Politics and Power (Boston: Allyn and Bacon, 1974), pp. 125–33.

29. Letter no. 191 from Wh. Bond to the British secretary of state for foreign affairs, 20 July 1929; Letter no. 205 from Bond, 10 August 1929. India Office Records, file R/15/5/32. The Shīʿtes of al-Qaṭīf complained of their treatment at the hands of the Saʿūds who forced them to follow at prayer times one of the imāms whom the Shīʿtes contemptuously called "a boy." India Office Records, R/15/2/74: letter from Shīʿtes to the deputy ruler of Bahrayn, 20 al-Muḥarram 1346.

30. For an excellent discussion of Nāṣirism, see Malcolm H. Kerr, The Arab Cold War, (3d ed. London: Oxford University Press, 1971).

31. Richard H. Nolte, "From Nomad Society to New Nation: Saudi Arabia," in K. H. Silvert, ed., Expectant Peoples: Nationalism and Development (New York: Random House, 1963), p. 92. Also see the "anti-capitalist" interpretation of Fred Halliday, Arabia Without Sultans (New York: Vintage Books, 1974), pp. 65–66.

32. Quote in The New York Times, 11 March 1962, p. 2; The New York Times, 17 March 1962, p. 6. For an example of al-Tāriqī's thinking, though written after his departure from Saʿūdī Arabia, see Shaikh Abdullah Tariki, "Oil in the Service of the Arab Cause," Middle East Forum 42, no. 1 (Winter 1966): 23–35.

33. The Times (London), 11 May 1962, p. 13; The New York Times, 10 June 1962, p. 3.

34. Ṭalāl quote in The Times, 16 August 1962, p. 10. For other statements by Ṭalāl, see The Times, 18 August 1962, p. 5; 22 August 1962, p. 7; and 19 October 1962, p. 5. "Free Saudi Arabia" cited in The New York Times, 10 November 1962, p. 5.

35. The New York Times, 8 November 1962, p. 7.

36. The Times, 24 January 1964, p. 11; 21 February 1964, p. 12; quote in latter. Also see Malone, Arab Lands, pp. 161–62.

37. The Times, 15 December 1965, p. 8; 29 January 1966, p. 7; 1 February 1966, p. 8; and 11 February 1966, p. 9.

38. The Times, 12 February 1966, p. 7; The New York Times, 19 June 1966; p. E3. For quotations from some of Nāṣir's speeches condemning the Islamic pact, see: Salāh al-Dīn al-Munajjid, al-Tadāmun al-Mārksī wa al-Tadāmun al-Islāmī; ʾArd lil-Ahdāth wa Wathāʾ iq (Beirut: Dar al-Kitāb al-Jadīd, 1967), pp. 66-88.

39. Al-Ahrām, 21 December 1966 (9 Ramaḍān 1386), p. 1. The headline read: "The Oil Pipeline 'Tapline' Was Blown up Inside Saudi Arabia."

40. Malone, Arab Lands, p. 163. Malone's conclusion, as stated elsewhere, that pan-Islam was "really unnecessary" is based on his evaluation of it as a foreign policy. See Joseph J. Malone, "Saudi Arabia," "Islam in Politics; a Symposium," The Muslim World 56, no. 4 (October 1966):290.

41. Al-Ahrām, 21 December 1966, p. 1; quote in The Times, 7 March 1967, p. 5. It

should be noted that *al-Ahrām* reported in its edition of 22 January 1967 (11 Shawāl 1386) that approximately four hundred people were arrested after a variety of explosions in Saudi Arabia (p. 1).

42. *The Times*, 24 April 1967, pp. 1, 4; 25 April 1967, p. 4; and 22 May 1967, p. 4.

43. J. Gaspard, "Feisal's Arabian Alternative," *New Middle East*, no. 6 (March 1969): p. 16.

44. *The New York Times*, 10 February 1968, p. 17.

45. Gaspard, "Feisal's Alternative," pp. 16–17; *The Times*, 25 August 1969, p. 4.

46. *The New York Times*, 9 September 1969, pp. 1, 6; 10 September 1969, p. 3; and 4 December 1969, p. 20.

47. *The New York Times*, 27 December 1969, p. 3. Haykal wrote on Nāṣir's reassurance to Fayṣal in an article entitled "The Crisis in Achieving Arab Unity" in *al-Ahrām*, 9 January 1970 (1 Dhū al-Qiʿda 1389), p. 3. Also see Mohamed Heikal, *The Road to Ramadan* (Glasgow: William Collins Sons, 1975), pp. 75–77.

48. *The New York Times*, 18 February 1971, p. 6; see Fayṣal's interview with Dr. Amīn al-Ḥāfiẓ, *al-Anwār*, 16th year, no. 4975, 13 September 1974, pp. 1, 16. In another Beirut newspaper interview, while the king urged Arabs to unify in order to rid themselves of foreign intrusions, he suggested that, by way of contrast, "Islamic solidarity is already an existing fact and an internationally recognized institution." See *The Daily Star*, no. 8224, 12 October 1974, p. 1.

49. Statement by *shaykh* Kamal Adham, royal counselor in *Arab News*, 15 June 1975, p. 9.

50. Broadcast on Riyadh Domestic Service, 1800 GMT, 31 March 1975, as monitored by the *Foreign Broadcast Information Service (FBIS)* 5, 1 (April 1975): C2.

51. *Al-Muṣṣawar*, no. 2650, 25 July 1975 (16 Rajab 1395), unnumbered, but sixth and last page of interview with King Khālid.

52. *Kul Shayʾ*, 22nd year, no. 1085, 9 August 1975 (2 Shaʿbān 1395), pp. 17–18. Prince Fahd has spoken more directly on Arab solidarity:

> Permit me to say that, here in the kingdom of Saudi Arabia, we do not make a distinction between the confrontation states and other countries. According to our faith and conviction, we are one nation and are like one body. . . . Rumours will never divert us from our links with the Arab people. We shall remain attached to the Arab people and to the Arab citizen wherever he may be.

See *The Journal Rabetat al-Alam al-Islami* 5, no. 3 (January 1978, Safar 1398): 5. For another statement on Arab unity by another member of the royal family, see Prince Sulṭān's comments in *al-Anwār*, 16th year, no. 4977, 15 September 1974, pp. 1, 18.

53. "L'ombra dell' Arabia Saudita sul futuro dell' Opec," *Politica Internazionale*, no. 2 (Febbraio 1977): 6.

54. *Le Monde Diplomatique*, 24th year, no. 279 (June 1977): 22.

55. William Rugh, "Emergence of a New Middle Class in Saudi Arabia," *The Middle East Journal* 27, no. 1 (Winter 1973): 7–20, especially pp. 18–20.

56. Judith Miller, "Americans in Arabia: Keys of the Kingdom," *The Progressive* 41, no. 4 (April 1977): 47.

57. A. A. Mughram, "Assarah, Saudi Arabia: Change and Development in a Rural Context" (Ph.D. diss., Durham University, 1973), p. 202.

58. Levon H. Melikian, "The Modal Personality of Saudi College Students: A Study in National Character," in L. Carl Brown and Norman Itzkowitz, eds., *Psychological Dimensions of Near Eastern Studies* (Princeton, N.J.: The Darwin Press, 1977), p. 169.

59. *The Times*, 13 August 1970, p. 7.

60. The advent of a national television network, presumably also enhances the development of a national perspective. See Herman F. Eilts, "Social Revolution in Saudi Arabia, Part II," *Parameters* 1, no. 2 (Fall 1971): 28.

61. Sixteen tribes were listed as appertaining *(al-tābiʿa)* to the Saʿūdī government in a formal letter from the minister of foreign affairs to the British representative acting on behalf of Kuwayt in treaty negotiations in 1940. The Saʿūdīs had, in addition to these sixteen, earlier laid claim to parts of two others. See India Office Records, R/15/5/115, and compare with Manfred W. Wenner's figure of "one hundred tribes" in "Saudi Arabia: Survival of Traditional Elites," in Frank Tachau, ed. *Political Elites and Political Development in the Middle East* (New York: Schenkman Publishing, 1975), p. 167.

62. Donald Powell Cole, *Nomads of the Nomads* (Arlington Heights, Ill.: AHM Publishing, 1975), p. 94.

63. William Gifford Palgrave, *Personal Narrative of a Year's Journey Through Central and Eastern Arabia (1862-1863)* (London: MacMillan and Co., 1871), p. 23.

64. Cole, *Nomads*, p. 109.

65. Louise E. Sweet, "The Arabian Peninsula," in Sweet, ed., *The Central Middle East* (New Haven: HRAF Press, 1971), p. 237.

66. I need to make clear that the Saʿūds do not, properly speaking, constitute a tribe. Rather, they are a family unit in the al-Masalīkh lineage of the ʿAnayza tribe.

67. See, for example, *al-Jazīra*, 9 Muḥarram 1400 (28 November 1979). The *fatwā* is found in *al-Riyāḍ*, no. 4387, 6 Muḥarram 1400 (25 November 1979), p. 3.

68. See, for example, G. H. Jansen, *Militant Islam* (London: Pan Books, 1979), especially pp. 194-95.

69. Crawford Young speaks of "political" and "social" identity in *The Politics of Cultural Pluralism* (Madison: University of Wisconsin Press, 1976). See especially pp. 23-47.

70. See Lewis, *The Arabs in History*, pp. 25, 47; and Albert Hourani, *Arabic Thought in the Liberal Age, 1798-1939* (London: Oxford University Press, 1970), p. 10.

71. Majid Khadduri, *Modern Libya* (Baltimore: Johns Hopkins Press, 1963), pp. 9-10.

72. Michael C. Hudson, *Arab Politics: The Search for Legitimacy* (New Haven: Yale University Press, 1977), p. 18.

73. Nolte, "From Nomad Society," pp. 89-90.

74. Halliday, *Arabia Without Sultans*, p. 87.

75. Hudson, *Arab Politics*, p. 181.

76. Malone, *The Arab Lands*, p. 168.

77. The Israeli government, for one, reportedly believes that the Saʿūdī royal family is close to collapse. See *The Daily Telegraph* (London), December 27, 1979, p. 4.

78. Robert O. Keohane and Joseph S. Nye, Jr., eds., *Transnational Relations and World Politics* (Cambridge: Harvard University Press, 1971), p. 388.

PIERRE-MICHEL FONTAINE*

Transnational Relations and   6
Racial Mobilization: Emerging
Black Movements in Brazil

As the subtitle suggests, this chapter is about incipient black protest movements in Brazil, which is an apparent incongruity—
some would even say absurdity—in view of Brazil's die-hard reputation as a "racial paradise" or "racial democracy." Actually, such
movements are not as absent from Brazilian history as most people
think; one need only mention the various black civil rights movements
of the 1920s and 1930s, such as the *Frente Negra Brasileira*, based in
São Paulo but with branches in other cities,[1] and the movements of
the 1940s and 1950s associated with the *Teatro Experimental do
Negro* and the First Congress of the Brazilian Black.[2]
    Still, these movements have failed to change the image of Brazil as
the land where the racial problem either does not exist or has come
closest to being solved, a land of racial peace and harmony, a
paradise for blacks and whites alike. So pervasive and powerful is the
myth that no amount of scientific studies disproving it or of black
protest efforts challenging it have affected its enduring nature and
the Brazilians' almost unshakable faith in it.[3]

    *This essay is part of a project on Afro-Brazilian Social Mobility and Mobiliza-
tion supported by a grant from the Ford Foundation Fund of the UCLA Committee
on Comparative and International Studies (CICS) and by supplementary travel support from the UCLA Institute of American Cultures through the Center for Afro-
American Studies. The author is grateful for this aid and also for the valuable assistance of Clotilde Blake and Lawrence Day.

In fact, in the face of all this, and of the more recent empirical evidence of pervasive and persistent racial discrimination against blacks adduced by Carlos A. Hasenbalg,[4] the sociologist Gilberto Freyre,[5] generally acknowledged as the earliest and most articulate propagator of the myth, has risen to the intellectual challenge by rejecting racial statistics as irrelevant. He attacked certain São Paulo sociologists—presumably Fernando Henrique Cardoso, Octávio Ianni, and Florestan Fernandes, especially the latter—as being "archaicly Marxist or Communist" and "even more militant Marxist than knowledgeable *Paulista*." At the same time, he wrote of the increasing Brazilian consciousness of being a "meta-race," of the increasing "browning" ("*amorenamento*") of the population, and of this process being socially, economically, and politically democratizing.[6] Presumably, *amorenamento* is the new term coined to replace "*embranquecimento*" ("whitening") as the racial ideal of Brazil.

Even such an ardent mythmaker as Gilberto Freyre, however, soon had to recognize and lament the fact that there was not a single black in President Geisel's cabinet, though there was a Japanese-Brazilian, and also that there was no significant black presence in the "state assemblies, the National Congress, the upper hierarchy of the Church, the military command or in various types of leadership positions."[7]

Essentially, this means that, numerous cases of racial discrimination and persistent patterns of racial exclusion notwithstanding, the racial ideology of Brazil is culturally assimilationist, socially integrationist, and biologically miscegenationist. The behavioral counterpart of this ideology is a pattern of social relations characterized by the absence of overt racial conflicts and tensions and the cultivation of outward peace and harmony among the races, thanks to the legitimation, or at the very least, the explaining away, of racial inequalities.

For this reason, the myth of "racial democracy" and "racial paradise" has been readily accepted by Brazilians and by foreigners and even repeated by black Brazilians themselves, the very victims of it. Indeed, the absence of overt conflicts and tensions and the absence of overt segregation and openly sanctioned or legalized discrimination is the very essence of the Brazilian concept of racial or ethnic democracy.[8] The point is significant and needs to be elaborated, for it constitutes the basis for the primary proposition of this paper—namely, that the stability structures are so effective as to make it nearly impossible for the society to generate socioracial change "internally." A corollary proposition is that such pressures for change need to be either generated "externally" or supplemented by "external" forces in order to overcome the resistance of these stability and maintenance mechanisms.

Although the reality of the Brazilian situation, which is only a special case of the general Latin American condition, has been analyzed in the works of above-mentioned Bastide, Cardoso, Fernandes, Hasenbalg, and Ianni, and other writings by Anani Dzidzienyo, Pierre-Michel Fontaine, Jean-Claude Garcia-Zamor, and Luiz Pinto, it is useful to present a taxonomy of these stability structures to illuminate the present discussion.[9] It will be argued, thereafter, that these structures are being undermined by a set of transnational forces whose sources are to be found in the realm of international political economy.

STRUCTURAL DIMENSIONS OF RACE RELATIONS

The first, and most obvious, mechanism of system maintenance is the *ambiguity* of the racial situation and of racial attitudes; it is the very essence of the Brazilian system, this mixture of "tolerance" and suppression, of intimacy and contempt, of friendliness and discrimination.[10] The situation is such that the Brazilians themselves, when pressed, claim that they do not quite understand it—that is, after they have made the standard speech about the absence of any racial problem *"aqui no Brasil."* At the limit, inequalities between blacks and whites are attributed to class, which is very difficult to prove or disprove.

One element of ambiguity is precisely the difficulty of placing an individual along the long and complex spectrum of color, especially since the spectrum itself has been shifting over time. Marvin Harris has analyzed this ambiguity and its consequences in the calculus of racial identification.[11] One is not simply black or white; there are various intermediate categories. Furthermore, the concept of whiteness has expanded over time to include more and more shades of darkness and, therefore, more and more people, thereby gradually fulfilling the ideal of "whitening," the Brazilian solution to the race problem. Under such conditions, of course, the same person can be put in two or more different categories, depending on who is making the judgment (or performing the calculus), especially since there are various social and cultural factors to be taken into account. It is this *fluidity* that led José Clarana to assert that "Brazilians could not draw the color line for they would not know where to begin."[12] The result is a *residual category*, where, theoretically, only the very dark and the very poor are relegated. A black identity becomes, then very problematic and very difficult to achieve. Thus, the country that has the largest African-descended population in the world outside of Nigeria can safely claim that blacks are a minority there. More significantly, this black "minority" is made more powerless by the co-optation of its potential leaders into higher, socially determined color categories. This process of negative elite recruitment—which one might call "disrecruitment"—is a powerful deterrent to mobilization.[13]

Not only are the ranks of officially black people substantially reduced by the ideal of *"embranquecimento"* that compels dark men to prefer lighter women in order to produce lighter offsprings, but also these residual blacks are constrained to a life of accommodation and acquiescence or, alternatively, to withdrawal, abstention, or flight. The ideal is *peace and harmony*. The overall preoccupation is to avoid confrontation. The goal of the well-bred gentleman is amiability and cordiality, which are fundamental rules of etiquette. And an attitude of moderation and decorum is especially expected from a person of color.[14] This has a direct bearing on our contention of the difficulty of racial mobilization. This is not to say, of course, that racial violence does not occur. More often than not, it takes the form of police violence, which is rather widespread. Occasionally, it takes on very bizarre and seemingly aberrant turns, such as the case of the white woman who, despondent over the imminent prospect of her white son having mulatto children, shot her pregnant, black daughter-in-law in the stomach, thereby killing the fetus. Somewhat more frequent are the cases of verbal violence, such as referring to a black person as *"negro sujo vagabundo"* ("dirty black bum"), but this is often an instrument used to control "uppity" blacks—that is, those who violate the etiquette of accommodation and cordiality.

When verbal abuse and other obvious forms of structural violence, such as employment discrimination or prevention of access to hotels, night clubs, or restaurants, occur and are denounced, they are generally treated as *individual cases* of inexplicably *aberrant behavior*, not as regular manifestations of systemic tendencies. Usually, both the press and the public authorities, including, in recent times, even the president of the republic, are mobilized to castigate the alleged culprit verbally, though, characteristically, no serious sanctions are taken against him. It is as if the very thought of pervasive racial discrimination should be exorcised from the public mind at home and abroad, without any effective action being taken to redress the grievance.

When all else fails, of course, the racial order is maintained by the political system, which is a major independent variable in the determination of the nature and development of the racial order. A populist government would seek the co-optation of the black masses through patronage and other means of controlled mobilization. This was apparently the relationship between the Brazilian Labor party (PTB) and the black electorate under President Getulio Vargas.[15] Under such conditions, black collective protest was channeled and fused into guided mass mobilization in support of a coalition of mainly urban and industrial interests.

Under the post-1964 military regime, which Guillermo O'Donnell calls a "bureaucratic-authoritarian" regime, the emphasis is put on demobilization, following the destruction of the old populist coalition.[16] The new ruling coalition is bent on enforced consensus to achieve accumulation and growth through a depoliticized and technocratic process. Here, mass mobilization is dysfunctional, and racial protest is, like other protests, subversive. In this context, one readily sees the logic of Freyre's response to Fernandes and other revisionist students of race in Brazil. Equally understandable is the reaction of the president of the Tietê Yacht Club of São Paulo in the spring of 1978 when he filed charges of subversion of the public order with the Department of Public Order and Security (DOPS) against the four volleyball coaches who had accused the club of racism when four black, teenage players were excluded from the premises and from the team because of their color. Thus, under both of these regimes, and even more so under the earlier, oligarchic regime, black protest is viewed as illegitimate and hence is rendered exceedingly unlikely, if not impossible.

This being the case, it is not surprising that Brazil, just as most of the rest of Afro-Latin America for that matter, has, until very recently, remained safely outside the great transnational currents of black thought and action.[17] Similarly, in a major essay on the internationalization of black power in which the author made repeated references to the United States, the Carribbean, and Africa, he did not name Brazil, or any other Latin American country for that matter, even once.[18]

The key question is, Under what conditions are movements of racial protest likely to reappear in Brazil? Or, in a more "sophisticated" jargon, What are the conjunctural requisites for racial mobilization in an assimilationist social order? In the past, such movements have emerged in Brazil at times of internal crises or changes that were, in part, repercussions of major international crises or changes. The *Frente Negra Brasileira* was founded in September 1931, two years into the Great Depression, which had significant repercussions throughout the capitalist "center" and its "periphery." The *Clarim d'Avorada*, the major black-activist newspaper of the time, was founded in 1924, the same year as Marcus Garvey's Universal Negro Improvement Association (UNIA), and it gave periodic coverage to the activities of Garvey and the UNIA and to other world and U.S. black news. It was a time of fascism, economic uncertainties, and social ferment in the United States, Europe, and Latin America. And, like the UNIA, the *Frente Negra* had its paramilitary organization, its white shirts, and its rigid discipline.[19] In Brazil, the golden immigration era was over, and the immigrants were moving, or preparing to move, into the middle class, leaving the blacks behind, while in the political realm, the old republic was in a state of advanced decomposition, soon to give way to the new republic and eventually to Vargas's *Estado Novo*. The movements of the late 1940s and early 1950s coincided with the immediate post—World War II period, the cold war, and, later, the Korean War. Internally, it was the period of the consolidation of the populist coalition and of the import-substitution industrialization policies that it personified.

The movements of the 1920s and 1930s signaled the emergence of a black proletariat and the early gestation of a middle class, the passage from a paternalistic outlook to an increasingly competitive vision.[20] They were strongly and aggressively integrationist and nationalistic (pro-Brazilian) in outlook. They were more mass-mobilization oriented than the later movement, perhaps because the black community in this early stage of socioeconomic development was less differentiated and therefore less "incohesive."

Yet, these movements achieved little in the way of direct, discrete impact on the larger society, especially in the form of legislation. In this context, it is interesting to note that, when President Vargas established his *Estado Novo* (new state) in 1937, he abolished all political parties, including the *Frente Negra Brasileira*, which had registered itself as a political party the previous year. Its reemergence soon afterward as the *União Negra Brasileira* could not save it, and the organization collapsed by May 1938, soon after the celebration of the fiftieth anniversary of the abolition of slavery. The populist state could not accommodate alternative and competitive structures of mass mobilization.

However, the creation of the PTB (Brazilian Labor party) and Vargas's massive labor and welfare legislation had significant effects in bringing increasing numbers of blacks out of marginality into the mainstream of the proletariat and a very few into the middle class. However, the principal effects of the movements of the 1920s and 1930s may have been to reinforce black integrationist feelings by emphasizing self-improvement and the need to adopt the values of the dominant society.[21] Thus, they sowed the seeds of their own demise by fostering an individualistic outlook and approach to social mobility.

The movements of the 1950s, especially the *Teatro Experimental do Negro*, signaled the advent and aspirations of a black intellectual class, where the impulse was less integrationist in outlook and more self-centered. It was epitomized in Guerreiro Ramos's radical criticism of white social science, both Brazilian and foreign, as being inappropriate and harmful to the cause of blacks because it reinforced and legitimized the status quo, and in his call for a study of the black condition by black sociologists.[22] The *Teatro Experimental do Negro*, under Abdias do Nascimento, took a vigorous stand and had a measure of success in promoting the development of a serious, committed, and high quality black theatre as a vehicle for black consciousness raising and mobilization.[23] Nascimento also organized the first congress of the Brazilian black, which, while it was not the first Afro-Brazilian congress ever held—Gilberto Freyre had done just that in 1934 in Recife and in 1935 in Bahia[24]—was remarkable in that it was the first to be organized and controlled by black intellectuals.[25]

By their very nature, these movements were less oriented toward mass mobilization than was the *Frente Negra*. They even had a certain elitist character. Yet, they may have played a role in generating the Afonso Arinos Law against racial discrimination in 1950. Although Afonso Arinos himself attributes his submission of the bill to the fact that his black driver had been barred from an ice-cream parlor while his blue-eyed wife, the daughter of German immigrants, and their children were allowed in;[26] an alternative version of the story had it that Afonso Arinos had submitted the bill in response to the exclusion of famed, black American dancer Katherine Dunham from a Rio de Janeiro hotel. And he is reputed to have taken the initiative at the insistence of a number of black intellectuals and professionals.

In the case of these movements, too, the maintenance function of the political system can be seen in the fact that, subsequent to the 1964 military takeover, both Abdias do Nascimento and Guerreiro Ramos went into exile in the United States, where the former has continued and escalated his racial-protest activism, while the latter has completely dropped out of Afro-Brazilian studies or activism.

To understand the causes and emergence of the present-day black protest movement in Brazil within the context of a bureaucratic-authoritarian regime, we need to adopt a model that takes into account the political regime. This regime is, in turn, embedded into a system of relations of production that determines it and that is, in turn, influenced by it. This system transcends the national boundaries of Brazil, and its study is to be placed in the realm of transnational relations or, better yet, international political economy. In other words, this chapter analyzes emerging black movements in Brazil in a multicausal framework of political economy, emphasizing both its internal and transnational dimensions. Moreover, it will focus on the political system, the system and relations of production that form its underpinning, and the inter- and transnational exchanges that derive therefrom. Thus, the analysis is at once historical, institutional, behavioral, and procedural.

TRANSNATIONAL RELATIONS AND THE GLOBAL POLITICAL ECONOMY

So far, we have tried to demonstrate the eminent stability of the Brazilian system of race relations. We have argued that, for reasons relating to ambiguity of behavior, fluidity of the color line, residuality of blackness, the consequent deterrence to a black identity, enforced pacifism, and the authoritarian nature of the society and policy, overt racial protest and racial-protest movements have been rare, though by no means nonexistent. And, no less importantly, such movements, when they have arisen, have failed to have a significant, direct impact on the system of race relations. The new movements that we are concerned with here are unlike anything that has happened in Brazil in the past: they are more like the American system of race relations than that of Brazil, and that is the way most Brazilians (black and white) treat them.

It is being argued that these movements are the product of a crisis in the Brazilian "miracle," or model of development, a crisis that is grounded in international economic relations, and that the forces generated thereby are being reinforced by transnational processes, some of which are also the products of the relations of production in the Brazilian system. To understand this, one must first explain the model and what has been called "the crisis,"[27] "the limit,"[28] or "the test"[29] of the Brazilian "miracle."

Briefly, the Brazilian "model" that produced the so-called Brazilian miracle was implemented by the various military governments that have ruled Brazil following the *coup d'état* that overthrew João Goulart in 1964. After a series of fits and starts, the model was consolidated and began bearing enormous fruits by 1968: control of inflation and annual rates of economic growth of 10 percent or more. This was achieved by massive doses of direct foreign investment and foreign loans and no less massive doses of public-sector investment and by strict controls on monetary policy.[30] These measures were, in turn, made possible by the obliteration of the labor movement to assure labor peace;[31] the abolition of the old political parties and, in a sense, of politics itself, in favor of "bureaucratics"; the elimination of the peasant leagues; the destruction of the urban guerrillas; the jailing, torturing, exiling, banishing, and *cassação* of radical, leftist, obstreperous, or merely objecting politicians and others. Many were deprived of their political rights for as much as ten years in application of Institutional Act No. 5 (AI-5). Political peace was imposed; an authoritarian technocracy was established for the purpose of achieving economic growth and development. The motto, "*Ordem e Progresso*," on the Brazilian flag was being enforced to the hilt.

To be sure, it was not the first time that Brazil had adopted a developmentalist ideology and model. The Juscelino Kubitschek government in the 1950s was nothing if it was not developmentalist.[32] Nor was the involvement of foreign capital a new phenomenon.[33] Nor, again, can it be said that a high rate of economic growth was something new in Brazil. Brazil had known high rates of growth during most of the postwar period, and certainly throughout the 1950s. What was new was the higher level of intensity of all these themes. Developmentalism became the exclusive governmental claim to legitimacy since political freedom and social rights had been put on the back burner. The infusion of foreign capital was greater than ever, resulting in substantial denationalization of marginal and even some not-so-marginal industries. As for the rate of growth, it was unprecedentedly high, even as the standard of living of the masses steadily declined.

This seeming paradox was no paradox at all, since a principal tenet of the model was that this rate of growth could only be achieved through high rates of accumulation in the capitalist sector, which, in turn, meant systematic shifting of income from the masses to the bourgeoisie. A new coalition thus came to the fore, including the local industrial bourgeoisie, the transnational corporations, and the state, in the hands of the armed forces. The state, meanwhile, became the major source of industrial investment in the economy.[34] Thus, the old populist coalition of industrialists, urban labor, and some rural elements was broken. It was the attempt by urban labor to increase its returns from the coalition, and the efforts on the part of the peasant sector, through the *Ligas Camponesas* (peasant leagues), to join the coalition because it had been left out of the benefits of it, that created the crisis of the early 1960s that the military ended by overthrowing Goulart in 1964. These developments had several implications for black Brazilians and for the potential for socioracial change.

1. The removal of the PTB from the political scene eliminated an avenue of mobility for individual blacks and mulattoes, albeit in a pattern of infiltration under the paternalistic wings of a white politician. Thus, while the majority of Brazilians suffered from the banning of the old parties, the loss was probably greater for blacks.

2. The disbanding of the *Ligas Camponesas* (peasant leagues) removed from the scene a major mechanism of social and political mobilization from the very area, the rural northeast, where the black population is most heavily concentrated.

3. The reversal of the labor and social-welfare conquests of the populist period could only greatly affect black social mobility and standards of living.

4. The general decline in the standard of living of the masses, which resulted from the intensive capital accumulation policy of the regime, affected blacks especially strongly, as the vast majority of them belong to the lower class.

5. The establishment of the "national security state" meant that racial protest became more unthinkable than ever, as it could be equated with subversion. Any racial protester could be faced with an impressive array of entities in a most complex apparatus of repression: the military police, the civil police, the technical police, the security units of the army, the navy, and the air force, the DEOPS (State Department of Public Order and Security), and, if all else failed, the extralegal *"Escuadrões da Morte"* ("death squads"), most of whose assassination victims are thought to be poor blacks (petty criminals, allegedly). And, of course, there is the censure that dutifully excises controversial reporting of the black conditions from the media for reasons of both internal security and international image. An example of this was the suppression by the *Newsweek*-style news magazine *Veja* of an article on the black condition by one of its own star reporters, Cláudio Bojunga, under pressure from higher-ups in Brasilia. The article was subsequently published in another journal.[35]

6. At the same time, the increasing bureaucratization of society and the increasing modernization of the bureaucracy mean enhanced opportunities for educated blacks in terms of career upward mobility.[36]

7. Finally, it may be that the Brazilian literacy campaign, Alfabetização Movimento (MOBRAL), if it has had any success, has been helpful to blacks, the majority of whom are illiterate. But I have no reliable information on MOBRAL.

It is significant in this context that two related processes have begun to appear among Afro-Brazilians, especially in São Paulo and Rio de Janeiro, which, although still weak and in an embryonic stage, constitute the attitudinal and organizational infrastructure or bases of the movements considered in this chapter.

Attitudinally, there appears to be developing a barely perceptible change in black Brazilian self-perception, or at least in racial identity, in those areas mentioned. Because of the absence of comparable and reliable longitudinal data on this aspect, it is hard to be sure about it. Yet, recent surveys among upwardly mobile, black, corporate professionals has shown a level of alienation from blackness perceptibly below what was expected on the basis of previous work and conventional wisdom.[37] Interracial marriage, in particular, seems to have lost some of its appeal; in fact, even a 1975 respondent who had deemed it beneficial to the career advancement of a black manager[38] was no longer so sure at the end of 1978.[39] Even the conservative, middle-class *Aristocrata Clube* of São Paulo is reported to be thinking of changing its name to the more appropriate *Afro-São Paulo*. Also, the majority of the black professionals interviewed were more prone to classify themselves as *negro* and/ or *preto* (black) than might have been expected.[40]

Organizationally, in the past few years, there appears to have been a veritable explosion of associations, social clubs, cultural centers, study and research societies, and other such entities. They include: CACUPRO (House of the Culture of Progress—a euphemistic name chosen to avoid the words "black" or "Afro-Brazilian" and thereby avoid the inevitable accusations of racism) in São Paulo in the mid-1970s (now defunct); CECAN (*Centro de Cultura e Arte Negra*), also in São Paulo; the Institute of Research on Black Cultures (IPCN) in Rio; the GTPLUN (Group of United Black Professional Workers) in São Paulo. This last group is led by a black woman physician, Dr. Iracema de Alameida, and is dedicated, not only to the training and mentoring of young blacks, but also to the strengthening of black cultural awareness, for instance, by sponsoring lectures on precolonial African history. These organizations, unlike the long-established, traditional *irmandades* (brotherhoods), usually do not last very long, partly because of lack of funds to support such efforts on a sustained basis, and partly because of the scattered patterns of black housing. Actually, contrary to general belief, black Brazilians have a moderately extensive network of organizations. What is lacking is a national civil rights organization of the stature of the NAACP, the Urban League, or even the old SNCC or CORE.

Along with the proliferating organizations fed by it, and in turn reinforcing it, have been efforts to revive the black press, which goes back to the second decade of the century. The first issue of the newspaper *Liberdade* appeared in 1919. The *O Clarim d'Alvorada*, the most prestigious among them, survived from 1924 to 1948, and the last black newspaper closed in 1960. In the past few years, efforts have been made toward a comeback. At the moment, there is a newspaper called *Jornegro*, which is precariously published monthly by the Federation of Afro-Brazilian Entities of the State of São Paulo (FEABESP). Generally, these newspapers do not last very long. It is perhaps because of this that a group led by Hamilton Bernardes Cardoso and linked to the United Black Movement Against Racial Discrimination (MNUCDR) has found a niche in a regular section, entitled "Afro-Latino America," in the alternative monthly paper *Versus* of São Paulo.

It is in the context of these developments that the two major black movements have appeared, primarily in Rio de Janeiro and São Paulo: the Black Soul Movement—with the terms "black" and "soul" used in English; and the United Black Movement Against Racial Discrimination (MNUCDR). The two are not linked together, although, ideally, they should be. As a matter of fact, some of the MNUCDR view the "soul" members with much suspicion, to put it mildly.

THE BLACK SOUL MOVEMENT

The Black Soul Movement is a lower-class movement that recruits its membership from among the young men of the *favelas* (slums): uneducated, underemployed, unemployed, or holding menial jobs such as office boys, messenger boys, and so on. Essentially, they are avid fans of American soul music, of black films such as *Wattstax, Claudine, Sounder,* and of "blaxploitation" (black exploitation) films such as *Superfly.* They call themselves, and are called by others, the "blacks" (in English) or the "soul" or "black-power kids" (with the key words in English). They have a passion for soul dancing, which is their main form of entertainment. They wear outlandishly colorful and elaborate clothes and use equally elaborate handshakes among themselves. They do not drink, smoke, or take drugs, unlike the rock kids—the white boys from the *Zona Sul* (southern zone of Rio de Janeiro). The soul boys are from the *Zona Norte* (Rio's northern zone), the *favelas*, and soul music is to them and the *Zona Norte* what rock-and-roll is to the whites and the *Zona Sul*. There is a dialectic even in music.

The soul kids' heroes are James Brown, Isaac Hayes, Aretha Franklin, and the Reverend Jesse Jackson of Operation PUSH, after whom they repeat, in unison, "I am somebody" (in English), with the appropriate clenched-fist black-power gesture when they watch him on the screen in the movie *Wattstax*. They see the movie repeatedly; it is their bible (an audiovisual bible is more suited to their low level of education), and the Reverend Jesse Jackson's declamation is their manifesto.

It may be true that these young people are alienated from Brazilian culture. For instance, they refuse to dance the samba, which they consider to have been excessively commercialized for the benefit of whites. It may be true also that they are being exploited by the dance, movie, and concert promoters, many of whom are white, who cater to their taste. But I do not think the phenomenon can be dismissed as merely a big—and profitable—commercial hype by money-hungry promoters, as some suggest, for the following reasons.

First, the poor black youth's passion for soul music is, as indicated above, and as they are well aware, the equivalent of the well-to-do white youth's dedication to rock music. In fact, rock-and-roll and other forms of American music constitute the bulk of the music played on the radio and even in the Musak systems in the principal cities of Brazil. Thus, it is an expression of Brazilian cultural dependency and is therefore structural in nature.

Second, black reliance on separate, segregated dances is a response to the discrimination and other indignities they have suffered in attempting to enter white night clubs.

Third, the predisposition to choose their heroes from among United States blacks is consistent with the well-known tendency toward what I call "disrecruitment" in the Brazilian black "community," that is, the co-optation of potential leaders out of the black group by virtue of their personal success.

Fourth, members of the Black Soul Movement seem to have taken seriously the meaning of the words they repeat in unison with such conviction: "Black is beautiful," "I am somebody." Thereby they acquire a sense of black identity and community so far denied or deterred by the prevailing racial ideology. Areas of confusion appear to remain, however, as some are reported to have bleached their hair in their pursuit of the outlandish accoutrement.

Finally, the whole exercise is a massive rejection of cultural accommodation and the traditional etiquette of black behavior. It is a violation of one of the principal props of the Brazilian racial order— the constant reaffirmation of the uniqueness of the Brazilian experience—and above all, of the imperative necessity to avoid emulating black American behavior whether at play, in business, or in protest. For blacks and whites in the Brazilian racial order, contempt for black American behavior and beliefs is indeed the beginning of wisdom.

Thus, the Black Soul Movement acquires the seeds of a veritable cultural revolution. for this very reason, however, it has little chance of acquiring legitimacy in the eyes of the rest of the society or of appealing to the black middle class. This is why the middle-class elements are generally opposed to it, whereas the MNUCDR people are, at best, ambivalent toward it.

For the purpose of our discussion, however, the dynamics of the Black Soul Movement have to be found in transnational relations between Brazil and the United States. Young, lower-class blacks, faced with deprivation, humiliation, and constant police harassment at home, are exposed to soul music and movies by virtue of Brazil's overall cultural dependency on the United States. These blacks embrace and absorb the music, which sings of black people's miseries and triumph, and the movies, which glorify or idealize the black experience. This is a product of the free flow of goods and services from the United States to Brazil. While the Brazilian government has persuaded the Nigerian government to thwart Abdias do Nascimento's participation as the Brazilian delegate to the Second World Black and African Festival of Arts and Culture (FESTAC) in 1977;[41] while the same government prevented or failed to help the departure of several Brazilian delegates to the First Congress of Black Cultures in the Americas (Cali, Colombia, 1977) and later interfered with the activities of a festival sponsored by a group of black Americans in Salvador and Rio;[42] that government did not think of banning records, movies, and singers, and the subservice message they carried. For the young blacks of the *favelas*, the Black Soul Movement is the Brazilian equivalent of the U.S. ghetto riots of the 1960s.

THE UNITED BLACK MOVEMENT AGAINST RACIAL DISCRIMINATION

The United Black Movement Against Racial Discrimination (MNUCDR) was created in April 1978 as a result of two incidents. The first was the barring from the Tietê Yacht Club in São Paulo of four black teenagers who had been selected by the coaches of the club's volleyball team to play on the team. The other catalyst was the murder, under torture in a police station, of a young black worker. The MNUCDR is a movement of intellectuals, students, and some professionals that tries to achieve mass mobilization by appealing to all the black strata. Typically, it was triggered by both a middle-class incident (the Tietê affair) and a lower- or working-class incident (the police murder of a black worker).

In an increasingly competitive social order, where the old clientelist process seems to be losing its effectiveness under the impact of bureaucratization and standardization, and where the process of accumulation at the top with increasing deprivation at the bottom threatens to squeeze them or pull them down, these educated blacks see their opportunities blocked by racism and racial discrimination, and they turn toward mass mobilization as an alternative route to mobility. This situation is aggravated by the deceleration of the economic growth process, which makes the squeeze even more imminent. They use a multipronged approach, including street demonstrations, legal representation of persons facing racial discrimination, and infusing black history into Brazilian culture and education. Another approach is the manipulation of symbols, whereby they have rejected May 13, the anniversary of the abolition of slavery, as the traditional Day of the Blacks, and have proposed, instead, the celebration of the anniversary of Zumbi, the hero of the seventeenth-century Republic of Palmares, which they call "the first free territory in post-Columbian America." They want Zumbi to be made a Brazilian national hero.

The MNUCDR also engages in effective political action. Its objective is to turn the black population into active, independent political agents, instead of being manipulated by white politicians. To this effect, the MNUCDR undertook to negotiate with individual politicians to obtain their support in making racial discrimination and black marginalization a political issue. In return, the MNUCDR would attempt to deliver the black vote at the November 1978 elections. Apparently, all the black politicians refused, but some whites accepted and were supported. Some were elected, others were not. In his senatorial campaign, the sociologist Fernando Henrique Cardoso, who was not elected but who got more than 1.5 million votes, discussed the issue at some length during his campaign interviews.[43]

A major element of the MNUCDR's strategy is to link the black struggle with the general struggle for democratization in Brazil. The point is made repeatedly in their pamphlets and other publications, as well as in their charter of principles. After the election, they participated in the National Meeting for Democracy in Rio de Janeiro on December 8–10, 1978, and raised these points again.

Nevertheless, their struggle remains an uphill battle because black activism—and black soul—violates the racial etiquette and all the other rules of the game. Even though activism has happened and is happening, it is theoretically, technically impossible. This is why, in a survey conducted by the author from December 1978 to January 1979 among black professions in corporate settings, the majority believed that movements of racial protest were impossible in Brazil and that there were no such movements in existence.[44] Among those who answered affirmatively, there was a prominent black journalist in Rio who, nonetheless, could not give the exact name of the movement, in spite of the fact that the MNUCDR has chapters in the principal cities of Brazil, aside from São Paulo and Rio, and propogates its views through leaflets and the "Afro-Latino America" section of the magazine *Versus*. Among the respondents, there was not an overwhelming majority in favor of the MNUCDR. The movement, at any rate, is publicly opposed by some prominent blacks, such as the poet and journalist Oswaldo de Camargo and the *vereador* (city councilman) Mario Américo, who fears reprisals and accusations of subversion.

How was such a movement possible in the first place? The deceleration of the rate of economic growth due to the limits and contradictions of the developmentalist model—namely, the reduction of the purchasing power of the masses due to the accumulation principle (an "internal" factor) and the oil crisis of 1973 (an "external" factor)—reduced the legitimacy base and, therefore, the self-confidence of the regime. Another internal contradiction that has undermined the regime is the phenomenal expansion of the state sector, which brought it into sharp competition with the local private sector. While the São Paulo industrialists have not gone to war against the multinational corporations—the Parliamentary Commission of Inquiry (CPI) headed by Sen. Herbert Levy (ARENA), São Paulo entrepreneur, was not much more than window-dressing—they have complained bitterly against *estatizaçao* and have vigorously pushed for a reduction of the state sector to their benefit.[45]

The strain within the ruling coalition, plus the faltering of the model, made possible an increasing boldness from outside the coalition. For instance, significant labor activity and labor unrest was recorded in 1978, a phenomenon unheard of since the late 1960s. Some of these events tended to weaken the position of the hard-liners in the military. President Geisel's policy of *distenção* (détente) was followed by the *abertura* (opening), the removal of the AI-5, the reduction of the censure, the return of the exiles (though not all of them), and the elimination of banishment and some of the other elements of the state of emergency. In the electoral field, the sound victory of the opposition MDB (Brazilian Democratic Movement) against the government party, ARENA (National Renovation Alliance), had expressed the people's repudiation of the regime. The Redemocratization Front, which emerged from this, provided the opportunity for the black activists to insert themselves into its interstices and try to gain as much as they could from the *abertura*.

Still, this does not necessarily fully explain the MNUCDR, in view of the strong cultural taboos constraining political activism. Perhaps the following factors help to explain the evolving transnational nature of the movement.

First, when the developmentalist model began to falter, Brazil resolved to salvage the situation by increasing exports, and it turned to Africa as the most propitious market. It even argued that Brazilian technology was more appropriate to African conditions than was European or American technology. It was hoped, at the time, that Brazil's increasing relations with Africa would enhance the status of Afro-Brazilians. But, though it was widely rumored that African countries were pressuring Brazil to appoint black negotiators and diplomats to deal with Africa, no African diplomats interviewed in January 1979 could confirm that claim. They all agreed that it would be presumptuous on the part of any government to tell another what type of person to send as diplomat. In addition, the Brazilian social structure and the status of diplomats are such that African diplomats rarely meet and interact with Afro-Brazilians. Besides, the rejection of Abdias's paper from FESTAC II by Nigeria is symptomatic that the effect may be negative. In another area, at least some of the Afro-Brazilians connected with the Leopold Senghor Center in Rio de Janeiro are among the most conservative of middle-class blacks. Thus, the direct contact with Africans is problematic.

A more likely factor facilitating racial transnationalism is the receptivity to the idea of African power and thus of black power in Brazil. Abdias do Nascimento has been a vital link with the U.S. black milieu, and he was in Brazil with the U.S. black group that organized the festivals in Bahia and Rio. Although there have been exchanges of ideas, those contacts do not appear to have been very smooth or fruitful.[46] The attempt to send a delegation to the First Congress of Black Cultures in the Americas in 1977 was thwarted by the government. Yet, black people in Brazil have finally been made aware of, and have made some contact with, the ideas, styles, tactics, and strategies of other Western Hemisphere blacks, which may have been the crucial catalyst. Surely, the tactics, strategy, terminology, and slogans of the MNUCDR are highly suggestive of a North American influence.

CONCLUSION

The Brazilian government's persistent efforts to minimize contacts between the Afro-Brazilians and other black activitist of the Americas suggests that is appreciates the potential of transnational

relations to undermine the existing socioracial order, as does its
insistence on sending carefully selected official Brazilian delegations to black and African cultural festivals. But this also shows a
determination to achieve an "African presence." Herein lies the
dilemma of Brazil's African offensive: how can it intensify and
exploit relations with Africa and, at the same time, avoid the destabilizing effects of transnational relations on the socioracial
status quo?

NOTES

1. Florestan Fernandes, *The Negro in Brazilian Society* (New York: Columbia
University Press, 1969), pp. 187–233; Quintard Taylor, "Frente Negra Brasileira: The
Afro-Brazilian Civil Rights Movement, 1924–1937," *Umoja: A Scholarly Journal of
Black Studies* (1978).

2. Abdias do Nascimento, *Relações de Raça no Brasil* (Rio de Janeiro: Biblioteca do
Teatro Experimental do Negro 1950); Abdias do Nascimento, ed., *O Negro Revoltado*
(Rio de Janeiro: Ediéxões GDR, 1968); Charles Anderson Gauld, "Brazilian Negroes
Seek Greater Rights," *Interracial Review* 22 (July 1949):107.

3. Roger Bastide and Florestan Fernandes, eds., *Relações Raciais entre Negros e
Brancos em São Paulo* (São Paulo, 1955); Roger Bastide and Florestan Fernandes,
Brancos e Negros em São Paulo 2d ed. (São Paulo: Companhia Editôra Nacional,
1959); Fernandes, *The Negro in Brazilian Society*; Florestan Fernandes, *O Negro no
Mundo dos Brancos* (São Paulo: Difusão Europeia do Livro, 1972); Fernando
Henrique Cardoso, "Colour Prejudice in Brazil," *Présence Africaine* 25, no. 53 first
quarter (1965): 120-28; Fernando Henrique Cardoso and Octávio Ianni, *Cor e
Mobilidade Social em Florianópolis* (São Paulo: Companhia Editôra Nacional, 1960).

4. Carlos A. Hasenbalg, "Desigualdades Raciais no Brasil," *Dados* (Rio de Janeiro),
no. 14 (1977):7–33.

5. Gilberto Freyre, *O Mundo que o Portugues Criou* (Rio de Janeiro: Livraria José
Olimpio Editôra, 1940); Gilberto Freyre, *The Masters and the Slaves: A Study in the
Development of Brazilian Civilization* (New York: Alfred A. Knopf, 1946); Gilberto
Freyre, *New World in the Tropics: The Culture of Modern Brazil* (New York: Alfred A.
Knopf, 1959).

6. Gilberto Freyre, "O Brasileiro como uma Além-Raça," *Folha de São Paulo*,
May 21, 1978.

7. It is interesting that Freyre wishes that President Emilio Garrastazu Medici had
followed Carlos Lacerda's "lucid suggestion" of appointing Pelé as Brazilian ambassador to Paris. Gilberto Freyre, "Brasileiros de Origem Afro-negra," *Folha de São
Paulo*, August 1, 1978.

8. Thales de Azevedo, *Democracia Racial: Ideologia e Realidade* (Petrópolis:
Editôra Vozes, 1975). Giberto Freyre, "Ethnic Democracy: The Brazilian Example,"
Americas 15 (December 1963):1–6.

9. Anani Dzidzienyo, *The Position of Blacks in Brazilian Society* (London:

Minority Rights Groups, 1971); Pierre-Michel Fontaine, "The Dynamics of Black Powerlessness in Brazil: The Case of São Paulo," mimeographed (Washington, D.C.: African Heritage Studies Association, April 3-6, 1975); Pierre-Michel Fontaine, "Aspects of Afro-Brazilian Career Mobility in the Corporate World," mimeographed (Symposium on Popular Dimensions of Brazil, UCLA, February 1-2, 1979); Jean-Claude García-Zamor, "Social Mobility of Negroes in Brazil," *Journal of Inter-American Studies* 12 (April 1970): 242-54; Carlos A. Hasenbalg, "Race Relations in Post-Abolition Brazil: The Smooth Preservation of Racial Inequality" (Ph.D. diss., University of California at Berkeley, December 1978); Luiz de Aguiar Costa Pinto, *O Negro no Rio de Janeiro: Relações de Ra;a numa Sociedade em Mudança* (São Paulo: Companhia Editôra Nacional, 1953).

10. Carl N. Degler, *Neither Black Nor White: Slavery and Race Relations in Brazil and the United States* (New York: Macmillan, 1971), p. 277.

11. Marvin Harris, "Referential Ambiguity in the Calculus of Brazilian Racial Identity," *Southwestern Journal of Anthropology* 24 (Spring 1970):1-14; also in Norman E. Whitten, Jr. and John F. Szwed, eds., *Afro-American Anthropology: Contemporary Perspectives* (New York: The Free Press, 1970), pp. 75-85.

12. José Clarana, "Getting Off the Color Line," *Crisis* 6 (September 1913):244-46.

13. Fontaine, "The Dynamics of Black Powerlessness."

14. Thales de Azevedo, *Les élites de couleur dans une ville brésilienne* (Paris: UNESCO, 1953).

15. Amaury de Souza, "Raca e Política no Brazil Urbano," *Revista de Administração de Empresas* 11, no. 4 (December 1971):61-70.

16. Guillermo A. O'Donnell, *Modernization and Bureaucratic-Authoritarianism: Studies in South American Politics* (Berkeley: Institute of International Studies, University of California, 1973).

17. Pierre-Michel Fontaine, "Pan-Africanism and the Afro-Latin Americans," mimeographed (Queens College, City University of New York, Symposium on Pan Africanism: New Directions in Strategy, May 8-10, 1975).

18. Locksley E. G. Edmondson, "The Internationalization of Black Power: Historical and Contemporary Perspectives," in Orde Coombs, ed., *Is Massa Day Dead? Black Moods in the Caribbean* (Garden City, N.Y.: Doubleday, 1974), pp. 205-43.

19. Fernandes, *The Negro in Brazilian Society*, pp. 211-12.

20. Ibid.

21. Ibid., pp. 200-201.

22. Alberto Guerreiro Ramos, "O Problema do Negro na Sociologia Brasileira," *Cuadernos de Nosso Tempo* 2 (1954):189-220; Alberto Guerreiro Ramos, *Patologia Social do "Branco" Brasileiro* (Rio de Janeiro: Jornal do Commercio, 1955).

23. Abdias do Nascimento, *Drama para Negros e Prólogo par Brancos: Antologia do Teatro Negro-Brasileiro* (Rio de Janeiro: Teatro Experimental do Negro, 1961).

24. Gilberto Freyre et al., *Estudos Afro-Brasileiros* (Pref. E. Roquette-Pinto. Rio de Janeiro: Ariel Editôra Ltda., 1935); Gilberto Freyre et al., *Novos Estudos Afro-Brasileiros* (Pref. Arthur Ramos. Rio de Janeiro: Civilização Brasileira, S. A. Editôra, 1937).

25. Nascimento, *O Negro Revoltado*.

26. "Desapontado, Arinos Acusa a Indiferenca pela sua Lei," *O Estado de São Paulo,* May 14, 1978.

27. Theotonio Dos Santos, "La Crisis del Milagro Brasileño," *Comercio Exterior* (Mexico), 27, no. 1 (1977):23–80.

28. Marcel Niedergand, "I Limiti del 'Miracolo' Brasileiro," *Affari Esteri* 7 (October 1975):618–28.

29. Alain Rouquié, "Le modéle' brésilien à l'épreuve," *Etudes* (May 1977):625-40.

30. Maurício Días David, "Algunos Aspectos del 'Model' Brasileño," *Desarrollo Indoamericano* 12 (June 1977):17–18.

31. Carlos Marques Pinho, *A Macropolítica Econômica e os Sindicatos Operários* (Revista de Historia coleção, vol. 62, Faculdade de Filosofia, Lehas e Ciencias Hamanas, São Paulo, 1975).

32. Miriam Limoeiro Cardoso, *Ideologia do Desenvolvimento - Brasil: JK-JQ* (ColeçãoEstudos Brasileiros, vol. 14, Rio de Janeiro: Paz e Terra, 1977); Thomas Skidmore, *Politics in Brazil, 1930-1964: An Experiment in Democracy* (New York: Oxford University Press, 1967).

33. Carlos von Doellinger, "Política, Política Econômica e Capital Estrangeiro: As Decadas de 30, 40, 50, *Revista Brasileira de Mercados de Capitais* 3 (May–August 1977):231–60.

34. IPEA, *Aspectos da Participação do Governo na Economia,* IPEA Monograph No. 26 (Rio de Janeiro: IPEA/IPNES, Servico Editorial, 1976); Carlos Estevam Martins, ed., *Estado e Capitalismo no Brasil* (Humanismo, Ciencia e Tecnologia, São Paulo: CEBRAP, 1977).

35. Cláudio Bojunga, "O brasileiro negro, 90 anos depois," *Encontros com a Civilização Brasileira,* no. 1 (July 1978):175-204.

36. Fontaine, "Aspects of Afro-Brazilian Career Mobility in the Corporate World."

37. Ibid.

38. Pierre-Michel Fontaine, "Multinational Corporations and Relations of Race and Color in Brazil: The Case of São Paulo," *International Studies Notes* 2 (Winter 1975): 1–10.

39. Fontaine, "Aspects of Afro-Brazilian Career Mobility in the Corporate World."

40. Ibid.

41. Abdias do Nascimento, *O Genocidio do Negro Brasileiro: Processo de um Racismo Mascarado* (Pref. Florestan Fernandes. Rio de Janeiro: Editôra Paz e Terra, 1978).

42. Hoyt W. Fuller, "Brazil: The Struggle for Equality Begins," *First World* 2, no. 2 (n.d.):17–20.

43. Fernando Henrique Cardoso, *Democracia para Mudar: 30 Horas de Entrevista* (São Paulo: Editôra Paz e Terra, 1978).

44. Fontaine, "Aspects of Afro-Brazilian Career Mobility in the Corporate World."

45. FIESP, "Industriais criticam a política econômica," *Revista Bancaria Brasileira (Federação das Industrias do Estado de São Paulo)* 44 *(August 1976):20–22*; Roberto Saturnino, *Política Econômica e Estatização: Debates Parlamentares* (Rio de Janeiro: Editôra Civilização Brasileira).

46. Fuller, "Brazil: The Struggle for Equality Begins."

DAVID B. KANIN*

Ethnicity and the Politics of Cultural Exchange: Transnational Sport in the International System

7

A great many activities are lumped together under the term "cultural exchange." Every transfer of artifacts, dance troops, and intellectuals can be grouped into this area at the discretion of analyst, art critic, or government agency. What sets these forms of transnational relations apart from the rest is their purpose. Cultural exchange takes place when interactions of people, objects, or ideas are arranged with a sympathetic, personal relationship as their goal. It is hoped that contact will breed understanding, and perhaps friendship, between the direct participants of the transaction, who are then expected to go home and tell their countrymen of their experiences.

The "attitude change" that Keohane and Nye see as an effect of transnational relations[1] becomes, in these instances, the explicit goal of the interchange.

The political content of these exchanges is usually seen in the same positive light. Cultural exchange is looked to for opening moves in diplomatic rapprochement, and for alteration (or reinforcement) of mass- or elite-audience perception of the temper of relations between the countries involved. These exchanges are expected to transcend ethnic and political animosity rather than to end them. Cultural

*This manuscript was prepared prior to the author's employment at CIA. His current employment there neither constitutes CIA authentification of factual material nor implies CIA endorsement of the author's views.

treaties are so often a part of diplomatic traffic because the participating governments can use them to provide some atmospheric
benefit while not forcing consideration of the harsh reality of the
political issues that divide them in the first place.

While such limited accomplishments satisfy the state, there are
those who suggest more embracing effects of cultural exchange on
the international system. Those who believe in the therapeutic
powers of these transnational relations follow Deutsch's sociocausal
paradigm.[2] His view of political integration postulates a world where
social integration can be accomplished only after the creation of a
homogeneous transnational culture. Thus, it is only through repeated
doses of mass social integration that state-cultivated nationalism can
be broken down.

Historically, cultural exchange has been a powerful, if unobtrusive,
force in the international system. Yet, cultural exchanges have
facilitated both global integration and patterns of fragmentation.
For example, when the Kant-Massini view of nationalism posited a
solution to ethnic discord through the self-determination of nations
in state form, such phenomena as *Grimm's Fairy Tales*, the *Philike
Hetaira*, and the Bohemian *Sokol* athletic movement became rallying
points designed to educate people about their national identity.
While we think of cultural expression as a means of transcending
cultural exclusivity, in fact, these artistic endeavors have as often
been important tools in its reinforcement.

THE TRANSNATIONAL SPORT PROCESS

Sport is inherently a mass phenomenon, appealing to the broadest
audience of any cultural exchange. Since cultural exchange is undertaken with audience attitude in mind, it is reasonable to examine
the effects of such events as the Olympic Games and World Cup
soccer, where thousands of direct participants perform for the
entertainment and/or edification of hundreds of millions of spectators.[3]

Sport gains its significance from its mass public appeal, its perceptual
relationship to the question of aggression, its organization into
units corresponding in name and in territorial jurisdiction to states,
and its peripheral relationship to "high politics." Whether sport

transactions between different ethnic groups result in social integration, structured conflict, or focused animosity is a question that can be approached by examining these factors.

At the outset, it should be noted that integration is a problem on many levels. Although this discussion concentrates on transnational sport, ethnic competition between representative teams takes place within state boundaries as well. Various ethnic groups from metropolitan areas will often have one or more teams in a favored sport. Identification with such teams can be one way of preserving a sense of cultural exclusivity in an urban polyglot. Competition between Glasgow Ranger and Celtic football teams can focus local religious questions as effectively as "Ping-Pong diplomacy" did to international political issues. The analysis might be applied locally, especially where sport is organized into recognizable ethnic units.

In sport at all levels, the spectator is a more important part of the political process than is the athlete. The mass public appeal of sport is what makes it attractive to those who seek direct political return from the transaction. There are more spectators than there are athletes, and it is the reaction of the former to representative competition that draws the attention of governments in the first place.

Olympic scoring on a national basis, for instance, is not legal in terms of Olympic rules. Such computations are always done, in any case, because it is in the interest of governments and their national presses to create a perceptual connection between athletic victory and patriotic identification. This is not an intrusion of politics into sport, for the Olympic system encourages such comparative nationalism by restricting sanctioned participation to units that correspond to those of the surrounding political system. As will be shown, this fact is just as important to ethnic groups opposed to the celebration, through sport, of certain states.

Spectator reaction to political sport has been made even more important in the contemporary era by the explosion in mass-media technology. The boundaries of cultural exchange have been extended so that they involve people in a process that they need not travel to in order to take part in. While most of those who viewed the tour of treasures from the tomb of Tutankhamen had to wait in line for hours to get into a museum, sport fans need only turn on a television or radio if they wish to be indirect participants in the sporting process.

These fans can usually articulate reactions to the event. There is no secrecy in this process, as there is in much of international politics. No athlete or referee can claim that a particular action should not be explained on the grounds of "national security." President Nixon could put forth a "secret plan" to end the Vietnam War and expect his countrymen to allow its details to remain a secret from them. Sport fans, however, do not assume that referees or athletes know more about the activity than they do, and they will react with overt hostility if they perceive action that does not correspond to their (more or less) developed sense of what constitutes "proper" conduct.

IS SPORT A "SAFETY VALVE"?

The number and importance of individual sport participants brings into question certain assumptions concerning the cathartic effect of sport on individual and societal aggression. Sport is, after all, an inherently competitive process, unlike many forms of cultural exchange. Artworks can be exchanged without necessitating a zero-sum comparison between representative national heritages. Evaluations of comparative culture are common, but they are not required of most transactions themselves.

But competition is ingrained in sport: no international meet is held without somebody keeping score. Why is a form of transnational interaction that stresses winning and losing looked on as a palliative in international relations? The answer to this lies in society's frequent preoccupation with athletes. Sport is often assumed to be a means to structure conflict through participatory competition. Aggression is to be released in a healthy manner under the restraints of time, space, rules, and referees. This "tea kettle" school suggests that sport serves as an organized safety valve for pent-up emotions. In addition, sport is perceived to have educational properties. Thomas Arnold reorganized English upper-class education with his concentration on required sport and strenuous physical activity. His ideas about educational sport greatly influenced Baron Pierre de Coubertin, the founder of the modern Olympic Games.[4]

A major assumption behind such ideas is the universality of aggression. For sport to serve as a catalyst for acceptable behavior on a global level, the problem it seeks to alleviate must be just as widespread. Thus, according to Konrad Lorenz, aggression must be a universal phenomenon of biological origin.[5] Lorenz credited safety-valve sport with a significant role in human development. "It educates man to a conscious and responsible control of his own fighting behavior."[6]

Sport has even been seen as having a beneficial effect on war itself. Johan Huizinga lamented the passing of the play element in traditional warfare.[7] Rules and honor used to mitigate conflict. Huizinga decided that the nuclear age has no such rules, and that human beings were worse off because of it. Actually, "mutual assured destruction," the "hot line," and other forms of inter-superpower communication have put a significant gloss of game and rule on the nuclear rivalry.

The mythology of sport is based, not only on its universal appeal, but also on its universal service. Biological drives, like rules and standards of play, must be uniform. A UNESCO conference study summed up many of these views.[8] Sport, as nonlingual communication among the world's youth, is made available to all people through the good offices of the Olympic Movement. According to this study, sport serves as an outlet for aggression and as a meeting place for the rising generation (for example, the Olympic villages of each Olympic Games).

The only problem is, according to UNESCO, that politics intrudes on the process and threatens its peaceful mission. The prominent place of national flags, anthems, and other state or national symbols in international sport causes the appearance of political problems where they supposedly have no right to be. Bad feeling and violence are thus considered intrusions on a supposedly apolitical process. Sport itself does not originate hostility and hatred or magnify existing bad feeling. Politics creates the problem from the outside.

Richard Sipes called the safety-valve concept the "drive-discharge model,"[9] He contrasted this to the "culture-pattern model," which asserted that aggression is learned behavior. The presence of cultural aggression is what determines the warlike behavior of a society or an ethnic subgroup of that society. Sport and war, as cultural phenomena, will tend to reinforce and overlap each other. Warlike (combative or contact) sport can as easily increase as decrease levels of aggressive feeling and behavior. Sipes tested for the relationship of combative sport and warlike behavior in aboriginal societies,[10] and the test results leaned toward the culture-pattern model. Combative sport was more prevalent in warlike societies.[11] There was no evidence that any universal aggressive instinct was blurred by sport activity.

Sipes linked sport and war to the larger question of cultural heritage. Transnational relations are, of course, cross-cultural interchanges. Different people, even those playing the same sport under the same rules, may have different ideas about what constitutes acceptable conduct in that sport. According to the culture-pattern model, since amounts of combativeness in sport will vary as a function of learned behavior in different societies, acceptance levels of physical contact in certain sports will differ from area to area and within multiethnic societies on the basis of cultural differences.

The rules of most sports have certain gray areas, where conduct in specific situations is not explicitly defined. Indeed, many actions in sport *must* not be constrained so that players do not become robots functioning automatically. It is the variety of action, as well as the identification with athletes, that keeps sport interesting to its audience. But when a society accepts one level of physical contact in a sport and its opponent expects another, play between them may result in differing interpretations of fair play and in significant misperceptions concerning opponent intentions. Referees from one cultural or ethnic heritage may not be qualified to control matches between contestants from another.

The importance of spectators makes this issue more complex. They do not get the same physical release that is considered so important by the safety-valve school of sport. Partisan spectators, and those who believe in their ability to discern the difference between fair play and foul, will not grant to authorities the same latitude as they might to political leaders regarding international issues considered to be the province of "experts." Sport serves as a simple drama in which heroes compete against villains. Transnational sport organization is arranged so that the athletes are usually representative of their states. Even those who are not, such as urban soccer contestants for the European Cup, often represent ethnic groups within major metropolitan centers. Reactions to representative national clashes often reflect feelings concerning national issues. While there is some evidence that combative sport increases crowd hostility relative to noncombative sport,[12] all sports can serve as conduits for national rivalry.

Even the sport of badminton sparked a major riot in 1967. Indonesia, the host, was in danger of losing the Thomas Cup for the first time in nine years. Its opponent was a team from Malaysia, a state that had been the target of a massive political and propaganda offensive under the Sukarno regime. Despite the fact that Sukarno was out of power, the matches focused a smoldering hostility, and the spectators rioted rather than allow the match to be completed. When the International Badminton Federation moved the match site to New Zealand, Indonesia refused to send its team, reasoning that it could not be defeated if it did not show up. General Suharto eventually surrendered the Thomas Cup, but he gave it to the federation, not to Malaysia.[13]

A more serious example of an athletic event that focused political violence was the so-called soccer war between El Salvador and Honduras in 1969. The World Cup elimination round between the two sides was not the cause of the war, but it did provide an arena for the representation of national feeling at a specific time and place. Resentment relating to Salvadorian settlers in Honduras, and to their ouster under an agrarian-reform law designed to meet the requirements of the Alliance for Progress, was centered on soccer matches that brought together thousands of national fans who could play out their own hostility while backing their national team. War broke out in an atmosphere exacerbated by athletic rivalry.

The benefits assigned to transnational sport interactions are therefore open to debate. When such a reevaluation is made in the context of sport organization, patterns of national identification of ethnic conflict begin to emerge.

ETHNICITY AND TRANSNATIONAL SPORT ORGANIZATION

Most international sport is under the control of organizations within an old and complex transnational system, the international Olympic system, which includes the International Olympic Committee (IOC), national Olympic committees (NOCs) in control of Olympic team selection, and federations with jurisdiction over the rules and conduct of individual sports. Teams for federation-sponsored championships are chosen by sanctioned national units in each sport. The IOC, the NOCs, and those federations in control of sports in the Olympic Games are considered the International Olympic Movement. Other federations can be included in the Olympic *system* when they are organized along lines similar to Olympic sport federations and when they have some sort of "amateur" rule regarding participation. They need only celebrate their sport in the Olympics in order to join the movement.

The political content of this system comes from its own organization. The prominence of national (that is state) teams and flags is reinforced by a jurisdictional division that permits NOCs and national units of federations wide latitude in their definition of sport participation. National-team members must be citizens of the state and be accredited by the NOC and/or the local unit of the federation in control of their sport.

This system is transnational by definition of both the IOC and the state. IOC rules require that NOCs be independent of state control, but the IOC has not chosen to enforce this code in those countries where functional power is held by state sport ministries. States are content to exercise policy through "independent," but entirely representative, NOCs. Athletic requirements of state citizenship ensure state control over visa and passport traffic. Prestige can be won without the direct application of state power or the risk of interstate conflict.

Individuals who seek to enter events without a country identification are often denied admission. Even when such requests support IOC disapproval of actions by certain NOCs, the IOC will not challenge NOC jurisdiction. In 1976, for example, the IOC was faced with African, Asian, and Latin American boycotts of the Olympic Games over the issue of New Zealand's participation.[14] James Gilkes, an athlete from Guyana, sought to compete on his own. The IOC, which had encouraged such requests, turned him down.[15] Similar considerations affected Hungarian athletes who defected after the Soviet invasion of 1956. When they gave up their relationship to the Hungarian Olympic Committee, they lost their right to enter most world-class sporting events. They were unable to enter future Olympic Games as individuals, except in those cases where an athlete changed citizenship, thus making him eligible for membership in another NOC.

Defection can be ineffective when it is used for publicity purposes by athletes whose ethnic group does not possess a state. They cannot hope to compete as members of an emigré-state unit. They can either submerge their ethnic identification in another, alien NOC or they can remain aloof, using the press and their fellow nationals as sounding boards. Few athletes are so reknowned as to keep up public interest for very long in this manner. In the state that was deserted, meanwhile, new athletes will emerge, and the disenfranchised ethnic group will be no better represented than before. Indeed, one of their symbols will now be beyond the reach of national spectators, unless the new home seeks propaganda points against the old one. Whether such a campaign would involve a public insult from one country to another would be determined by the states involved. The individual athlete and his or her fans would have very little say in the matter.

SPORT AND STATE POLICY

Such campaigns are rare, but other uses of sport in state and national politics are not. Sport serves as a useful tool in international politics because it is peripheral to the international political system. Sport is simply not as important as are the issues of "high politics" —economics and national security. A defeat in a match will not normally be avenged in a military, economic, or political sense by the state whose transnational athletic representatives have lost. Even the soccer war was not caused by sport; it merely focused existing international tensions. Sport is thus a safe forum for expressing diplomatic policy.

On the other hand, a demonstration of friendship through sport does not always indicate a real improvement in relations between the states involved. The peripheral relationship of sport to the central issues of international politics means that the atmosphere of sporting interchanges need not signal substantive changes in policy. Asymmetries of perception can result when previously hostile states enter into sport relations for different reasons. The visit of the U.S. Table Tennis Team to China in 1971 was significant in the extent to which it altered American public perceptions of Red China. It was not, however, a shortcut to the kind of relationship where such issues as Taiwan and Soviet-American détente could be ironed out. Ping-pong diplomacy could only provide a basis for future contacts; it could have no more substantive effect than to establish a precedent for future diplomatic and cultural meetings.

When the SALT treaties and continued American support for Taiwan dimmed the Sino–American relationship between 1974 and 1977, repeated uses of sport had little effect. Track-and-field and gymnastic exchanges proved to be less significant than the initial contact since the public was by now used to Sino-American sport. The mass audience of sport lost interest, so the political utility of sport diminished.

The use of sport as a diplomatic and political tool is now a regular process in international politics. States have an advantage in its use because they have corresponding units in the transnational sport system. For dissatisfied ethnic groups to take advantage of political sport, they must not only learn the operation of the system, they must also enlist the support of member states in their campaigns. Only through the aid of visible national teams can the sporting process become a forum for national policy, except when terrorist tactics are chosen such as the massacre of Israeli athletes and coaches at the 1972 Olympic Games.

Sport, as an activity has no political *value*: that is to say, anyone, representing any ideology or ethnic heritage, is equally capable of throwing a ball or running a race. As a *process*, however, sport can be given any ideological interpretation imaginable. The all-American boy, the new Soviet man, and athletes competing for the sake of proletarian politics or the Aryan race can compete on the same field under the same rules. There is no limit to the use of sport as a rallying point for ethnic pride, provided that such a campaign is carried out by people who understand how to use the transnational sport system.

ETHNIC POLITICS AND THE STRUGGLE FOR RECOGNITION

Ethnic-sport politics are usually contested over the issue of recognition. Ethnic groups seeking statehood find sport a useful public forum as a political expression of national consciousness.

Despite the fact that states hold a near monopoly over transnational sport identification, they are often put on the defensive by ethnic units that gain wide publicity for their causes through sport.

The peripheral nature of the phenomenon creates special problems for both sides. States find it difficult to prevent ethnic-sport publicity campaigns since the use of force to stop such political sport is rarely considered. This is a problem especially when the ethnic insurgents have other states as sponsors. The risk of war with these states over political sport just does not seem worth the effort.

Nonstate movements, on the other hand, must cope with the fact that sport recognition does not lead automatically to statehood and to the rights of sovereignty under international law. The most that can be claimed is tacit diplomatic recognition, which may be enough to annoy an adversary, but it will only be a stage in the drive for international political status. The insurgent seeks to end his or her transnational political designation and enter the world of interstate relations, while the status-quo power wants just the opposite.

Since transnational sport is organized along the same lines as the rest of international politics, campaigns for recognition center on the goal of becoming an equal participant in political sport. The simple question of membership will often be the center of the dispute.

A variation on this theme is the linkage between international recognition and domestic legitimacy. A shaky government, or a regime in control of a state that includes a large number of ethnic groups to be appealed to, will use sport in an attempt to bind pride in athletic victory to feelings of patriotism. Just as ethnic identification is attacked by changing regional boundaries and provincial names, the presence of a national team at an Olympic Games, regional Games, or federation world championship can become a focus for the attempted separation of people from their ethnic heritage.

The following analysis illustrates the uses of political sport described above. It demonstrates that sport has been a political force since at least 1896, and suggests links between the transnational and interstate systems. Each event can only be understood in the light of the diplomatic and political situation around it. Therefore, the balance of the chapter places the international sporting process within a number of distinct historical and political settings. The role played by ethnicity in both the transnational and interstate dimensions of world politics will be examined in detail.

THE FIRST OLYMPICS: ROYAL FAMILY AS ETHNIC MINORITY

Both domestic and international propaganda campaigns accompanied the awarding of the Games of the First Olympiad to Greece. The 1896 Olympics were the focus of a drive for national unity by a dynasty under pressure. The Greek royal family was actually a Danish princely house placed on the throne by the European powers after the long struggle for Greek independence from Turkey. The Olympic concept provided the opportunity for the dynasty to tie its fortunes to the glories of ancient Greece, while the Olympic system permitted celebration of a team representative of the modern Greek state.

The award was not greeted with universal enthusiasm in Athens. Prime Minister Trikoupes opposed the idea because he felt his country could not afford to pay for it.[16] Financial problems haunted the Olympic preparations then as today. Crown Prince Constantine used his personal prestige to save the Games from collapse. He took charge of the Games Organizing Committee and found private financial backing for Olympic stadium construction after a public appeal failed.[17]

Once under way, the Games provided an arena for public appearances by the royal family. Since, in the early Olympics, judging and rulemaking were left to the hosts, dukes involved themselves as referees, and princesses handed out awards. If the crown prince did not succeed in making himself popular, he and his family at least got themselves noticed. National pride was fittingly served by a Greek shepherd's victory in the most prestigious event of the early Olympiads, the marathon run.

The designation of "marathon" as the name of the climactic Olympic event had significant political content. Greece, Europe was reminded, had saved European civilization from an Asian onslaught. Greek publicists sought to use this image in the context of continuing strife with Turkey over territory in the eastern Mediterranean.

In an article in *Harper's Weekly* in September 1895, Demetrius Kalopathakes expressed what some Greeks hoped the First Olympiad would provide.[18] He began by saluting the Anglo-Saxon peoples for being the athletic race par excellence, and sought to draw a connection between them and the ancient Greeks. The British and Americans were the most enthusiastic participants in international sport[19] and thus became the targets for prototypical Olympic propaganda.

Kalopathakes contrasted Greece, as a classical Western civilization, with the specter of Turkish tyranny still extant in the Balkan and Aegean areas. He also compared the traditions of Greece with what were described as the more recent claims of Serbs and Bulgars in Macedonia. Competing national claims were presented in the context of classical ethnic imagery. In short, the 1896 Olympic Games were the focus for an attempt to present Greece as a barrier against Turks and Slavs in modern times, as it was against the Persians at Marathon. Turkey sent no team to the 1896 Games; the two countries were at war over Crete two years later.

Greece sought to become the permanent host of the Olympics.[20] Had this campaign succeeded, the Olympic Games might have become a forum for the Cyprus dispute, as it had been for Greco-Turkish problems before World War I. The political content of transnational sport remains constant. Changes in its application result from the influence of the diplomatic and political environment upon transnational, but representative, sport organization as well as upon each event.

The reason Greece did not receive permanent award of the Games was that Olympic organizers wanted to rotate the prestige of sport among the large capitals of the world.[21] Coubertin was most interested in Paris, the 1900 host, but it was recognized that this transnational organization would have to appeal to the political interest of states it wanted represented at its events.

SUBSOVEREIGN SPORT PARTICIPANTS

The state-unit basis of transnational sport is reinforced by exceptions that prove the rule. Those nonstate actors that do achieve recognition in organs of political sport can use publicity and participation to press for sovereignty in the rest of the international system.

Only *full* membership will do; there is little use for observer status in sport since only the players on the field receive the spectator attention so significant in the political content of this process. The German Democratic Republic, for example, achieved conditional Olympic status in 1955, when its NOC was granted some separate representation.[22] Since this did not mean separate status for East German teams in international sport, GDR committees continued the fight in each sport federation as well as in the IOC.

Palestinian claims have just begun to affect international sport. There was no Arab Palestinian Olympic Committee created to counter the political claims of Israel to sport legitimacy after the end of the British mandate, even though Arab states did oppose Israeli Olympic participation in 1948 and 1952. No campaign for Palestine accompanied Indonesia's refusal to admit an Israeli team to the Fourth Asian Games held in Djakarta in 1962. No invitation was extended to Palestine to join the Games of the Newly Emerging Forces in Djarkarta the next year.[23]

A positive appeal for such legitimacy did not begin outside the Arab world until after the death of Israeli athletes in Munich in 1972 and after the 1973 war. To date, it has been limited to states sympathetic to the Arab cause. In 1975, India refused to issue visas to the Israeli team sent to the World Table Tennis Championships in Calcutta. A group from Palestine-Gaza was, on the other hand, allowed to compete.[24]

Israel was barred from the 1978 World Karate Championships and the 1977 Asian Games on the grounds that security would be too costly in the wake of both the Munich violence and the money spent in Montreal to prevent its recurrence.[25] As yet, there has been no effort to place a Palestinian team in either of these events.

Those nonstate actors that have taken full advantage of political sport have often found themselves opposed by the same states that block their recognition in the rest of the international system. Bohemia had a stong athletic tradition by virtue of the *Sokol* (Falcon) gymnastic movement. The political importance of this organization, which urged Czech national rejuvenation through physical vitalization, was recognized by Austria, which passed legislation banning any central *Sokol* organization in 1867 (the year of the Austro-Hungarian *Augsleich*) and in 1872.[26]

Athletic tradition led Bohemia to become a founding member of the Olympic system, complete with its own NOC. Equality with Austrian and Hungarian NOCs reflected *Sokol* policy favoring trialism, a policy designed to make the dual monarchy into the triple monarchy by granting ethnic Slavs (in this case, West Slavs) political autonomy. The rallying of ethnic pride behind this team led Austria (Bohemia was in that part of the monarchy under Austrian control) to push for the ouster of Bohemia from Olympic politics after 1908. In 1912, the Czechs were forced to march as part of the Austrian team. Two years later, the *Sokol* movement reacted to World War I by changing its allegiance from trialism to independence. The rubble of that war brought the accomplishment of this goal, and Czechoslovakia was prominent in both the 1919 Inter-Allied Games and the 1920 Olympics.

Finland, part of the Russian Empire after 1809, did not have its own NOC and still used Olympic publicity to gain international attention before World War I. Finnish attempts for separate team status in London in 1908 presented that Olympic host with a problem. As a member of the shaky Triple Entente, Britain cared a great deal about Russian feelings. Dogger Bank was not forgotten, and the Bosnian test of the entente was just around the corner. British Olympic organizers complied with Russian demands that Finnish athletes march with the Russian team and that the Finnish flag not be flown over the Olympic site.

Finnish claims had better success in 1912, when the Olympics were celebrated in neighboring Sweden. The issue was the same: Russia insisted that Olympic politics reflect Finland's lack of sovereignty; meanwhile, the Finns pressed for separate status. Although Finland did not get to raise its flag in Stockholm, its athletes did march as a unit behind a sign reading "Finland."[27]

At present, Puerto Rico is the only subsovereign unit with its own NOC. Sport has not, as yet, been a forum for the expression of separatist desires, but it could be in the future. If the movement can enlist the support of Puerto Rican athletes, ethnic spectators may some day be treated to a public demonstration for independence at the Olympics or, more likely, at the Pan-American Games. The latter have been a showcase for Cubans seeking to overcome the psychological effects of hemispheric isolation. Solidarity between Cuban and Puerto Rican athletes would receive significant transnational publicity.

In other branches of transnational sport, Great Britain does not exist. The Act of Union has no effect on separate Scottish, Welsh, and Northern Irish (Ulster) teams. Matches between English teams and these others are officially termed "international." Scotland made it to the World Cup soccer finals in 1974, an event that served as a rallying point for fans who were voting nationalist in increasing numbers. In this case, as with the others, sport does not *cause* such independence movements, but separate status in transnational sport provides a potential forum for ethnic feeling once it is mobilized by other factors.

THE NAZI OLYMPICS: WEIMAR'S FOREIGN POLICY AND HITLER'S RACIAL POLITICS

German Jews did not follow the pattern of the ethnic groups analyzed above. Unlike the others, Jews made no attempt to create a state for themselves outside of German territory. Indeed, Reformed Judaism owed some of its impetus to the desire of certain Jews to assimilate into their German environment. Germany's Jewish policy during the 1936 Olympic Games was, therefore, based on purely ethnic (defined as "racial") issues and was prepared on an *ad hoc* basis, since the Games were, at first, an afterthought to the Nazi regime.

The 1936 Olympics were awarded, not to the Nazis, but to the Weimar Republic at the 1930 Berlin Olympic Congress. Germany had felt the ties between sport and politics since 1920, when it was denied participation in the Olympic Games. The same things happened in 1924 and affected most individual sport contacts with former enemy states. The prohibition of German participation in sport was a facet of what the victors called the "league system." As long as Germany was a political pariah, its athletes were outcasts from political sport.

But Germany had contacts with athletes from its former allies and from neutral states. Soccer was played with Switzerland, Austria, and Hungary as early as 1920; by 1923, sport relations were also restored with the Dutch.[28] The first German contact with entente athletes was through a soccer match with an Italian team in 1923. Italy was no longer a member of the enemy coalition. It had been disappointed by the treatment of Italian claims at Versailles, and, under Mussolini, had become frankly revisionist. Not until Germany was accepted back into international politics were its athletes permitted to reenter mainstream political sport. Locarno diplomacy brought Germany back into the League of Nations and back into the transnational sport system as well.

The 1930 award of the 1936 Olympics to Germany was thus an expression of the international political environment. The Weimar Republic hoped to use the Games as a festival to celebrate German return to respectability. The goals of those who were awarded the 1936 Olympics were remarkably similar to those who planned the 1972 Games. Both visions were shattered by issues relating to Jewish politics. Unlike the Munich murders , the alteration of the 1936 Games was part of official German policy. While Himmler opposed the Games, and Streicher called them an "infamous" festival dominated by Jews, Propaganda Minister Goebbels recognized the opportunities posed by the Olympics and gained Hitler's support.[29]

Sport had been used in appeals to German national consciousness since the war of liberation from Napoleon. Father Jahn's *Turnvereine* had been the prototype for national gymnastics movements.[30] The 1936 Olympic Games were used as an arena for an appeal to German *Volk* consciousness. Sport was put under the control of a *Reichssportfuhrer*, as it became a tool in the coordination (*Gleichshaltung*) of all aspects of social life. These preparations demonstrated the effectiveness of an appeal to the ruling ethnic group designed to tie together concepts of nation, state, and race.

Jews were not viewed as part of this process and were excluded from active participation in Olympic preparations. While the German government delayed application of the most virulent anti-Jewish laws in order to quell international threats to boycott the Berlin Olympics,[31] internal pressure on Jews continued throughout the period before the Games. Jews were forbidden from displaying German colors if they wanted to celebrate the Olympics, so they flew the Olympic flag instead.[32]

While German Jews tried to show their loyalty to the Reich, their troubles prompted a significant transnational ethnic campaign against Germany. Nazi anti-Semitic policies combined with prevailing anti-Semitism in eastern Europe to drive many in the Jewish cultural and economic elite to the United States. America was already a center of Jewish life, but now it became the headquarters of Jewish political activities directed against Hitler and toward the creation of a Jewish state in the Middle East.

The campaign to prevent American participation in the 1936 Olympic Games was an early manifestation of transnational Jewish organization in the contemporary world. At the end of May 1933, the American Jewish Committee declared itself in favor of an Olympic boycott.[33] In November, the Amateur Athletic Union, which was the leading U.S. sport organization in transnational sport politics by virtue of its sport franchises from many federations, came out in favor of that position and threatened to prevent an American team from going to Berlin unless Germany changed its attitude toward Jews.[34]

The boycott movement failed because of the intervention of newly elected AAU president Avery Brundage and the pressure of German-Americans, who had a transnational ethnic organization of their own, the *Bund*. Brundage believed his organization's position amounted to a capitulation of sport to politics. Brundage went to Germany and received assurances that Jews would be allowed to compete on German teams.[35] For Brundage, this was the key issue. As long as official German sport policy did not reflect its political policy, he felt that Olympic requirements were satisfied. Since sport and politics should be kept separate, Olympic consideration (and jurisdiction) should not extend to political matters.

The AAU accepted Brundage's reasoning and reversed its stand. Brundage was able to keep the argument defined as one between politics and something above politics, so international sport was perceived as aloof from the political strife of the day. This attitude was reinforced as Brundage rose through IOC ranks to become its president in 1952.

CONTEMPORARY CONSIDERATIONS OF THE RECOGNITION ISSUE

Part of the political content of placing sport above politics is the advantage thus dealt to states. As members of the transnational sport system, they have access to sport and its publicity. Ethnic groups opposing a state will find the system to be an adversary and sporting events to be a celebration of the status quo. When terrorists killed Israeli athletes in Munich, IOC "shock" was directed against the action as much on the grounds that it assaulted the system as on the basis that athletes were murdered.[36]

The IOC defines itself outside politics, while the Olympic organization underscores the political role of transnational sport by linking national pride to athletic achievement. Those whose ethnic pride is not celebrated in the Games can be expected to continue to use transnational sport as a representative, mass-based political forum.

Such considerations affected both the policies of the Soviet Union and the actions of a number of other states during the 1980 Olympic games. The USSR attempted to keep political and ethnic dissidents away from the thousands of press personnel invading the country for the 1980 Games. The low profile of Soviet dissidents during the Summer Games was clearly an attempt by the Soviet government to forestall Western criticism of human rights violations in the internal politics of the USSR. The relative absence of domestic ethnic protests in the Soviet Union amid tight security measures during the mer Games is not at all surprising in the wake of the Soviet invasion of Afghanistan and the American-led fifty-five state boycot of the Moscow Games.

LEGITIMACY AND RACE: THE THIRD WORLD, GANEFO, AND SOUTH AFRICA

The rest of the world is now awakening to the use of cultural exchange according to Western rules and institutions, and of sport as a means of demonstrating its power. New states can use sport as easily as can old ones; on the playing field, a representative of a new state can defeat one from a stronger political power without fear of international reprisal.

Indeed, for a new state, sport can be even more important than for an older one. Many new states have complex legitimacy problems resulting from borders that are based on colonial administrative lines rather than on traditional ethnic considerations. Creating identification with the state, in the minds of people with a more particularist heritage, can be difficult. States composed of different nations, and lacking legitimacy that is gained through many years of authority and identity, need tools with which to build a patriotic consciousness.

Sport can be one of these tools. Citizens can be trained to be fans, and successful athletes can be used to the benefit of a new regime in search of popularity. Since sport activity has no intrinsic political value, the new leaders can advertise any ideology or cult of personality they choose. That which the Greek royal family found useful in the Olympic myth in 1896 has been attractive to many newly emerging states in contemporary transnational sport. They have simply altered the propaganda to appeal to different ethnic traditions.

An example was President Mobutu's utilization of the Muhammad Ali–George Foreman title fight in Zaire in 1974. Mobutu spent millions of dollars to host the event in order to weld together the many ethnic groups in the country. He created a cabinet-level post to organize the fight. Māndugu Bula, the national coordinator of the event, expected to draw both investment to his country and patriotism from within: "Whatever the cost it will be worth it. I will make Zaire's 200 ethnic groups into one great Zaire."[37]

Mobutu made public appearances with both fighters in all parts of the country. Every ethnic group was visited by the president in the months before the match, and he had his picture taken with regional and local leaders. On the night of the fight itself, the government flew in leaders from each ethnic group and gave them honored places at ringside. Fans and citizens could watch on strategically installed television sets while their national leaders took part in a festival celebrating "one great Zaire." The fight was preceded by a dance festival that involved most of Zaire's peoples. A huge portrait of Mobutu presided over the entire affair.

After Ali defeated Foreman, Mobutu claimed continental, as well as national, leadership. "Muhammad Ali has regained his glory, but we showed to our people and the Africans and the world that black Africans can produce an international event that brings the world to us."[38]

Afro-Asian national emergence has raised issues that have defined Third World cohesion relative to transnational sport and traditional sport powers: anti-Westernism and race. Many of the states that have swelled the ranks of international politics, and therefore of the transnational sport system, are based on traditions without debt either to Greek civilization or to Western philosophy. The Olympic myth has as little meaning for these governments as artificial state boundaries have for their people.

At one time, there was a movement by some states to create a separate transnational sport institution that would rival the Olympic system and rally Third World identification. This developed when President Sukarno of Indonesia was threatened with Olympic and Asian Games Federation sanction after he barred Israeli and Taiwanese teams from participating in the Fourth Asian Games held in Djakarta in 1962. Sukarno called for a new organization based on the needs of emerging states.[39] To be sure, Sukarno used this call to focus his ongoing campaign against Malaysia, which he called an outpost of imperialism in the Third World. But the structural significance of this movement was that, for the first time, the developing states threatened to create a transnational cultural-exchange movement completely separate from that of Western societies.

The Games of the Newly Emerging Forces (GANEFO) had their first celebration in 1963, but then foundered due to the instability of the leading participants. Sukarno was ousted from power, China began its convulsive Great Proletarian Cultural Revolution, and Egypt was shattered in the 1967 Six Day War. Since then, Third World states have been content to use traditional institutions of transnational sport to further patriotism and to promote those policies that the developing states could hold in common.

Racial policy was not a major factor (though perhaps an undertone) in the formation of GANEFO, but the use of sport as a weapon against racism has proven effective within the Olympic system. The campaigns against Rhodesia and South Africa have been the most successful uses of sport as a political sanction. The states and ethnic groups leading this movement have found sport to be a means of assaulting the legitimacy of states they have so far been incapable of destroying militarily.

The leaders of this campaign, though they worked within transnational sport organizations, were not content to appeal to units of the Olympic system. Rival groups were formed, which challenged the jurisdiction of South African sport federations and of the South African Olympic Games Association. This movement crystallized in the 1950s as a result of explicit South African policies, making interracial sport an international political issue.

The crux of athletic apartheid was a law passed in 1956 that reversed the strong tradition of interracial sport in South Africa. When these restrictions caused international protests, the South African government spelled out its policy in such a manner as to include the organs of transnational sport. Not only was domestic sport segregated, but no mixed teams could be sent abroad, and no such teams would be admitted to South Africa. The government reserved the right to refuse travel visas to anyone who wanted to leave the country and then use sport of campaign against South Africa.[40]

Of greatest institutional importance was the requirement that all nonwhite sport organizations affiliate through recognized white federations. Only the latter were permitted to seek jurisdiction over transnational sport. Units that granted affiliation to a South African organization were allowing the perpetuation of apartheid outside South Africa itself.

Opponents of apartheid within South Africa organized on the basis of equal access of all races to sport equipment, playing fields, and competition. From the beginning, the movement was nonracial rather than antiwhite. The South African Sport Association (SASA) was founded in the late 1950s to concentrate on setting up nonracial institutions within South Africa. In 1962, a subcommittee of SASA was created to spread this campaign abroad. The South African Non-Racial Olympic Committee (SANROC), in turn, concentrated its efforts in all sports. This movement was effective because it recognized: (1) the necessity of carrying out policy in all levels of the transnational sport system; and (2) that sport is a political process because of its organizational structure.

Therefore, nonracial committees fought South African recognition in each sport federation, attempting to isolate South Africa as widely as possible. These groups did not merely challenge apartheid on moral grounds; they claimed to represent the majority of South Africans and thus to have the right to replace white organizations as representatives of South Africa in political sport.

The race issue, like other ethnic problems, is not, by itself, enough of a platform on which to mount a sporting challenge to state legitimacy. Since sport affiliation is a form of tacit diplomatic recognition, organizations seeking to displace sport units must take state form. They can appeal for sport jurisdiction only through a claim to sovereignty as international political entities.

Antiapartheid forces recognized this fact and proceeded accordingly. Sport officials, however, still followed the Brundage position, denying the link between sport and politics, despite their own organizational structure. Ruford Harrison, past president of the International Table Tennis Federation (one of the first federations to revoke white South African affiliation) did not consider his organization responsible to anyone but table-tennis players.[41] Since most of the best South African players were white, and were affiliated with the white South African Table Tennis Union, Harrison felt more responsibility toward that organization than to its rival, the nonracial South African Table Tennis Board.

Such an approach was duplicated by the leaders of many sport organizations, who pleaded that their continued support of South African sport organs had nothing to do with their personal feelings about apartheid. Despite their efforts, however, transnational sport became a focus for the anti-apartheid movement. The opponents of South Africa were sophisticated in their use of sport. When nonracial organizations used the publicity of sport to make mass appeals against apartheid, units of transnational sport found themselves unable to keep their activities from the intrusion of politics.

Because the sport system depended on units corresponding to states, state reaction to anti-South African protests spilled over into Olympic politics. With increasing international concern for the rights of racial minorities, governments used sport to deflect some of the pressure put upon *them* to break ties with South Africa. Governments could favor (or accept) an end to sport ties with South Africa without fear of political reprisal. Public demonstrations of sympathy could be made without necessitating an end to diplomatic or economic ties. A state like Mozambique, for example, could retain ideological purity in sport organizations (as in the United Nations) without altering its policy of permitting citizens to work in South Africa.

By 1964, South Africa had been ousted from the Olympic Games and from the competitions of several sport federations as well. Rhodesia's Unilateral Declaration of Independence was met by similar sport isolation. The latter was made easier by the precedent of the struggle against South Africa and by Britains's opposition to the challenge to its authority posed by the UDI.

These successes coincided with the emergence of the civil rights movements in the United States and Great Britain. In both countries, civil rights was an issue permeated by race, and, in both countries, local issues became interwoven with the transnational movement for racial equality. Not only did the anti-apartheid campaign provide a successful organization to be emulated, but the apartheid policy itself proved to be a common rallying point for transnational allies who had little in common except the color of their skin and the oppression they felt. The Pan-Africa movement spread beyond that continent to encompass people whose ancestors had long ago left their ethnic homelands. Unlike other issues considered here, the race question involved conflict based on transnational color lines rather than on ethnic identification. Indeed, the common experience of oppression was looked to for relief from traditional conflicts between different African tribes.

Out of this movement grew a loose conglomeration of transnational organizations devoted to stopping specific sport contacts with South Africa. Each proposed tour of that country, or visit by a South African team somewhere else, would spark demonstrations and organized protests.[42] Favorite South African sports, such as rugby or cricket, were special focuses of campaigns based in the homelands of traditional rivals. Sport was effectively used to demonstrate to a mass South African audience the increasing isolation of their regime.

South Africa complicated the situation for itself by leaving the Commonwealth in 1961. It found itself outside Commonwealth sport organization, while trying to retain sporting relations with Commonwealth countries. Further sport matches had to be arranged on an *ad hoc* basis, allowing boycott advocates to concentrate on individual events rather than on organizational legitimacy. It proved easier to break up a match than to raise organizational majorities until nonwhite states outnumbered the founding members of the United Nations and the transnational sport system.

South African contacts with Commonwealth states tapered off in the 1970s. New Zealand, however, continued its sport ties to South Africa and became the center of a new stage in the anti-apartheid campaign. Now that South Africa was ousted from most sport organizations, the movement shifted its attention to those states not following the trend. Asian, African, and Latin American teams left the 1976 Olympic Games because New Zealand was allowed to compete. The IOC threatened to retaliate against NOCs participating in the boycott, as they were deemed to have violated Olympic principles. Nothing was done, however, as the IOC could not afford another GANEFO.

Many of the offending NOCs were under orders from their governments to leave the Games, yet the IOC did not choose to act on its long-standing rule that NOCs be independent of government control. Since the IOC is powerless to attack NOC jurisdiction in team selection and control, and since the IOC needs the allegiance of NOCs no matter who controls them, future NOCs can be expected to follow foreign-policy guidelines with little interference from Olympic authorities.

This trend has already reached the United Nations. The contention that sport organizations control transnational events outside UN jurisdiction is being challenged. Mexico, for example, based its boycott of the 1975 South African Davis Cup team on General Assembly Resolution 3324, urging an end of sport ties between member states and South Africa.[43] The head of the Special Committee Against Apartheid praised those boycotting the Olympics, and, in November 1976, the General Assembly passed a resolution calling for a conference to consider future sport action against apartheid.[44]

The overlap between transnational sport and intergovernmental relations can be examined by the example of Arthur Ashe. After many years of trying, Ashe was invited to break the color line of the 1973 South African Open Tennis Tournament. This was widely viewed as an attempt by South Africa to stem its sport isolation. SANROC and many American blacks urged Ashe not to compete, as his presence would lend perceptual legitimacy to the regime. Ashe chose to go and serve as a model of an independent black for young South African nonwhites to emulate. Ashe insisted on criticizing the regime and on having personal contact with his fans. He also chose to play Davis Cup matches against South Africa. Tennis is unusual in sport in that its organization is largely outside the Olympic system, insisting neither on amateur participation nor on adherence to Olympic tradition. The unit of identification for the spectator is the individual, and tennis audiences might be seen as examples of the sort of mass socialization sought by Deutsch.

Davis Cup, on the other hand, is an explicitly political competition based on national tennis teams. Corresponding more to the Olympic model, Davis Cup tennis encompasses much the same political content. While Ashe might have claimed to represent no one but himself in the South African Open, he was definitely representing his state when he served on the Davis Cup team. In the latter context, his participation underscored a direct grant of tacit recognition of South African jurisdiction by the United States. To allow representative international play is as clearly an act of policy as is a boycott, even if the representative national team is officially independent of government organs.

CONCLUSION: CULTURAL EXCHANGE IN ITS TRANSNATIONAL POLITICAL ENVIRONMENT

Each state and ethnic group using sport against South Africa used the same transnational organization to do so. As in other issues involving ethnic identification, transnational and intergovernmental policy operated within the same organizations, using the same strategy. In their studies of transnational relations, Keohane and Nye advanced conceptual division of the international system into "issue areas" in order to challenge traditional perceptions concerning homogeneity in the international system.[45] While it is true that variations from the state-centric model necessitate such analysis, rigid compartmentalization threatens oversimplification of transnational concepts.

When the culture-pattern model is considered, it can be shown that behavior of states and of transnational organizations will both be affected by the prevailing cultural environment. The dominance of Western culture (including Marxism), with its concentration on struggle (by state, class, or ethnicity), is reflected at all levels of international relations.

Transactions involving cultural exchange, therefore, cannot be considered independent of the political environment that spawns them. It is not enough that transnational interchanges are *intended* to promote attitude change or cultural enrichment. Political problems may find expression in such interchanges, particularly when the units of culture coincide with the jurisdiction of states.

The surprise that is often registered when UNESCO conclaves or Olympic Games turn out to be extensions of Security Council debates is, therefore, unwarranted. The audience of cultural exchange may have its own national pride reinforced through the transaction rather than gain a new appreciation of someone else's artistic achievement. While the mechanism of most transnational exchanges does not require spectator comparison of national heritage, such comparisons are quite common. The increasing number of transnational competitions in many art forms makes them even more likely.

Sport exchange is especially liable to have these results because its own mechanism does require winners and losers within a representative political structure. Transnational sport focuses political problems for a mass audience. It serves to strengthen ethnic particularism rather than to further the cause of transethnic socialization.

NOTES

1. Robert Keohane and Joseph Nye, *Transnational Relations and World Politics* (Cambridge: Harvard University Press, 1971) p. xvii.

2. Karl Deutsch, "Integration and Arms Control in the European Political Environment," *American Political Science Review* 60, 1 (March 1966):354–65.

3. Since it is more difficult to examine mass social attitudes than it is to concentrate on a specific public, elite social integration has more often been subjected to careful study. Interchanges directed at specific publics are only expected to affect the attitudes of certain individuals, and can be separated from the rest for purposes of study. Joseph S. Nye's discussion of regional integration is a good example. See "Comparative Regional Integration," *International Organization* 22, 4 (Autumn 1968): 855–80. He divided elite from mass social integration (SIe and SIm). Only the former was analyzed in depth by type and by category. SIm was relegated to the conceptual receptacle of "other." (ibid., p. 875.) This analysis is concerned with questions relating to SIm.

4. John Lucas, "Baron Pierre de Coubertin and the Formative Years of the Modern Olympic Movement" (Ed.D.. diss., University of Maryland, 1962).

5. Konrad Lorenz, *On Aggression* (New York: Bantam Books, 1971), p. 271.

6. Ibid., p. 271.

7. Johan Huizinga, *Homo Ludens* (Boston: Beacon Press, 1955), p. 210.

8. UNESCO, *Sport, Work, Culture: Report of the International Conference on the Contributions of Sports to the Improvement of Professional Abilities and to Cultural Development* (Helsinki, 1960), pp. 159–70.

9. Richard Sipes, "War, Sports, and Aggression: An Empirical Test of Two Rival Theories," *American Anthropologist* 70, 1 (February 1973):64.

10. "Warlike" was defined in terms of aggressive attacks on neighbors; combative sports were those in which there was physical contact and evidence of simulated combat.

11. Sipes, "War, Sports, and Aggression," p. 71.

12. Robert Goldstein and Robert Arm, "Effects of Observing Athletic Contests on Hostility," *Sociometry* 34, 1 (March 1971):83–90.

13. *Sports Illustrated* 27, 5 (July 31, 1967):9.

14. New Zealand refused to heed United Nations resolutions concerning the end of sport ties to South Africa. When the IOC supported New Zealand, many Third World delegations walked out of the Montreal Olympics.

15. *Boston Globe*, July 23, 1976.

16. Lucas, "Baron Pierre de Coubertin," p. 114.

17. Central Committee in Athens, *The Olympic Games: BC 776–AD 1896*, 2 vols. (Athens: Charles Beck & Co., 1896), 1:19–20.

18. Demetrius Kalopathakes, "The New Olympic Games," *Harper's Weekly* 39 (September 25, 1895):919–24.

19. It was even suggested that the modern Olympics be strictly an Anglo-Saxon affair, quite in line with the ethnic exclusivity of the ancient Greek Games. J. A. Cooper, "An Anglo-Saxon Olympiad," *The Nineteenth Century* 32 no. 187 (September 1892): 380–88.

20. Greece hosted an interim Games in 1906, following the failure of the 1900 and 1904 Olympics. The Greeks contrasted their enthusiasm with other peoples' apathy in a further attempt to win permanent award of the Games.

21. Central Committee in Athens, *The Olympic Games*, 2:81.

22. From 1952 to 1968, Germany was represented by a single Olympic committee under West German control. The single German team marched behind a compromise flag and had its victors saluted to the strains of a Beethoven hymn rather than by either national anthem. This unified sport tradition (which ended in several federations before 1968) underscored Adenauer's claims to German unity without requiring force to prove his point.

23. See Ewa T. Pauker, *GANEFO: Sports and Politics in Djakarta* (Santa Monica, Calif.: RAND, 1964).

24. *The New York Times*, January 15, 1975.

25. Ibid., July 25, 1976, and July 3, 1977.

26. See Ladislav Jandasek, "The Sokol Movement in Czechoslovakia," *The Slavonic Review* 11, 31 (July 1932):65–80.

27. Swedish Olympic Committee, *The Olympic Games of Stockholm, 1912* (Stockholm: Swedish Olympic Committee, 1913), plate 108.

28. Kurt Doerry and Wilhelm Dorr, *Das Olympia Buch* (Munich: Olympia Verlag, 1927), p. 92.

29. Bill Henry, *An Approved History of the Olympic Games* (New York: G. P. Putnam's Sons, 1948), p. 230.

30. *Turnvereine* served as a link between Germany and Germans emigrating to the

United States. Ethnic sport was used as a transnational link between the fatherland and those Germans who were feared lost to it.

31. *The New York Times*, December 1, 1935.

32. A. Weyand, *The Olympic Pageant* (New York: Macmillan, 1952), p. 251.

33. *The New York Times*, May 31, 1933.

34. Ibid., November 21, 1933.

35. Rudi Ball, a Jewish ice-hockey player, and Helene Mayer, a fencer with one Jewish parent, did compete for the Reich.

36. *Olympic Review* (IOC organ), #62–63 (January-February 1973):16–18.

37. *The New York Times*, August 18, 1974.

38. Ibid., October 31, 1974.

39. Pauker, *GANEFO*, p. 4.

40. Richard Lapchick, "The Politics of Race and International Sport: The Case of South Africa" (Ph.D. diss., University of Denver, 1973), pp. 36–37.

41. Author interview with Dr. Harrison, December 13, 1973.

42. For example, Peter Hain, *Don't Play with Apartheid* (London: George Allen & Unwin, 1971).

43. *The New York Times*, March 11, 1975.

44. Ibid., July 28, 1976.

45. Keohane and Nye, *Transnational Relations and World Politics*, pp. 169–71.

JOHN F. STACK, JR.

Conclusions   8

Three central issues raised throughout this volume need to be addressed by way of conclusion: (1) the interplay between the state and transnational forces; (2) the significance of ethnicity as a transnational force; and (3) the structural inequalities of the contemporary global system as they affect states, transnational relations, and ethnic groups. In each case, the analysis of ethnicity from a transnational perspective helps us to understand more clearly the international dimensions of ethnicity and the transnational aspects of contemporary world politics.

THE STATE AND TRANSNATIONAL ORGANIZATIONS

This volume raises, if only by implication, a central conceptual problem relating to the study of contemporary world politics: How do we assess the role of transnational actors vis-á-vis the influential position occupied by states? The conventional wisdom of international relations argues that transnational actors are not very important or even novel actors. Hedley Bull states this perspective most clearly and cogently in his analysis of world politics, *The Anarchical Society*. Bull dismisses the importance of transnational actors on four counts. First, Bull disputes the fact that contemporary examples of transnational relations—the existence of a global political system defined by the activities of state and nonstate ac-

tors—are a "new or recent development."[1] Second, he challenges
the assumption that transnational actors and forces play a more important role in the contemporary international system than was the
case in Europe before World War I or in the residual trappings of a
medieval world of the sixteenth and seventeenth centuries. Third,
Professor Bull rejects the idea that transnational relations "assure
the emergence of an integrated world society."[2] Finally, Bull asserts
that, where transnationalism appears to limit the freedom of action
of states, the impact of transnational relations has occurred in an
uneven fashion at best and has a purely regional influence.
Transnational relations, therefore, do not contribute to the explicit
goal of "global social integration."[3]

On the surface, Professor Bull's critique of transnational relations appears to be devastating. He is correct in pointing out that
transnational relations played a more important role in sixteenth-
and seventeenth-century European history than they do in the last
quarter of the twentieth century. The common language, values,
and customs that unified European aristocracy were truly transnational. Moreover, Bull's contention that there are no appreciable
trends toward greater levels of world socioeconomic and political
integration based on transnational relations is also quite accurate.
The establishment of the European Economic Community, for
example, was the result of the consent of states (and the continuing
agreement of states) rather than the by-product of sublimely
transnational forces.

The purpose of this book is not to dismiss the assessments of international politics proposed by Hedley Bull and others; rather, it is
to augment them. States continue to be central actors in the con-
.emporary global environment. States, however, clearly do not act
in a vacuum and tend to interact with a variety of transnational actors and processes in important ways. Thus, this volume challenges
the dogmatic assumption that states constitute the only legitimate
actors in world politics and, consequently, that the only fruitful
method of political analysis must emphasize a "state-centric"
perspective. It is precisely Professor Bull's state-centric orientation
that arbitrarily restricts his analysis of transnational relations.

Unfortunately, Professor Bull misperceives the recent flurry of
scholarship analyzing transnationalism. While Bull concedes that

global communication and transportation networks provide transnational actors with the wherewithal for greater penetration of societies throughout the world, international politics rermains the product of state interaction in global and regional balances of power, international organizations, international law, diplomacy, and war. In reminding us that states continue to play a major role in world politics, Professor Bull belabors the obvious.

The significant contribution that the study of transnationalism makes to contemporary world politics is the recognition of its complexity. The overwhelming thrust of studies of transnational relations has been to offer careful conceptual and empirical analysis of the nature of world politics. There are no implicit predictions about the withering away of the state system in these studies. Further, the analysis of transnational relations overwhelmingly focuses on the interplay between states and transnational actors, as exemplified in Joseph Nye and Robert Keohane's *Power and Interdependence*. From this perspective, the state system helps to structure the nature of relationships. For example, Nye and Keohane demonstrate how bureaucracies frequently play significant roles in altering relations between states that traditional indices of power (economic strength, military force, and diplomatic weight) could not adequately analyze. The study of transnational relations, therefore, broadens the analysis of international politics in much the same way that Graham Allison and Morton Halperin's work on the influence of domestic bureaucracies enriched the analysis of American foreign policy.[4] Indeed, Hedley Bull's central assumption that the study of transnational relations precludes an understanding of interstate politics is disputed throughout this book.

As each of the preceding chapters illustrates, transnational actors must be viewed in the context of interstate relations. It is suggested, moreover, that preoccupation with the activities of states should sensitize the student of international relations to less obvious manifestations of world politics. Two chapters in particular put forth this theme. John P. Paul's chapter, "The Greek Lobby and American Foreign Policy," illustrates how states provided the framework whereby Greek-Americans could interact directly in the international arena. As Paul is so careful to point out, Greek-Americans were not responsible for the implementation of the arms embargo against Turkey in 1974. The uneasy balance of power between suspicious Congress and an imperial presidency defined the principal lines of conflict. Greek-Americans, however, were clearly visible actors whose domestic and, to some extent, international political prestige was enhanced by the outrage of the Nixon administration, the machinations of the governments of Greece and Turkey, and the political and military turmoil in Cyprus. In this case, states helped increase the influence of a transnational actor, thus heightening the complexity of a conflict overwhelmingly defined by state activities.

A somewhat different perspective—the tensions between states and transnational actors that sometimes reinforce and restrict state activities—is the subject of Pierre-Michel Fontaine's analysis of black ethnic mobilization in Brazil. On the one hand, transnational processes—communication linkages via books, movies, and music—heightened the awareness of Brazilian blacks to the discriminatory treatment confronted by blacks in the United States and elsewhere. The seeds of political discontent, therefore, are a putative aspect of the increasing penetration of Brazilian culture by an aggressively marketed version of American popular culture, itself an expression of transnationalism. On the other hand, the Brazilian economic "miracle" is the product of significant transnational economic support of the Brazilian state's elite class by multinational corporations, international organizations, and advanced industrial societies. Thus, transnational relations reinforce state power in Brazil through Brazil's growing political and economic influence in the Western Hemisphere and the world while, at the same time raising the possibility of growing racial dissatisfaction among Brazil's large black population. The irony is that two transnational forces simultaneously reinforce and restrict the power of the Brazilian state.

TRANSNATIONAL RELATIONS AND ETHNICITY

The state system constitues a key variable that helps to define transnational relations. A second important area of inquiry concerns those global structures and processes, independent of explicit state control, that foster the transnational manifestations of ethnicity. We can identify at least four conditions that contribute to the transnational dimensions of ethnicity since World War II.

First, the diffusion of states outside of Europe and the Western Hemisphere broadened the global political system by emphasizing political, economic, and legal rights and responsibilities that were previously reserved only for a small group of Western and non-Western states. The process of Afro-Asian decolonization affected, to some extent, every major international institution associated with the state system—ranging from patterns of participation in international organizations to the conduct of war, especially wars of national liberation. The irony of the decolonization process was that, at the very moment the international system was most responsive to many of the economic, social-welfare, and ideological concerns of the "new" states, pervasive conditions of economic, political, and technological dependence on advanced industrial societies severely restricted the actual extent of their independence and sovereignty.

State borders were remarkably fluid, especially when the activities of international organizations and nonstate actors were involved. The permeability of states illustrates rising currents of systemic interdependence as well as an increasing network of transnational relations affecting every significant dimension of a state's internal politics. In this environment, ethnicity becomes a particularly salient aspect of the internal and external politics of Third World countries.

The interplay between ethnicity and transnationalism is most visible in the politics of those ethnic groups that comprise the decision-making elites of developing states in stratified, multiethnic societies. Internal cleavages are exacerbated by fundamental asymmetries in global political and economic relationships that tend only to exaggerate the importance of transnational relations in the absence of stable, homogeneous, historically-defined political cultures. The interplay between ethnicity and transnational relations constitutes a fundamental aspect of the difficult and by no means unilinear process of state-building in the developing societies of Africa, Asia, and the Middle East.

As James P. Piscatori's chapter illustrates so vividly, transnational relations have a major impact on the continuing viability of

Islamic states, especially the preeminent oil-exporting country of the Middle East—Saudi Arabia. Ethnicity and transnational relations may be seen to comprise two neglected, but significant, dimensions of the ongoing process of state-building in the Third World.

A second crucial factor accelerating the interplay between ethnicity and transnational relations is the creation of supranational organizations, the most successful being the European Economic Community. Whereas the decolonization process resulted in a weakening of sovereignty within a number of developing countries because of the absence of viable administrative infrastructures, trends to supranationalism in Western Europe encouraged the weakening of state sovereignty through the evolution of influential political and economic supranational bureaucracies. Through the creation of impressive levels of interdependence among the members of the Common Market, individual state autonomy is restricted in a number of specifically defined economic and, to a lesser extent, political areas. As Martin Slater's "International Migration and French Foreign Relations" implies, the acceptability of foreign workers in France (from its former colonies, Algeria and Tunisia; from members and associate members of the EEC, Greece; and from other countries, Spain, Yugoslavia, or Turkey) is dependent on transnational economic conditions that are, in part, shaped by regional and global forces—for example, the growth rate of the EEC or the stability of the global economic system.

Indeed, the presence of large numbers of foreign workers in unskilled jobs that are no longer attractive to increasingly affluent and highly skilled Europeans in the United Kingdom, France, Switzerland, and Germany underscores a significant arena of transnational relations. The heavy industries of Western Europe require the presence of low-skilled workers drawn from underdeveloped countries. A significant percentage of the salaries of foreign workers is returned home to the families of workers, thus constituting a significant aspect of the foreign exchange and economic stability of the labor-exporting states. Increasing levels of economic and political dependence are thereby created between the affluent societies of Western Europe and the underdeveloped states of the Middle East and North Africa.

The significance of the interplay between ethnicity and transnational relations is best seen in the increasingly explosive political and economic setting of the advanced industrial states of Western Europe—the brooding presence of ethnically distinct and hence unassimilable foreign workers amid rising currents of xenophobia as economic growth stagnates and financial resources become strained. The political and economic effects of European nativism, as Slater clearly points out, affect, not only the nature of the democratic process in Western European countries, but also the stability of the political, economic, and ideological systems of the labor-exporting states. Heightening levels of supranationalism in Western Europe illustrate the crucial interface between ethnicity and rising currents of dependence between advanced industrial societies and adjacent underdeveloped states. Ethnic cleavages, therefore, are reinforced by class conflicts amid networks of transnational economic relations.

A third aspect of the interplay between ethnicity and transnationalism is the revolutionary emergence of science and technology as a fundamental dimension of international politics.[5] The most specific manifestations of this process are the worldwide proliferation of communication and transportation systems. Instantaneous communication has politicized ethnicity as a global force and projected the image of the ethnic nationalist-terrorist as one of the primary ideological symbols of the 1970s. Whether it is the image of the Palestinian skyjacker or the kidnapping-murders of the Red Brigade, the upsurge of ethnic terrorism is facilitated by global communication and transportation systems. As I argue in "Ethnic Groups as Emerging Transnational Actors," accelerating levels of systemic interdependence promoted by transnational communication and transportation networks help explain the worldwide activism of ethnic groups.

The interdependence of the global mass media is not limited to incidents of ethnic terrorism, however. David B. Kanin's analysis of the transnational nature of the International Olympic Movement cogently illustrates how states and international organizations are significant variables in the ethnic and racial dimensions of international sport. Despite the explicitly universalistic and apolitical rhetoric of the Olympic Movement, the politics of international sport are intimately tied to the state system and hence the national jealousies and rivalries of individual states.

As the U.S. boycott of the 1980 Summer Olympic Games in Moscow demonstrated, international sporting events cannot be divorced from the political objectives of states. It is apparent that the United States intended to inflict ideological and financial damages on the USSR in the wake of the Soviet invasion of Afghanistan by withdrawing from the Summer Olympiad. More importantly, perhaps, the withdrawal of the United States and a number of countries was intended to convey a significant transnational message to the Soviet people and to mobilize world public opinion generally. The United States hoped to use the glare of worldwide press coverage to transmit a fundamental political and ideological message in the same way that ethnic groups have attempted to make political statements throughout the modern history of the Olympic Games, as Kanin points out. Thus, networks of transnational relations via global communication and transportation systems become the effective instruments of state and nonstate actors under specific circumstances.

Emphasis on the revolutionary manifestations of science and technology as epitomized in global communication and transportation networks suggests a fourth significant dimension of the interplay between ethnicity and transnational relations—the role played by systemic interdependence. It is now a truism to point to ever increasing levels of interdependence in economic, technological, and cultural areas as an indication of the structural change taking place in the global environment, especially among advanced industrial societies and between developed states and underdeveloped countries. Unprecedented levels of systemic interdependence bring the world's distinctive cultures psychologically and physically closer together. The process of psychological and physical integration need not result in the disappearance of ethnic diversity nor bring about the crystallization of global understanding. A significant body of political science and sociological literature predicting the assimilation and/or withering away of

ethnic diveristy based on increasing levels of worldwide modernization and development was discredited by subsequent conceptual and empirical analysis.[6] Despite rising degrees of systemic interdependence, ethnic diversity has increased, not attenuated,
while trends to ethnic or cultural pluralism have accelerated
everywhere from Britain to Bangladesh.

If the implicit assimilationist biases of the development literature
are discarded, then the significance of conditions of systemic interdependence on the resurgence or revitalization of ethnicity
becomes apparent based on the presence of ubiquitous transnational networks. Three aspects of systemic interdependence are
especially relevant to our discussion.

The first aspect is the worldwide process of modernization—the
creation of highly integrated, mass-consumption societies; high
levels of urbanization; and increasing reliance on technology as an
integral part of daily life.[7] Modernization did not diminish ethnic,
regional, cultural, or linguistic differences in more fully centralized
nation-states. Rather, it increased intergroup awareness of ethnic
differences, it highlighted basic inequalities within and between
states, and it provided the wherewithal for the ideological rationale
for the politicization of ethnicity in the old states of the North, in
the new states of the South, and amid the demands for global
redistribution of wealth, status, and privilege between the South
and the North. As the chapters by Stack, Piscatori, Slater, and Fontaine argue, the continuing penetration of states, societies, and
ethnic groups, brought about by transational relations, illustrates
the dynamic force that modernization plays resulting from unprecedented conditions of systemic interdependence.

A second dimension of worldwide interdependence is a more
specific manifestation of modernization—the vastly expanded scale
of change in world politics brought about by the cumulative impact
of technology. Pierre-Michel Fontaine is quite correct in pointing to
the potentially revolutionary impact of American popular culture
on the consciousness raising and hence politicization of Brazil's
blacks. A similar observation is made by James P. Piscatori in his
careful assessment of the role of transnational relations in Saudi
Arabia. Indeed, the presence of an enormous contingent of foreign
workers in Saudi Arabia raises a number of questions about the

political, social, cultural, and religious viability of the Saudi state elite. The rise of Islamic conservatism and political turmoil in Iran amid the monarchy's self-conscious attempts to modernize the state casts a pervasive shadow across the Islamic states of the Middle East, Africa, and Asia. As the seizure of the Grand Mosque in Mecca and the consequent storming of the American Embassy in Islamabad, Pakistan, vividly illustrate, technology magnifies the shock waves that result from a rapidly changing global system.

Finally, we can point to two political manifestations of systemic interdependence: the increasing scope of international organizations; and the role of ideology in legitimating ethnicity as a major transnational force. Indeed, as my analysis of ethnic groups as direct participants in world politics argues, the increasing involvement of ethnic groups with international organizations (intergovernmental, the UN, EEC, and the Arab League; and transnational, the International Olympic Movement, and the Ford Foundation) suggests an important area of further research.

The foregoing analysis of the interplay between transnational relations and ethnicity raises an additional perspective, however. How does the study of transnational relations address the structural inequalities of the contemporary global system as it relates to states and ethnic groups?

ETHNICITY, STATES, AND TRANSNATIONAL RELATIONS IN CONTEMPORARY WORLD POLITICS

The concept of transnationalism is central to the empirical and theoretical concerns of this study. There is a large and growing literature devoted to every conceivable dimension of transnational relations. What is increasingly clear is that transnationalism is not a neutral concept. Its explicit and implicit meanings range from neoliberal to neo-Marxist interpretations. Conceptual clarity and the self-conscious awareness of the implications of the use of the term "transnationalism" are especially important concerning the structural inequalities of the contemporary global system. In other words, the interplay between ethnicity and transnational relations must be analyzed from the perspective of advanced industrial societies, underdeveloped states, and the crucial interaction between the North and the South.

Initially, the notion that transnationalism included just about everything involved in "the transfer of tangible or intangible items across state lines" was reduced in scope and limited to the realm of transgovernmental relations between advanced industrial states.[8] The study of transgovernmental relations had the advantage of pointing to direct political linkages and providing researchers with hard data, but it may very well have had the negative consequences of reinforcing a distinctly neofunctionalist orientation. As illustrated in Keohane and Nye's most ambitious conceptual effort to date, *Power and Interdependence,* advanced industrial societies may in fact be increasingly drawn into an embracing network of functional relationships as a consequence of complex interdependence—the absence of military force, shifting hierarchies of issue areas, and multiple channels of diplomatic interaction by a variety of actors. The basic difficulty with this perspective is that it ultimately implies that transnational or transgovernmental processes will handle highly politicized issues in a dispassionate and cooperative manner. This technocratic framework, in the final analysis, is most conducive to relations between actors of approximate parity—those actors operating in advanced industrial societies, for example, multinational corporations, private foundations, international organizations, or state elites. This perspective, however, masks the fundamental cleavages that differentiate the technologically sophisticated societies of the North and the underdeveloped societies of the South.[9]

Conversely, the study of transnational relations has been broadened by the perspectives of the *dependencia* school, the neo-Marxists, and the structuralists. As the works of Johan Galtung, Immanuel Wallerstein, Theotonio Dos Santos, Harry Targ, and Richard Fagen illustrate, transnational relations are fundamental characteristics of the structural cleavages between the advanced, industrial societies of the center and the backward, underdeveloped societies of the periphery.[10]

It seems clear, therfore, that the study of transnational relations would benefit from conceptual and substantive frameworks that integrate studies of transgovernmental relations, patterns of complex interdependence between the actors of the world's center, with analyses of the structural manifestations of systemic dominance, dependence, and post-industrialism between the world's center actors and its underdeveloped peripheries. The chapters by Stack, Fontaine, and, to a lesser extent, Slater underscore the utility of studying ethnic transnational relations from the perspective of the structural inequalities of the global system.

Thus, the transnational dimensions of contemporary world politics provide ethnic groups with heightened visibility and perhaps even greater political clout under specific conditions. The studies that precede initiate the conceptual and substantive analysis of ethnicity and transnational relations in world politics.

NOTES

1. Hedley Bull, *The Anarchical Society: A Study of Order in World Politics.* (New York: Columbia University Press, 1977), p. 278.

2. Ibid., p. 279.

3. Ibid., p. 281.

4. See, for example, Graham T. Allison, *The Essence of Decision: Explaining the Cuban Missile Crisis* (Boston: Little, Brown, 1971); and Morton H. Halperin, *Bureaucratic Politics and Foreign Policy* (Washington, D.C.: The Brookings Institution, 1974).

5. Edward L. Morse, *Modernization and the Transformation of International Politics* (New York: The Free Press, 1976), pp. 7–11.

6. Walker Connor masterfully documented the conceptual and empirical deficiencies of those studies of modernization and development that predicted the disappearance of ethnicity particularly in the Third World. See "Nation-Building or Nation-Destroying," *World Politics* 24, no. 3 (April 1972): 319–55. Cynthia H. Enloe addresses this perspective with insight in *Ethnic Conflict and Political Development* (Boston: Little, Brown, 1973).

7. Morse, *Modernization and the Transformation*, especially pp. 1–21.

8. The empirical findings of these studies are consistently of a high quality. See, for example, Robert W. Russell, "Transgovernmental Interaction in the International Monetary System, 1960–1972," *International Organization* 27, no. 4 (Autumn 1973):431–64; Joseph S. Nye, Jr., "Transnational Relations and Interstate Conflicts: An Empirical Analysis," *International Organization* 28, no. 3 (Summer 1974):961–96; Robert O. Keohane and Joseph S. Nye, "Transgovernmental Relations and International Organizations," *World Politics* 27, no. 4 (October 1974):39–62; Peter J. Katzenstein, "International Relations and Domestic Structures: Foreign Economic Policies of Advanced Industrial States," *International Organiza-*

tion 30, no. 1 (Winter 1976):1-45; Annette Baker Fox, Alfred O. Hero, and Joseph S. Nye, Jr., eds., *Canada and the United States: Transnational and Transgovernmental Relations* (New York: Columbia University Press, 1976); and Peter J. Katzenstein, ed., "Between Power and Plenty: Foreign Economic Policies of Advanced Industrial States," *International Organization* 31, no. 4 (Autumn 1977): 587-920.

9. K. J. Holsti, "A New International Politics? Diplomacy in Complex Interdependence," *International Organization* 32, no. 2 (Spring 1978):523, 526-30.

10. Johan Galtung, "A Structural Theory of Imperialism," *Journal of Peace Research* no. 2 (1971):81-117; Immanuel Wallerstein, *The Modern World System: Capitalist Agriculture and the Origins of the European World-Economy in the Sixteenth Century* (New York: Academic Press, 1976); Theotonio Dos Santos, "The Structure of Dependence," in K. T. Fann and D. C. Hodges, eds., *Readings in U.S. Imperialism* (Boston: Sargent, 1971), pp. 225-36; Harry R. Targ, "Global Dominance and Dependence, Post-Industrialism, and International Relations Theory: A Review," *International Studies Quarterly* 20, no. 3 (September 1976):461-82; Richard R. Fagen, "A Funny Thing Happened on the Way to the Market: Thoughts on Extending Dependency Ideas," *International Organization* 32, no. 1 (Winter 1978):278-300.

Bibliography

Andemicael, Berhanykun. "Role of Non-Governmental Organizations in Economics and Social Development." *International Studies Notes* 4, no, 1 (Spring 1977): 17–22.

Apter, David E. "Political Life and Cultural Pluralism." In *Pluralism in a Democratic Society*, edited by Melvin M. Tumin and Walter Plotch, pp. 58–91. New York: Praeger Publishers, 1977.

Banton, Michael. *Race Relations*. New York: Basic Books, 1967.

Barth, Fredrik. "Introduction." In *Ethnic Groups and Boundaries*, edited by Fredrik Barth, pp. 9–38. Boston: Little, Brown, 1969.

Bayor, Ronald H. *Neighbors in Conflict: The Irish, Germans, Jews, and Italians of New York City, 1929–1941*. Baltimore: Johns Hopkins University Press, 1978.

Bell, Daniel. *The Coming of Post-Industrial Society: A Venture in Social Forecasting*. New York: Basic Books, 1973.

———. "Ethnicity and Social Change." In *Ethnicity, Theory and Experience*, edited by Nathan Glazer and Daniel P. Moynihan, pp. 141–70. Cambridge: Harvard University Press, 1975.

Bell, J. Bowyer. *The Secret Army: A History of the IRA*. Cambridge: MIT Press, 1970.

———. *On Revolt: Strategies of National Liberation*. Cambridge: Harvard University Press, 1976.

———. *Terror Out of Zion: Irgun Zvai Leumi, LEHI, and the Palestine Underground, 1929–1949*. New York: St. Martin's Press, 1977.

———. *A Time of Terror: How Democratic Societies Respond to Revolutionary Violence*. New York: Basic Books, 1978.

Bell, Peter D. "The Ford Foundation as a Transnational Actor." In *Transnational Relations and World Politics*, edited by Robert O. Keohane and Joseph S. Nye, pp.115–28. Cambridge: Harvard University Press, 1971.

Bell, Wendell. "Ethnicity, Decisions of Nationhood, and Images of the Future." In *Ethnicity and Nation-Building: Comparative, International and Historical Perspectives*, edited by Wendell Bell and Walter E. Freeman, pp. 283–300. Beverly Hills, Calif.: Sage Publicatons, 1974.

Bell, Wendell, and Freeman, Walter E., eds. *Ethnicity and Nation-Building: Comparative, International, and Historical Perspectives*. Beverly Hills, Calif.: Sage Publications, 1974.

Bergsten, C. Fred, Keohane, Robert O., and Nye, Joseph S. "International Economics and International Politics: A Framework for Analysis." *International Organization* 29, no. 1 (Winter 1975):3–36.

Bertelsen, Judy S., ed. *Nonstate Nations in International Politics: Comparative System Analyses*. New York: Praeger Publishers, 1977.

———. "The Palestinian Arabs." In *Nonstate Nations in International Politics: Comparative System Analyses*, edited by Judy S. Bertelsen, pp. 6–35, New York: Praeger Publishers, 1977.

Blake, David H., and Walters, Robert S. *The Politics of Global economic Relations*. Englewood Cliffs, N.J.: Prentice-Hall, 1976.

Blalock, Jr., Hubert M. *Toward a Theory of Minority-Group Relations*. New York: Capricorn Books, 1967.

Bull, Hedley. *The Anarchical Society: A Study of Order in World Politics*. New York: Columbia University Press, 1977.

Campbell, Ernest Q., ed. *Racial Tensions and National Identity*. Nashville: Vanderbilt University Press, 1972.

Caporaso, James A. "Dependence, Dependency, and Power in the Global System: A Structural and Behavioral Analysis." *International Organization* 32, no. 1 (Winter 1978):13–43.

———. "What Is the New Nationalism? Or Is There a New Nationalism?" In *The New Nationalism: Implications for Transatlantic Relations*, edited by Werner Link and Werner Feld, pp. 6–22. New York: Pergamon, 1979.

Cohen, Benjamin J. *Organizing the World's Money: The Political Economy of International Monetary Relations*. New York: Basic Books, 1977.

Connor, Walker. "Nation-Building or Nation-Destroying." *World Politics* 24, no. 3 (April 1972):319–55.

———. "The Politics of Ethnonationalism." *Journal of International Affairs* 27, no. 1 (1973):1–19.

———. "The Political Significance of Ethnonationalism within Western Europe." In *Ethnicity in an International Context: The Politics of Disassociation*, edited by Abdul A. Said and Luis R. Simmons, pp. 110–33. New Brunswick, N.J.: Transaction Books, 1976.

Cooper, Richard N. "Economic Interdependence and Foreign Policy in the Seventies." *World Politics* 24, no. 1 (January 1972):159–81.

Corrado, Ray. "The Welsh as a Nonstate Nation." In *Nonstate Nations in International Politics: Comparative System Analyses*, edited by Judy S. Bertelsen, pp. 131–92. New York: Praeger Publishers, 1977.

Cox, Robert W. "Labor and Transnational Relations." In *Transnational Relations and World Politics*, edited by Robert O. Keohane and Joseph S. Nye, pp. 204–34. Cambridge: Harvard University Press, 1971.

_____. "Labor and Multinationals." *Foreign Affairs* 55, no. 2 (January 1976): 344–65.

Cox, Robert W., and Jacobson, Harold K. "The Anatomy of Influence." In *The Anatomy of Influence: Decision Making in International Organizations*, edited by Robert W. Cox and Harold K. Jacobson, pp. 371–436. New Haven: Yale University Press, 1974.

Despres, Leo A., ed. *Ethnicity and Resource Competition in Plural Societies*. The Hague: Moulton Publishers, 1975.

_____. "Ethnicity and Resource Competition in Guyanese Society." In *Ethnicity and Resource Competition in Plural Societies*, edited by Leo A. Despres, pp. 87–177. The Hague: Mouton Publishers, 1975.

Deutsch, Karl W. *Nationalism and Social Communication: An Inquiry into the Foundations of Nationality*. 2d ed. Cambridge: MIT Press, 1966.

Dos Santos, Theotonio. "The Structure of Dependence." In *Readings in U.S. Imperialism*, edited by K. T. Fann and D. C. Hodges, pp. 225–36. Boston: Sargent, 1971.

Duvall, Raymond D. "Dependence and Dependencia Theory: Notes Toward Precision of Concept and Argument." *International Organization* 32, no. 1 (Winter 1975):51–78.

Edmondson, Locksley E. G. "Caribbean Nation-Building and the Internationalization of Race: Issues and Perspectives." In *Ethnicity and Nation-Building: Comparative, International, and Historical Perspectives*, edited by Wendell Bell and Walter E. Freeman, pp. 73–86. Beverly Hills, Calif.: Sage Publications, 1974.

Emerson, Rupert. *From Empire to Nation: The Rise to Self-Assertion of Asian and African Peoples*. Cambridge: Harvard University Press, 1960.

Enloe, Cynthia H. *Ethnic Conflict and Political Development*. Boston: Little, Brown, 1973.

_____. "Foreign Policy and Ethnicity in 'Soft States': Prospects for Southeast Asia." In *Ethnicity and Nation-Building: Comparative, International, and Historical Perspectives*, edited by Wendell Bell and Walter E. Freeman, pp. 223–31, Beverly Hills, Calif.: Sage Publications, 1974.

_____. "Internal Colonialism, Federalism and Alternative State Development Strategies." *Publius* 7, no. 4 (Fall 1977):145–60.

_____. "Multinational Corporations in the Making and Unmaking of Ethnic Groups." In *Ethno-Nationalism, Multinational Corporations, and the Modern State*, edited by Ronald M. Grant and E. Spenser Wellhofer, pp. 9-32. Denver: Graduate School of International Studies Monograph Series on World Affairs, University of Denver, 1979.

_____. *Police, Military and Ethnicity: Foundations of State Power*. New Brunswick, N.J.: Transaction Books, 1979.

_____. *Ethnic Soldiers: State Security in Divided Societies*. London: Penguin Books, 1980.

Erb, Guy F., and Kallab, Valeriana, eds. *Beyond Dependence: The Developing World Speaks Out*. New York: Praeger Publishers, 1975.

Evans, Peter B. "National Autonomy and Economic Development: Critical Perspectives on Multinational Corporations in Poor Countries." In *Transnational Relations and World Politics*, edited by Robert O. Keohane and Joseph S. Nye, pp. 325–42. Cambridge: Harvard University Press, 1971.

Fagen, Richard R. "A Funny Thing Happened on the Way to the Market: Thoughts on Extending Dependency Ideas." *International Organization* 32, no. 1 (Winter 1978):287–300.

Fann, K. T. and Hodges, D. C., eds. *Readings in U.S. Imperialism*. Boston: Sargent, 1971.

Fanon, Franz. *The Wretched of the Earth*. Translated by Constance Farrington. New York: Grove Press, 1965.

———. *Black Skin, White Masks*. Translated by Charles L. Markmann. New York: Grove Press, 1967.

Feld, Werner J. *International Relations: A Transnational Approach*. Sherman Oaks, Calif.: Alfred Publishing, 1979.

Field, Jr., James A. "Transnational and the New Tribe." In *Transnational Relations and World Politics*, edited by Robert O. Keohane and Joseph S. Nye, pp. 3–22. Cambridge: Harvard University Press, 1971.

Fontaine, Pierre-Michel. "Multinational Corporations and Relations of Race and Color in Brazil: The Case of Sao Paulo." International Studies Notes 2, no. 4 (Winter 1975):1–10.

Forsythe, David P. "The Red Cross as Transnational Movement: Conserving and Changing the Nation-State System." *International Organization* 30, no. 4 (Autumn 1976):607–30.

Francis, E. K. *Interethnic Relations: An Essay in Sociological Theory*. New York: Elsevier, 1976.

Frank, André Gunder. *Latin America: Underdevelopment or Revolution*. New York: Monthly Review Press, 1969.

Friedman, Irving S., and Costanzo, G. A. *The Emerging Role of Private Banks in the Developing World*. New York: Citicorp, 1977.

Galtung, Johan. "A Structural Theory of Imperialism." *Journal of Peace Research* 2 (1971):81–119.

Geertz, Clifford. *The Interpretation of Cultures: Selected Essays*. New York: Basic Books, 1973.

Glazer, Nathan. "The Universalization of Ethnicity." In *At Issue: Politics in the World Arena*, edited by Steven L. Spiegel, pp. 53–65. 2d ed. New York: St. Martin's Press, 1977.

Gordenker, Leon. *International Aid and National Decisions: Development Programs in Malawi, Tanzania, and Zambia*. Princeton: Princeton University Press, 1976.

Greeley, Andrew M. *Ethnicity in the United States: A Preliminary Reconnaissance*. New York: John Wiley and Sons, 1974.

———. *The American Catholic: A Social Portrait*. New York: Basic Books, 1977.

Hanrieder, Wolfram F. "Dissolving International Politics: Reflections on the Nation-State." *American Political Science Review* 72, no. 4 (December 1978):1276–87.

Hansen, Roger D. "The Political Economy of North-South Relations: How Much Change?" *International Organization* 29, no. 4 (Autumn 1975):921-47.

Haq, Mahbub Ul. *The Poverty Curtain: Choices for the Third World*. New York: Columbia University Press, 1976.

Harrington, Michael. *The Vast Majority: A Journey to the World's Poor*. New York: Simon and Schuster, 1977.

Hechter, Michael. *Internal Colonialism, the Celtic Fringe and British National Development, 1536-1966*. Los Angeles: University of California Press, 1975.

Heeger, Gerald A. *The Politics of Underdevelopment*. New York: St. Martin's Press, 1974.

Hoetink, Harmannus. "Resource Competition, Monopoly, and Socioracial Diversity." In *Ethnicity and Resource Competition in Plural Societies*, edited by Leo A. Despres, pp. 9-25. The Hague: Mouton Publishers, 1975.

Holsti, K. J. "A New International Politics? Diplomacy in Complex Interdependence." *International Organization* 32, no. 2 (Spring 1978):513-30.

Huntington, Samuel P. "Transnational Organizations in World Politics." *World Politics* 25, no. 3 (April 1973):333-67.

Isaacs, Harold. *Idols of the Tribe: Group Identity and Political Change*. New York: Harper and Row, 1975.

Juda, Lawrence. "A Note on Bureaucratic Politics and Transnational Relations." *International Studies Notes* 4, no. 2 (Summer 1977):1-3.

Kaiser, Karl. "Transnational Politics: Toward a Theory of Multinational Politics." *International Organizations* 25, no. 4 (Autumn 1971):790-817.

_____. "Transnational Relations as a Threat to the Democratic Process." In *Transnational Relations and World Politics*, edited by Robert O. Keohane and Joseph S. Nye, pp. 356-70. Cambridge: Harvard University Press, 1971.

Katzenstein, Peter J. "International Relations and Domestic Structures: Foreign Economic Policies of Advanced Industrial States." *International Organization* 30, no. 1 (Winter 1976):1-45.

Kelman, Herbert C. "The Conditions, Criteria, and Dialectics of Human Dignity: A Transnational Perspective." *International Studies Quarterly* 21, no. 3 (September 1977):529-52.

Keohane, Robert O. "International Organization and the Crisis of Interdependence." *International Organization* 29, no. 2 (Spring 1975):357-65.

Keohane, Robert O. and Nye, Joseph S. "Transnational Relations and World Politics: An Introduction." In *Transnational Relations and World Politics*, edited by Robert O. Keohane and Joseph S. Nye, pp. ix-xxv. Cambridge: Harvard University Press, 1971.

_____. "Transnational Relations and World Politics: A Conclusion." In *Transnational Relations and World Politics*, edited by Robert O. Keohane and Joseph S. Nye, pp. 375-89. Cambridge: Harvard University Press, 1971.

_____. "Transgovernmental Relations and International Organizations." *World Politics* 27, no. 4 (October 1974):39-62.

_____. *Power and Interdependence: World Politics in Transition*. Boston: Little, Brown, 1977.

Kilson, Martin. "Blacks and Neo-Ethnicity in American Political Life." In *Ethnicity,*

Theory and Experience, edited by Nathan Glazer and Daniel P. Moynihan, pp. 236–66. Cambridge: Harvard University Press, 1975.

———. *New States in the Modern World*. Cambridge: Harvard University Press, 1975.

Kilson, Martin L., and Rotberg, Robert I. *The African Diaspora: Interpretive Essays*. Cambridge: Harvard University Press, 1976.

Laqueur, Walter. *Terrorism*. Boston: Little, Brown, 1977.

Lemarchand, René. *Rwanda and Burundi*. New York: Praeger Publishers, 1970.

LeMelle, Tilden J., and Shepherd, Jr., George W. "Race in the Future of International Relations." *Journal of International Affairs* 15 (1971):302–13.

Lijphart, Arend. *Democracy in Plural Societies: A Comparative Exploration*. New Haven: Yale University Press, 1977.

Link, Werner, and Feld, Werner, eds. *The New Nationalism: Implications for Transatlantic Relations*. New York: Pergamon, 1979.

McLaughlin, Martin, ed. *The United States and World Development: Agenda 1979*. New York: Praeger Publishers, 1979.

Mason, Philip. *Patterns of Dominance*. London: Oxford University Press, 1970.

Mast, Robert H. "Some Theoretical Considerations in International Race Relations." In *Ethnicity and Nation-Building: Comparative, International, and Historical Perspectives*, edited by Wendell Bell and Walter E. Freeman, pp. 59–71. Beverly Hills, Calif.: Sage Publications, 1974.

Montagu, Ashley. *Statement on Race*. 3d ed. London: Oxford University Press, 1972.

Moran, Theodore H. "Foreign Expansion as an 'Institutional Necessity' for U.S. Corporate Capitalism: The Search for a Radical Model." *World Politics* 25, no. 2 (April 1973):369–86.

———. "Transnational Strategies of Protection and Defense by Multinational Corporations: Spreading the Risk and Raising the Cost for Nationalization in Natural Resources." *International Organization* 27, no. 2 (Spring 1973): 273–87.

———. *Multinational Corporations and the Politics of Dependence: Copper in Chile*. Princeton: Princeton Unversity Press, 1974.

———. "Multinational Corporations and Dependency: A Dialogue for Dependentistas and Non-dependentistas," *International Organization* 32, no. 1 (Winter 1978):79–100.

Mörner, Magnus, ed. *Race and Class in Latin America*. New York: Columbia University Press, 1970.

Morse, Edward L. *Modernization and the Transformation of International Politics*. New York: The Free Press, 1976.

Nachmias, David, and Rockaway, Robert. "From a Nonstate Nation to a Nation-State: The Zionist Movement, 1897–1947." In *Nonstate Nations in International Politics: Comparative System Analyses*, edited by Judy S. Bertelsen, pp. 36–68. New York: Praeger Publishers, 1977.

Obatala, J. K. "Black Consciousness and American Policy in Africa." In *Ethnicity in an International Context: The Politics of Disassociation*, edited by Abdul A.

Said and Luis R. Simmons, pp. 64–75. New Brunswick, N.J.: Transaction Books, 1976.

O'Donnell. Guillermo A. *Modernization and Bureaucratic-Authoritarianism, Studies in South American Politics.* Berkeley: Institute of International Studies, University of California, 1973.

Patterson, Orlando. "Context and Choice in Ethnic Allegiance: A Theoretical Framework and Caribbean Case Study." In *Ethnicity, Theory and Experience*, edited by Nathan Glazer and Daniel P. Moynihan, pp. 305–49. Cambridge: Harvard University Press, 1975.

Payer, Cheryl. *The Debt Trap: The International Monetary Fund and the Third World.* New York: Monthly Review Press, 1974.

Petersen, William. "On the Subnations of Western Europe." In *Ethnicity, Theory and Experience*, edited by Nathan Glazer and Daniel P. Moynihan, pp. 177–208. Cambridge: Harvard University Press, 1975.

Portes, Alejandro. "Modernity and Development: A Critique." *Studies of Comparative International Development* 8, no. 1 (Spring 1973):247–79.

Putnam, Robert D. "Interdependence and the Italian Communists." *International Organization* 32, no. 2 (Spring 1978):301–49.

Rabushka, Alvin, and Shepsle, Kenneth A. *Politics in Plural Societies: A Theory of Democratic Instability.* Columbus, Ohio: Charles E. Merrill Publishing, 1972.

Rosecrance R.; Alexandroff, A.; Koehler, W.; Kroll, J.; Laqueur, S.: and Stocker, J. "Whither Interdependence?" *International Organization* 31, no. 3 (Summer 1977):425–71.

Rosenau, James N. "Introduction: Political Science in a Shrinking World." In *Linkage Politics: Essays on the Convergence of National and International Systems*, edited by James N. Rosenau, pp. 3–14. New York: The Free Press, 1969.

Russell, Robert W. "Transgovernmental Interaction in the International Monetary System. 1960–1972," *International Organization* 27, no. 4 (Autumn 1973): 431–64.

Said, Abdul A. "A Redefinition of National Interest, Ethnic Consciousness, and U.S. Foreign Policy. In *Ethnicity and U.S. Foreign Policy*, edited by Abdul A. Said, pp. 1–15. New York: Praeger Publishers, 1977.

————, ed. *Ethnicity and U.S. Foreign Policy.* New York: Praeger Publishers, 1977.

Said, Abdul A., and Simmons, Luis R., eds. *Ethnicity in an International Context: The Politics of Disassociation.* New Brunswick, N.J.: Transaction Books, 1976.

————. "The Ethnic Factor in World Politics." In *Ethnicity in an International Context: The Politics of Disassociation*, edited by Abdul A. Said and Luis R. Simmons, pp. 15–47. New Brunswick, N.J.: Transaction Books, 1976.

Schermerhorn, R. A. *Comparative Ethnic Relations: A Framework for Theory and Research.* New York: Random House, 1970.

————. *Ethnic Plurality in India.* Tucson, Arizona: University of Arizona Press, 1978.

Shepherd, George W. *Anti-Apartheid: Transnational Conflict and Western Policy in the Liberation of South Africa.* Westport, Conn.: Greenwood Press, 1977.

————, ed. *Racial Influences on American Foreign Policy.* New York: Basic Books, 1970.

Shepherd, George W., and LeMelle, Tilden J., eds. *Race Among Nations: A Conceptual Approach.* Lexington, Mass.: D. C. Heath, 1970.

Shibutani, Tamotsu, and Kawn, Kian. *Ethnic Stratification: A Comparative Approach.* New York: Macmillan Co., 1965.

Smith, Anthony D. *Nationalist Movements.* London: MacMillan, 1976.

Smith, M. G. *The Plural Society in the British West Indies.* Berkeley: University of California Press, 1965.

Sondermann, Fred A. "The Linkage Between Foreign Policy and International Politics." In *International Politics and Foreign Policy: A Reader in Research and Theory,* edited by James N. Rosenau, pp. 9–29. New York: The Free Press of Glencoe, 1961.

Spero, Joan E. *The Politics of International Economic Relations.* New York: St. Martin's Press, 1977.

Stack, Jr., John F. "Ethnicity, Racism, and Busing in Boston: The Boston Irish and School Desegregation." *Ethnicity* 6 (March 1979):21–28.

————. *International Conflict in an American City: Boston's Irish, Italians, and Jews, 1935–1944.* (Westport, Conn.: Greenwood Press, 1979.

Suhrke, Astri, and Noble, Lela. "Spread or Containment: The Ethnic Factor." In *Ethnic Conflict in International Relations,* edited by Astri Suhrke and Lela Noble, pp. 213–32. New York: Praeger Publishers, 1977.

Targ, Harry R. "Global Dominance and Dependence, Post-Industrialism, and International Relations Theory: A Review." *International Studies Quarterly* 20, no. 3 (September 1976):461–82.

Tilly, Charles. "Reflèctions on the History of European State-Making." In *The Formation of Nation States in Western Europe,* edited by Charles Tilly, pp. 3–83. Princeton: Princeton University Press, 1975.

————. "Western State-Making and Theories of Political Transformation." In *The Formation of Nation States in Western Europe,* edited by Charles Tilly, pp. 601–38. Princeton: Princeton University Press, 1975.

Tumin, Melvin M., ed. *Comparative Perspectives on Race Relations.* Boston: Little, Brown, 1969.

Tumin, Melvin M., and Plotch, Walter, eds. *Pluralism in a Democratic Society.* New York: Praeger Publishers, 1977.

Uri, Pierre. *Development Without Dependence.* New York: Praeger Publishers, 1976.

Vallier, Ivan. "The Roman Catholic Church: A Transnational Actor." In *Transnational Relations and World Politics,* edited by Robert O. Keohane and Joseph S. Nye, pp. 129–52. Cambridge: Harvard University Press, 1971.

Van den Berghe, Pierre L. *Race and Racism: A Comparative Perspective.* New York: John Wiley and Sons, 1967.

————. *Race and Ethnicity: Essays in Comparative Sociology.* New York: Basic Books, 1970.

_____. "Ethnicity and Class in Highland Peru." In *Ethnicity and Resource Competition in Plural Societies*, edited by Leo A. Despres, pp. 77-85. The Hague: Mouton Publishers, 1975.

Van Dyke, Vernon. "Human Rights without Distinction to Language." *International Studies Quarterly* 20, no. 1 (March 1976): 3-38.

_____. "The Individual, the State, and Ethnic Communities in Political Theory." *World Politics* 29, no. 2 (April 1977): 342-69.

Wallerstein, Immanuel. "Social Conflict in Post-Independence Black Africa: The Concepts of Race and Status-Group Reconsidered." In *Racial Tensions and National Identity*, edited by Ernest Q. Campbell, pp. 207-26. Nashville: Vanderbilt University Press, 1972.

_____. "Dependence in an Interdependent World." *African Studies Review* 17 (April 1974):1-26.

_____. *The Modern World System: Capitalist Agriculture and the Origins of the European World-Economy in the Sixteenth Century* New York: Academic Press, 1976.

Weinstein, Franklin B. "Multinational Corporations and the Third World: The Case of Japan and Southeast Asia." *International Organization* 30, no. 3 (Summer 1976):373-403.

Wells, Jr., Louis T. "The Multinational Business Enterprise: What Kind of International Organization?" In *Transnational Relations and World Politics*, edited by Robert O. Keohane and Joseph S. Nye, pp. 97-114. Cambridge: Harvard University Press, 1971.

Wilkenfeld, Jonathan, ed. *Conflict Behavior and Linkage Politics*. New York: David McKay, 1973.

Young, Crawford. *The Politics of Cultural Pluralism*. Madison, Wis.: University of Wisconsin Press 1976.

Index

Contributors

CYNTHIA H. ENLOE is professor of government at Clark University. She is chairperson of the Social Science Research Council's Committee on Ethnicity. Among her publications are *Ethnic Conflict and Political Development* (1973), *Politics of Pollution in a Comparative Perspective* (1975), and *Ethnic Soldiers: State Security in Divided Societies* (1980).

PIERRE-MICHEL FONTAINE is an associate professor in the Department of Political Science and a faculty research associate in the Center for Afro-American Studies at the University of California at Los Angeles (UCLA). His current research interests focus on race, ethnicity, and political economy in Brazil and the Caribbean. His forthcoming book is entitled *The Black Experience in Brazil: From Powerlessness and Immobility to Incipient Mobilization*. He is also editing two volumes titled, respectively, *Aspects of the Political Economy of the Black World* and *Race and Class in Modern Brazil: New Areas of Inquiry*.

DAVID B. KANIN is a political analyst at the Central Intelligence Agency. Before joining the CIA, he taught courses on international politics at Boston College and Framingham State College. He is coeditor of *Sport in International Relations* (Stipes Publishing, 1975) and the author of several articles on sports in international politics.

JOHN P. PAUL is associate director of Fund Development at National Medical Fellowships. He is currently working on a book about the Greek lobby and American foreign policy.

JAMES P. PISCATORI is a member of the Royal Institute of International Studies, (Chatam House), London. He has contributed articles on the Middle East and on international law to several journals and books and is currently working on a book entitled *International Law and Culture: The Case of Saudi Arabia*.

MARTIN SLATER is lecturer in government and a member of the Center for European Affairs at Essex University. He is the author of several articles on ethnicity in Western Europe and is currently working on a book about migration and workers' conflicts in Western Europe.

JOHN F. STACK, JR., is assistant professor of political science and director of ethnic studies at Florida International University. He is the author of *International Conflict in an American City: Boston's Irish, Italians, and Jews, 1935–1944* (Westport, Conn.: Greenwood Press, 1979). He is working on a study of transnationalism within the framework of contemporary North-South relations.